Leading and Managing
Continuing Professional Development

Leading and Managing Continuing Professional Development

DEVELOPING PEOPLE, DEVELOPING SCHOOLS

PETER EARLEY AND SARA BUBB

P·C·P
Paul Chapman
Publishing

Paul Chapman Publishing
A SAGE Publications Company
1 Oliver's Yard
55 City Road
London EC1Y 1SP

SAGE Publications Inc
2455 Teller Road
Thousand Oaks, California 91320

SAGE Publications India Pvt Ltd
B-42, Panchsheel Enclave
Post Box 4109
New Delhi 100 017

Library of Congress Control Number 2003115349

A catalogue record for this book is available from the British Library

ISBN 0 7619 4321 8
ISBN 0 7619 4322 6 (pbk)

Typeset by Dorwyn Ltd, Rowlands Castle, Hants
Printed in Great Britain by Cromwell Press

Contents

1 Introduction: CPD Policy and Practice 1
People matter • What is continuing professional development? • Is the focus on CPD new? • Taking CPD seriously • An entitlement to CPD • Learning from other professions

PART I: PROFESSIONAL DEVELOPMENT FOR SCHOOL IMPROVEMENT

2 Learning People – Learning Schools 17
How adults learn • Professional learning communities • What is effective CPD? • The standards framework • Collaboration

3 Leading and Managing CPD 35
The professional development co-ordinator role • The training and development cycle • Investors in People • Balancing needs with the budget • Procedures to help CPD co-ordinators • Case study

4 Identifying Training and Development Needs 47
Individual or school needs • Taking account of workload and well-being • Finding out what CPD staff want and need • Catering for a range of people and learning styles • Performance management • Setting objectives

5 Meeting CPD Needs 59
Collating CPD needs • Finding what the CPD options are • Action plans

6 Monitoring and Evaluation: the Impact of CPD 77
Monitoring • Evaluating impact • Models of evaluating impact • Spreading the impact • How schools have evaluated impact

List of Figures

List of Tables

Acknowledgements

We would like to thank all those who helped and contributed in some way to the writing of this book, particularly Graham Handscomb for writing Chapter 7, and Kevan Bleach, Tony Hill, Peter Taylor and Barry Wylliams for information about the management of professional development in their schools. We would also like to thank all the teachers who come on our CPD and higher degree courses. They stimulate thought and help keep our feet on the ground!

Most of all, we must thank our families – especially Paul, Julian, Miranda, Oliver, John and Diana, and Jackie, Amy and Jess – for their encouragement and tolerance.

Preface

This book been written for those who lead and manage continuing professional development (CPD). Continuing professional development co-ordinators hold a key role and one that needs to be developed further in many schools. We hope that this book helps people think more deeply about the professional development and training of staff – all staff – in schools. We hope, too, that it will lead to even better practice.

The last decade or so has seen a growing recognition, in schools and other organizations, that people matter and that attention must be given to their needs, especially those for their professional and personal development and growth. This is perhaps best epitomized by the government's emphasis on lifelong learning and the introduction in 2001 of a strategy for continuing professional development. Alongside this recognition of the importance of people there has been a growing awareness that schools do not always manage their staff – their human resources – as well as perhaps they might. The quality and quantity of professional development that individuals experience is hugely variable, largely depending on what school they are in. We hope that this book will help human resource development and the management and leadership of continuing professional development so that more people get a better deal.

In writing this book we have tried to do two things. First, we have summarized the most recent relevant research – some of which we have been personally involved in – to highlight the issues and current state of affairs. This gives a firm foundation for CPD co-ordinators leading and managing professional development. Secondly, we have given examples and case studies of good practice drawn from a wide range of schools.

The book is made up of two parts. After an introductory chapter which examines the notion of continuing professional development, locating it within the wider context of human resource development, Part I is entitled 'Professional development for school improvement'. We argue that individual professional development is crucially important and that the professional growth and learning of staff is crucial to school improvement. How adults and schools learn is the focus of Chapter 2, which also examines the notion of the learning community and effective professional development. It is important to remember that development cannot be forced and that teachers and other staff who are excited and motivated by the experience of their own learning are likely to communicate that excitement to the pupils.

What we know about effective leadership and management of CPD is the theme of Chapter 3 where the training and development cycle is introduced. This cycle – of needs identification, meeting the training and development needs of staff, and monitoring and evaluating the impact of CPD – forms the substance of the next three chapters, whilst the final chapter of Part I, written by Graham Handscomb, examines the importance of collaborative enquiry, the sharing of practice and the growth of the self-researching or the 'research-engaged' school. In all of these chapters, indeed throughout the book, we draw upon latest research and examples of good practice, where possible giving case studies and pen portraits from schools.

Part II of the book – 'Leading and managing the CPD of specific groups' – examines the implications of the training and development cycle for those who work in schools. We look at specific groups or categories in schools – support staff, newly qualified teachers (NQTs), teachers in the first five years, supply teachers, middle managers, school leaders and governors. The issues around their roles and development needs are considered and we suggest ways in which they might be met.

Although our focus is predominantly on schools we argue throughout the book that for CPD to be effective it has to be well led and managed at three levels, that of the school, the LEA and at a national level. The key goal of all educational organizations is pupil learning, whereas the ongoing learning of teachers, support staff and other employees is not always prioritized or adequately resourced. Creating a culture of learning is crucial and this is shaped essentially by the attitude and approach of school leaders and governors towards CPD. There is a need to ensure that individual or personal development is not marginalized as it is crucial to teacher effectiveness and thus to the success of the school. Schools need to achieve a healthy complementarity or interrelationship between system and individual needs – something that has been absent over the past decade or so. The balance needs to be right.

We hope those in schools who are responsible for leading and managing CPD will find the book helpful. For if one of the keys to effective CPD is to ensure it is effectively led and managed, then the role of CPD co-ordinators needs to be given the kudos and time it requires to be done well. The book has been written with this in mind.

Sara Bubb and Peter Earley
Institute of Education, University of London
September 2003

Abbreviations

AST	Advanced skills teacher
ASTITT	Advanced skills teacher for initial teacher training
BECTA	British Educational Communications and Technology Agency
BTEC	Business and Technology Education Council
CEA	Cambridge Education Associates
CEDP	Career Entry and Development Profile
CIPD	Chartered Institute of Personnel and Development
CPD	Continuing professional development
DfEE	Department for Education and Employment
DfES	Department for Education and Skills
DRB	Designated Recommending Bodies
EAL	English as an additional language
EDP	Education development plan
EFQM	European Foundation for Quality Management
EPD	Early professional development
ESS	Education Standard Spending
FLARE	Forum for Learning and Research Enquiry
GTC	General Teaching Council
GTP	Graduate Teacher Programme
HEADLAMP	Headteacher Leadership and Management Programme
HEI	Higher education institution
HIP	Headteacher Induction Programme
HMCI	Her Majesty's Chief Inspector
HMI	Her Majesty's Inspectorate
HoD	Head of department
HRD	Human resource development
HRM	Human resource management
ICT	Information and communications technology
IEP	Individual education plan (for pupils with SEN)
IiP	Investors in People
ILP	Individual learning plan
INSET	In-service education and training
IPDP	Individual professional development plans
IPPR	Institute of Public Policy Research
ITET	Initial teacher education and training
ITT	Initial Teacher Training
LEA	Local education authority
LftM	'Leading from the Middle'
LiG	Leadership Incentive Grant
LMS	Local management of schools

LPSH	Leadership Programme for Serving Headteachers
LSA	Learning support assistant
LSC	Learning and Skills Council
MFL	Modern foreign languages
MPS	Main pay scale
NAGM	National Association of Governors and Managers
NAHT	National Association of Head Teachers
NARIC	National Academic Recognition Information Centre
NC	National Curriculum
NCSL	National College for School Leadership
NCT	Non-contact time
NERF	National Education Research Forum
NFER	National Foundation for Educational Research
NLC	Networked Learning Communities
NPQH	National Professional Qualification for Headship
NVQ	National vocational qualification
NQT	Newly qualified teacher
Ofsted	Office for Standards in Education
OSHLI	Out of School Hours Learning Initiative
OTT	Overseas-trained teacher
PDC	Professional development centre
PDP	Professional development profile
PGCE	Postgraduate certificate in education
PM	Performance management
PSLN	Primary School Learning Network
QTS	Qualified teacher status
RB	Recommending body
RE	Religious education
SCITT	School-centred initial teacher training
SDP	School development plan
SEN	Special educational needs
SENCO	Special educational needs co-ordinator
SHA	Secondary Heads Association
SMT	Senior management team
SNA	Special needs assistant
STA	Specialist teacher assistant
SWOT	Strengths, weaknesses, opportunities and threats
TA	Teaching assistant
TDLB	Training development lead body
TES	*Times Educational Supplement*
TIPD	Teachers' international professional development
TPLF	*Teachers' Professional Learning Framework*
TTA	Teacher Training Agency
VRQ	Vocationally relevant qualification

CHAPTER ONE

Introduction: CPD Policy and Practice

- People matter
- What is continuing professional development?
- Is the focus on CPD new?
- Taking CPD seriously
- An entitlement to CPD
- Learning from other professions

The improvement of training and development of heads, teachers and support staff is high on both national and local educational agendas, particularly as delegated budgets and devolved funding have enabled all schools to become self-managing and increasingly autonomous. Teachers, researchers, policy analysts and politicians argue that teacher professionalism must increase if education is to improve. Throughout the western world, the professionalism of teachers has been placed under considerable pressure by the move towards centralized curricula and assessment, and the use of performance data and outcome measures as a means to account for and improve what goes on in classrooms.

This chapter provides the context and rationale for the book arguing strongly that for schools to improve urgent attention must be given to its main resource – its people. It attempts to define professional development and to show how, despite the recent introduction of a CPD strategy from the government (DfEE, 2001a), the focus on it is not new. This introductory chapter also provides a strong case or rationale for taking the management and leadership of CPD seriously, whilst also offering a framework for understanding CPD. Finally, it briefly considers a range of practices outside education before concluding that an entitlement to CPD or lifelong learning is the proper way forward and that all employees have a right to work in a learning community.

PEOPLE MATTER

Educational reform, especially over the last 15 years, has made imperative the need for urgent and high-quality staff development and training. Teachers have delivered unparalleled curricular change including the introduction of a 'National Curriculum' in 1988; Key Stage 2 literacy and numeracy strategies ten years later and, more recently, the Key

Stage 3 strategy, thus placing well-documented strain on the profession, and promoting national concerns about teacher recruitment, retention and morale. The pivotal role of teachers in the delivery of the government's reform agenda was acknowledged with the introduction in England in March 2001 of the CPD strategy where it was clearly stated that 'all our ambitions for education depend on teachers doing well in the classroom' (DfEE, 2001a: 3).

There is a growing recognition that the management and development of people – human resource management (HRM) and human resource development (HRD) – is more effective in enhancing the performance of organizations, including schools and colleges, than any other factor. For example, the Chartered Institute of Personnel and Development (CIPD) argue for the careful management of people as the prime resource of the organization, claiming that managers get better results (in terms of productivity, customer satisfaction, profitability and employee retention) by managing and developing people better. Within the sphere of education, Riches and Morgan were probably the first to recognize that the truly key and scarce organizational resource was not finance or money but excellent people when they stated:

> Of all the resources at the disposal of a person or an organisation it is only people who can grow and develop and be motivated to achieve certain desired ends. The attaining of targets for the organization is in *their* hands and it is the way *people* are managed so that maximum performance is matched as closely as possible with satisfaction for the individuals doing the performing, which is at the heart of HRM and optimum management. (1989: 1 original emphases)

People and their training and development – their continuing professional development – must be seen as an investment and it is therefore essential that each school establishes not only a CPD or HRD policy but also the means of its implementation through effective management and leadership. As funds and responsibilities are progressively transferred to schools they can be deployed in more varied and creative ways, leading to more responsive and effective systems of CPD. Schools and their governing bodies take the main responsibility for developing the quality, motivation and performance of their people – for managing and developing the human resources. The approach to CPD and its management presented in this book is to regard the training and development of staff as both a collective and individual responsibility – institutional and individual needs have to be regarded in a complementary and holistic way. Schools operating in this way are likely to have a better motivated and higher-performing workforce.

Schools that do not look after their staff's professional development usually lose the best teachers. The arguments for professional development are clear. We believe that it:

- helps everyone be more effective in their jobs, so pupils learn and behave better and achieve higher standards;

- improves retention and recruitment – word gets around about the places where you are looked after, and where you are not;

- contributes to a positive ethos where people feel valued and motivated;

- makes for a learning community – the pupils are learning and so are the staff;

- is a professional responsibility and entitlement;
- saves money – the costs of recruiting and inducting a new teacher into a school can be about £4,000.

If the expertise and experience of staff is increasingly seen as a school's most precious resource then the management and leadership of CPD must be seen as an integral part of managing the total resources available to the school. Some have linked CPD to targets as identified in both school development and personal development plans. In this way it is likely that an appropriate balance will be retained between school (and group) needs and the personal and professional needs of the individual. Teachers and other staff will always feel the need to be valued, and this should not be forgotten when considering the balance between identifying and meeting individual and institutional needs. The effective management of CPD should ensure that support is available and conditions created which enable staff to work together and to develop and improve their workplace performance. By headteachers, CPD co-ordinators and other staff helping to create a climate or culture which is conducive to learning – of both staff and pupils – schools are well on the road to becoming learning communities where investment in people is given the priority it deserves. Student learning is a key goal of all schools, whereas often the ongoing learning of teachers and other paid employees is not always prioritized or adequately resourced.

WHAT IS CONTINUING PROFESSIONAL DEVELOPMENT?

One of the hallmarks of being identified as a professional is to continue to learn throughout a career. The professions, broadly defined, now cover over 20 per cent of the workforce – more if managers are included – and most are employed in large companies or the public sector. They range from the well established and powerful to those who are still trying to establish their professional status. The strongest are those of over 80 professions regulated by law, public authority and royal charter, where membership or registration is necessary to practise. Continuing professional development has become the term widely used for ongoing education and training for the professions. If teaching is seen as a profession – and a case for this has long been argued – an important characteristic or hallmark of a member of a profession is the commitment shown towards self-improvement or development. This is not, however, for its own sake but to ensure that the beneficiaries or clients – in our case pupils and parents – are provided with the best possible service. The prime responsibility for securing individual professional development of teachers is not, however, the exclusive concern of the employer – teachers themselves must expect to play a key role – and professional development opportunities must be available for individuals to help them become better practitioners.

But what do we mean by the term CPD and is it different from *personal development* or *staff development* or *in-service education and training* (INSET)? Broadly speaking, continuing professional development encompasses all formal and informal learning that enables individuals to improve their own practice. Professional development is an aspect of personal development and, wherever possible, the two should interact and complement each other. The former is mainly about occupational role development, whereas personal development is about the development of the person, often the 'whole' person, and it almost always involves changes in self-awareness. As Waters explains: 'It is the development that can occur when teachers are construed first and foremost as people, and is predicted on the premise that people are always much more than the roles they play.' (1998: 30)

A definition of CPD might refer to: 'any professional development activities engaged in by teachers which enhance their knowledge and skills and enable them to consider their attitudes and approaches to the education of children, with a view to improve the quality of the teaching and learning process' (Bolam, 1993). In this sense it is perhaps little different to how some have defined in-service training or staff development. The seminal James Report (DES, 1972) defined INSET as: 'the whole range of activities by which teachers can extend their personal education, develop their professional competence and improve their understanding of education principles and techniques'.

An analysis of the literature does, however, reveal a number of nuances and slight differences for the different concepts used. A simple but most useful conceptual breakdown is offered by Bolam (1993) in his publication for the General Teaching Council. Bolam makes use of a threefold distinction among:

- *professional training*, for example, short courses, workshops and conferences emphasizing practical information and skills;

- *professional education*, for example, long courses and secondments emphasizing theory and research-based knowledge;

- *professional support*, for example, activities that aim to develop on the job experience and performance.

Continuing professional development is an ongoing process building upon initial teacher training (ITT) and induction, including development and training opportunities throughout a career and concluding with preparation for retirement. At different times and at different stages one or other may be given priority, but the totality can be referred to as continuing professional development. Development – as noted earlier – is about improvement, both individual and school improvement

Continuing professional development embraces those education, training and support activities engaged in by teachers following their initial certification which aim to:

- add to their professional knowledge;

- improve their professional skills;

- help clarify their professional values;

- enable pupils to be educated more effectively (Bolam, 1993).

In their survey of continuing education for the professions, Madden and Mitchell (1993) state that CPD can fulfil three functions:

- updating and extending the professional's knowledge and skills on new developments and new areas of practice – to ensure continuing competence in the current job;

- training for new responsibilities and for a changing role (for example, management, budgeting, teaching) – developing new areas of competence in preparation for a more senior post;

- developing personal and professional effectiveness and increasing job satisfaction – increasing competence in a wider context with benefits to both professional and personal roles.

Day has noted how most definitions of professional development stress its main purpose as being the acquisition of subject or content knowledge and teaching skills, whereas for him it must go beyond these:

> Professional development consists of all natural learning experiences and those conscious and planned activities that are intended to be of direct or indirect benefit to the individual, group or school and which contribute, through these, to the quality of education in the classroom. It is the process by which, alone and with others, teachers review, renew and extend their commitment as change agents to the moral purposes of teaching; and by which they acquire and develop critically the knowledge, skills, and emotional intelligence essential to good professional thinking, planning and practice with children, young people and colleagues through each phase of their teaching lives. (1999: 4)

More recently, the government in launching its strategy for professional development offers a further, albeit succinct, definition when it states: 'By "professional development" we mean any activity that increases the skills, knowledge or understanding of teachers, and their effectiveness in schools' (DfEE, 2001a: 3). What is central to the success of the strategy is the need for staff to work in schools with collaborative cultures, where there is a commitment to improving teaching and learning and, in the words of the department, where there is 'learning from and with other teachers' (DfEE, 2001a: 6). Learning on the job and learning from the best are key characteristics of the CPD strategy – issues which are further explored in later chapters.

To summarize, CPD is an ongoing process of education, training, learning and support activities which is:

- taking place in either external or work-based settings;
- engaged in by qualified, educational professionals;
- aimed mainly at promoting learning and development of their professional knowledge, skills and values;
- to help decide and implement valued changes in their teaching and learning behaviour so that they can educate their students more effectively thus achieving an agreed balance between individual, school and national needs (based on Bolam, 2002).

It is clear that long gone are the days when initial training and induction were seen as a total or final preparation for a career in teaching; nowadays they have to be seen as merely providing a platform on which further or continuing professional development will be built. Nevertheless, the initial period in teaching is crucial as the experience of the first year is most formative. There is therefore a need to set high expectations and standards when there is the greatest receptiveness and willingness to learn and develop. It is during the induction period, for example, that the support of others is crucial if new entrants to the profession are to develop the competences, the confidence and the attitudes that will serve as the basis for ongoing professional development.

Perhaps the single most important feature of CPD is to encourage and promote a commitment on the part of the individual to professional growth. Leading and managing people development – making CPD work – therefore means providing structures and procedures to co-ordinate developmental opportunities so as to promote such growth and to help staff develop and improve their workplace performance.

IS THE FOCUS ON CPD NEW?

The formation in September 1994 of the Teacher Training Agency (TTA) and, more recently, the launch of the government's CPD strategy in March 2001, meant both initial teacher training or education and CPD have attracted much attention. But these ideas about the central importance of CPD to the teaching profession are not new, although they are of fairly recent origin:

> The first national enquiry into in-service education training was not mounted until 1970, which seems to suggest that it had broadly been assumed that initial education and training would suffice for a professional lifetime. It is an assumption rooted in a view, perhaps held subconsciously rather than formalized as 'policy', that the task of the teacher remained constant. (H. Tomlinson, 1993)

The James Report, published over 30 years ago, was aware of the need to change such outmoded views and recognize the social and cultural changes that were affecting the education system. As a result, the further professional development of teachers became a national issue. The report, which is perhaps best known for its suggestion that teachers should be entitled to the equivalent of one term's release for training and development every seven years, stressed the importance of in-service education and training, and stated that each school should regard the continued training of its teachers as an essential part of its task for which all members of staff share responsibility. Every school was seen as needing a 'professional tutor' to co-ordinate training and development, and to compile and maintain 'a training programme for the staff of the school, which would take account of the curricular needs of the school and of the professional needs of the teachers' (DES, 1972). As Williams (1993) notes in his overview of changing policies and practices, the strength of these proposals was their focus on teachers and schools, seeing responsibility for CPD to be that of individual teachers and the schools in which they worked.

The James Report also made reference to the now widely used and accepted continuum of professional development – the so-called 'three Is' of initial teacher training, induction and INSET. Continuing professional development should ensure that individuals progress from 'novice' or 'advanced beginner' status to that of an 'expert'. However, expert status is not a once and for all achievement. It is ongoing – new demands, a changing curriculum and various other changes mean that learning and development is never ending.

At the time of the James Report, training and development was seen very much as the individual's concern and it was not perceived as important by all teachers or their employers, the local education authorities (LEAs). The report was followed by a number of policy and discussion documents, culminating in what has been termed 'the INSET revolution' so that now CPD has 'gradually become a priority within the education system paralleling the rise of "human resource development" in other large organisations in the public and private sectors' (Oldroyd and Hall, 1991). The point has been made, however, that the predominant view of INSET over the recent past is that it is centrally funded and used largely to 'retool' and 'retrain' teachers so they can 'deliver' the government's reforms, particularly those associated with the 1988 Education Reform Act and the strategies for literacy, numeracy and Key Stage 3. John Tomlinson, for example, identifies the early 1980s as a turning point: 'between a time when INSET was almost entirely left to be pursued by the individual teacher and the present view that it must also, indeed predominantly, serve the needs of the schools and the system as well as the personal or professional development of the individual' (1993). We shall return in a later chapter to this shifting emphasis of CPD provision and consider how the needs of the 'system', the 'institution' and the 'individual' might be catered for.

TAKING CPD SERIOUSLY

Continuing professional development has to be seen as a collective responsibility – the responsibility of both individual teachers and the schools in which they work. Individuals and their places of employment should take joint responsibility for professional development and training, which should be for the benefit of both. Recently, growing attention has been given to organizational 'cultures' and the emphasis that may or may not be given to the training and development or the 'learning' of its members. The experience and expertise of staff – both teaching and support – is generally recognized to be the school's most important and most expensive resource (Earley, 1995). The term 'learning community' or 'learning organization' is becoming more commonly known and attempts are being made – through such initiatives as Investors in People and the most recent inspection framework (Ofsted, 2003a) – to ensure that more schools are aware of what this means for themselves. Leading and managing people and their development have to be seen as a central part of the responsibility of managing the school's total resources.

A learning community is sensitive to its environment and constantly evolving, making use of the skills and talents of all of its people to greatest benefit. As Watkins and Drury (1994) state it is:

> an organization which learns and which wants its people to learn, ensures that the conditions for learning and for response to change are such that the aspirations of the individual, the team, and the organisation are in tune. It develops a learning culture where learning and development are valued and seen as an integral part of effective performance, and where people are regarded as assets rather than costs to be reduced.

The term is particularly appropriate to education. In a school, for instance, the question has to be asked how can the idea of learning be central to it if its own staff are not engaged in that process themselves? There are two groups of learners within schools – young people and adults – and we neglect either at our peril. If teachers and other staff are not seen as continuous learners by the school itself, how can adults engage youngsters in any meaningful pursuit of learning?

As any teacher who has worked in more than one school will attest, the training and development culture may be quite different from one establishment to another. In some schools teachers' ongoing professional development is seen as integral, given great significance and very closely linked to the school development plan (SDP). In such places there is an expectation that individuals and their managers will take a collective responsibility for both individual and institutional development. In this sense 'good schools' are said to make 'good teachers' as much as the other way around. A school wishing to become a learning community would therefore take its CPD responsibilities most seriously and strive to secure effective learning for both its pupils and staff. It would subscribe heavily to a development culture and give training and development – and its effective leadership and management – a high priority.

Investors in People – a national standard for training and development – is at the fore-front in helping schools to embrace a development culture and become 'learning' communities or 'thinking' schools. The learning community is capable of developing itself and its workforce, and a culture of training and development – of CPD – will imbue the school and be embedded in both its structures and processes. By the end of 2002, that over 26 per cent of schools have been awarded Investors in People status is a formal recognition of this. Chapter 3 considers Investors in People in more detail.

AN ENTITLEMENT TO CPD

The notion of an entitlement to CPD is something that has been promoted in England and Wales by the General Teaching Council. It sees an entitlement to professional development as 'career long and sustained so that on entry to the profession a teacher has a clear expectation of continuing, relevant and planned professional development'. England's General Teaching Council (GTC) has drawn up an entitlement to professional learning within its *Teachers' Professional Learning Framework* (*TPLF*) that was published in March 2003 (GTC, 2003b). The GTC believes that there should be a personal entitlement to professional development throughout a teacher's career and one that is not linked solely to school targets.

Teachers need the opportunity to:

- Have structured time to engage in sustained reflection and structured learning;
- Create learning opportunities from everyday practice such as planning and assessing for learning;
- Develop their ability to identify their own learning and development needs and those of others;
- Develop an individual learning plan;
- Have school-based learning as well as course participation, recognized for accreditation;
- Develop self-evaluation, observation and peer review skills;
- Develop mentoring and coaching skills and their ability to offer professional dialogue and feedback;
- Plan their longer-term career aspirations. (GTC, 2003b: 6).

So, there is a great lever for professional development in the *Teachers' Professional Learning Framework* but, as noted earlier, any teacher who has worked in more than one school will know that the training and development culture may vary from one school to another. Carol Adams, the chief executive of the GTC (England), is clear about the need for a high quality CPD entitlement:

> First of all the GTC is arguing for a lifelong entitlement for teachers to replace the current, rather hit and miss arrangements. For this entitlement to be convincing to teachers, there needs to be recognition of the myriad of equal opportunity issues that affect teacher partici-pation e.g. if CPD is in twilight hours there needs to be provision or funding for childcare. If

CPD opportunities fall outside part timers' hours there needs to be flexibility to enable and encourage them to participate.

Next we need to transform the meaning of CPD so that teachers and providers come to see it as lifelong access to high quality experiences that enhance teaching for teachers and learning for learners; opportunities for teachers' needs to be met as and when they arise. This model stands in stark contrast with one of being 'sent' on a course. Activities like observing teaching and learning in a range of colleagues' classes is valued by teachers and those who lead them and is an important component in GTC's vision. (in Cordingley, 2001)

In Wales the GTC considers that teachers and employers have different but complementary responsibilities in relation to CPD (see Jones, 2003):

- *employers* – to provide professional development opportunities for teachers to support a broad range of priorities which occur during the normal work cycle and an entitlement to professional development which focuses on the individual professional and personal needs and objectives of the teacher is emphasized;

- *teachers* – to develop themselves as 'reflective professionals' by reflecting on their work and by identifying new ways of working. These activities should be undertaken as part of a teachers' work.

The GTC argues that teachers need CPD opportunities based on three priority areas (see Figure 1.1):

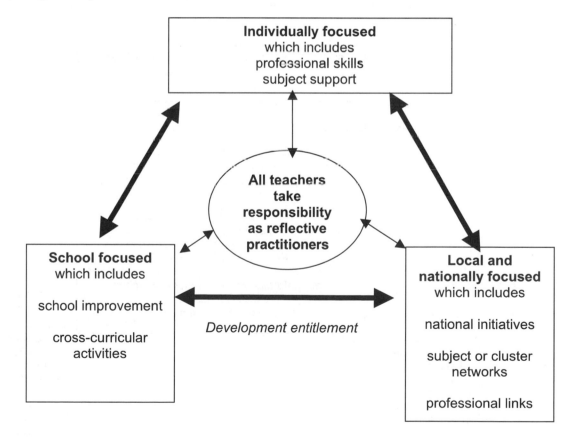

FIGURE 1.1 CONTINUING PROFESSIONAL DEVELOPMENT FRAMEWORK (JONES, 2003: 37)

■ *Individually focused* – these activities should focus on a teacher's own needs and be identified by the individual teacher as supporting their professional development and/or career objectives. Appropriate CPD activities might include attending courses, mentoring, developing a new teaching activity, exchanging ideas and good practice with colleagues, and exchange visits.

■ *School focused* – these activities should primarily be targeted at the requirements of the school that currently employs the teacher. The CPD requirements would be identified from the school development plan and relevant activities should largely be undertaken during the statutory non-pupil contact days, with any additional identified school-focused activities financed from school budgets.

■ *National/LEA (including diocesan authorities) focused* – these CPD activities would meet the demands of national and local initiatives. They could involve activities organized on cross-school basis such as cluster meetings or around a national priority.

As Jones notes, 'teachers require a career-long entitlement to professional development opportunities, with clear opportunities for teachers at different stages of their careers' (2003: 38). The advice from the GTC (Wales) proposes a continuum of opportunity from initial teacher education and training (ITET) throughout a teacher's career (see Figure 1.2).

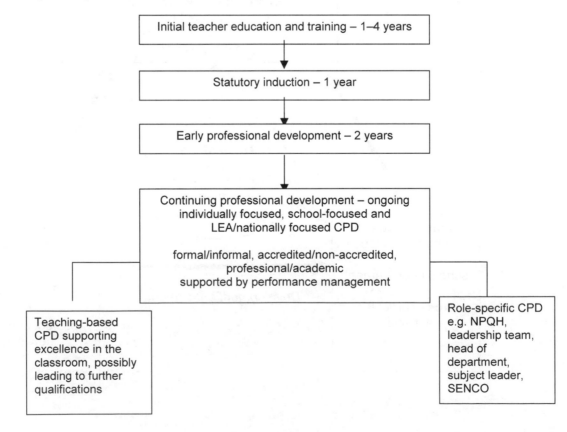

FIGURE 1.2 A CAREER-LONG PROFESSIONAL DEVELOPMENT ENTITLEMENT (JONES, 2003: 38)

An entitlement to CPD is a notion whose time has clearly come! The rest of this book is devoted to an analysis and portrayal of the key areas and issues around the successful leadership and management of continuing professional development, a better understanding of which it is hoped will help realize that entitlement.

RESPONSIBILITIES

Professional development is a responsibility throughout teachers' careers, as can be seen in the *Teachers' Standards Framework* (DfES, 2001a). One of the standards that people have to meet in order to get qualified teacher status (QTS) is that:

> 1.7 They are able to improve their own teaching, by evaluating it, learning from the effective practice of others and from evidence. They are motivated and able to take increasing responsibility for their own professional development. (TTA, 2002a: 6)

In order to pass induction teachers have to:

Show a commitment to their professional development by:

- identifying areas in which they need to improve their professional knowledge, understanding and practice in order to teach more effectively in their current post, and
- with support, taking steps to address these needs.

(DfES, 2003: 43)

The threshold standards require people to have 'wider professional effectiveness' and be able to demonstrate that they:

- take responsibility for their professional development and use the outcomes to improve their teaching and pupils' learning, and
- make an active contribution to the policies and aspirations of the school.

With the change of emphasis on the importance of training and development and the greater control from the centre, there has been a corresponding move towards a higher degree of prescription and statutory requirements regarding CPD. The late 1980s, for example, saw the introduction of the Teachers Pay and Conditions of Service Act (1987), which for the first time specified teachers' professional duties. These included, amongst many other things, 'participating in arrangements for his [sic] further training and professional development as a teacher'. It did not, however, make it a statutory requirement for teachers 'to show any official evidence of developing, updating or even maintaining their professional knowledge and competence' (Tomlinson, H., 1993). The legislation also introduced the notion of 'directed' time (1,265 hours) and 'non-contact' days. The latter – consisting of five days when teachers met without pupils being on site – were for the purpose of preparation, planning, assessment, review and in-service training. Research into the use of these five days – of which at least three are recommended to be used for CPD – suggests that, initially, they had not always been used productively by schools (Harland et al., 1999). Although matters have improved, there is still much variation in how effectively these training days are being used for development purposes, an area of interest to the TTA and the Department for Education and Skills (DfES) as it investigates the cost-effectiveness of the estimated £400+ million spent annually on teacher development.

How schools and teachers are making use of their non-contact or training days is one of the areas considered by the Office for Standards in Education (Ofsted) team during its inspection of the school. An examination of the framework for the inspection of schools or the inspection handbook shows that matters to do with CPD are included. Section 8 on 'How well is the school led and managed?' asks whether 'a commitment to staff development is reflected in effective induction, professional development strategies and, where possible, the school's contribution to initial teacher training' (Ofsted, 2003a: 34). However, CPD is still not given the prominence or priority it deserves. Perhaps Investors in People – which is exclusively about training and development (and not only for teachers) – provides a most useful complement to an Ofsted inspection. However, whereas the regular inspection cycle is compulsory and underpinned by legislation, involvement in Investors in People is entirely voluntary.

LEARNING FROM OTHER PROFESSIONS

What about other professions? What is their situation regarding CPD? In their survey of 20 professional bodies, Madden and Mitchell (1993) found that 14 of them had a policy on CPD. Only one, the Royal Institute of Chartered Surveyors, specified mandatory CPD for all its members, although others (for example, the Law Society) had consulted members and are likely to introduce mandatory CPD in the near future. Some bodies, such as the Royal Institute of British Architects, have an obligatory requirement that members undertake certain amounts of CPD each year. The survey found that 13 of the 20 professional bodies specified a certain number of hours of CPD – a median of 30 hours a year.

They highlight three main areas regarding effective CPD:

    A. Policy and conditions for CPD;

    B. CPD provision;

    C. Monitoring, quality assurance and evaluation.

Within the above they identify 12 key factors from which the following extracts are taken (see Figure 1.3). You might like to give consideration to each factor in turn as a way of auditing current practice in your school.

Professional bodies can be located on a continuum from full mandatory CPD requirements to individuals taking responsibility voluntarily for their own ongoing development. Teachers are perhaps found somewhere in the middle of the continuum. The 'old and established' professions are more likely to be at the voluntary end, emphasizing the autonomy and responsibility of their members. This led Madden and Mitchell (1993) to suggest that there were two main models of CPD in the professions – the sanctions and benefits models.

Within the teaching profession there has been no shortage of calls for CPD to be taken more seriously, whether as a reward (the benefits model) or compliance (the sanctions model) and for certain 'entitlements' to be enshrined in legislation. However, the problem with any voluntary scheme is that those with most to gain from CPD are often the least likely to do so, whilst mandatory policies may lead to a lack of individuality, although the latter do ensure all members have the opportunity to develop.

A. POLICY AND CONDITIONS FOR CPD

1. Policy
It is important to have a policy on CPD that defines its aims and describes how these will be implemented. Its content may vary greatly to suit particular needs but it is stronger where it provides for structured, systematic CPD throughout a professional's career, and where there is a continuum of initial and continuing professional education. It should also prepare practitioners for the changes facing their professions.

2. Analysis of professional competence
Analysis of professional competence, a generic term, is a useful basis for planned CPD.

3. Good CPD culture
This includes several factors which emerged as important in establishing an environment favourable to CPD:
i. the establishment of a positive CPD attitude by all parties and acceptance of the idea of CPD throughout the working life, i.e. lifelong learning.
ii. to inculcate the need for continuous learning into new practitioners during their initial professional education and, ideally, to establish a synthesis of initial and continuing education;
iii. to give practitioners the ability to learn effectively, i.e. by applying the knowledge of cognitive psychologists to the needs of the practitioner and CPD provision. Adult learning is about learning to learn rather than simply being taught.
iv. to provide expert support and guidance on CPD issues for all parties and especially for the practitioners.

B. CPD PROVISION

4. Range of CPD options
A wide range of CPD options should be recognized, both informal and formal.
Whatever the choice, it seems desirable that any CPD undertaken should be part of a structured CPD framework to meet longer-term professional goals.

5. Teaching
Teaching methods should be appropriate to the professional students and should incorporate the implications of the research into adult learning (e.g. the importance of reflecting and the experiential learning cycle). Emphasis should be placed on increasing practitioners' competence in practice and on the close interaction of CPD and work.

6. CPD content
Attention should be given to both updating and extending knowledge and to enhancing practitioners' skills to increase professional competence. While updating and extending knowledge is very important, CPD must also enhance skills. Analysis of professional competence can form the basis for decisions of CPD for all parties.

7. Providers and partners
CPD may be offered by a wide range of providers, especially the employer, the professional bodies, higher education and appropriate private providers.

8. Forms of CPD
Where, when and how CPD is provided must be determined to suit the professional practitioner. The emphasis is on flexibility.

9. Promoting and marketing CPD
It is important to persuade practitioners of the value of CPD. To show, for example, how it might meet individuals' requirements as well as those of employers and the professional bodies.

10. Cost
At one level it can be argued that this involves a straight-forward cost-benefit analysis, with on the one hand the cost of undertaking CPD (in money and time) and on the other the cost of not doing so both in terms of reduced professional effectiveness and even incompetence.

C. MONITORING, QUALITY ASSURANCE AND EVALUATION

11. Monitoring of practitioners' CPD
For professional bodies that operate a mandatory CPD policy there is a need for CPD activities to be recorded by those required to comply and for the amount and type of CPD undertaken to be monitored.

12. Quality assurance and the evaluation of CPD provision
Very few professional bodies make an attempt at serious evaluation of CPD providers or provision and devolve this responsibility to the practitioner (and so implicitly to the employer). Developments by professional bodies in CPD evaluation seem desirable

FIGURE 1.3 THREE AREAS OF CPD EFFECTIVENESS (AFTER MADDEN AND MITCHELL, 1993: 68-9)

CONCLUSION

Continuing professional development is about professional lifelong learning which will help us respond to ever-changing situations and exercise judgement in informed and creative ways but, as Pachler and Field remind us, it should also be seen as a means for us 'to rejuvenate practice, to expand our professional repertoire, increase our self-esteem, self-confidence and enthusiasm for teaching or, for example, our level of criticality and, thereby, achieve enhanced job satisfaction' (2004: 2). This book is about all of these and more!

PART I: PROFESSIONAL DEVELOPMENT FOR SCHOOL IMPROVEMENT

CHAPTER TWO

Learning People – Learning Schools

- How adults learn
- Professional learning communities
- What is effective CPD?
- The Standards Framework
- Collaboration

Professional development is crucial for organizational growth and school improvement. The professional growth of teachers and other staff is a key component of developing children's learning. Over a decade ago Roland Barthes a former US principal and well-known writer on school improvement remarked: 'Probably nothing within a school has more impact on students in terms of skills development, self-confidence, or classroom behaviour than the personal and professional development of their teachers' (1990: 49). This is quite an assertion, but the fundamental point he was making has been supported by research and inspection evidence. But how does adult development and learning occur and is there anything different about how adults learn compared to children? What do we know about how adults best learn? Also what sort of organizational settings and cultures are most conducive to adult or teacher development and growth? What do we know about learning organizations or communities of learners? How do staff and schools learn? These questions form the main themes of this chapter.

HOW ADULTS LEARN

Thinking about how adults learn is crucial for anyone involved in CPD. The way that we understand learning will affect the provision of activities we make for people to learn, and the accuracy of our understanding will affect the effectiveness of the learning that takes place. Those who work in schools and other educational organizations come from a variety of backgrounds and experiences. This needs to be recognized and built upon. Adults have a wide variety of previous experiences, knowledge, skills, interests and competences. Some prefer informal learning situations others more formal ones. So how teachers and other adults learn is therefore as important, if not more important, than what they learn. The American writer Knowles (1984) who was the first to use the term 'andragogy' (as opposed to pedagogy) noted the following characteristics of adult learners:

- They are largely self-directed and require a climate of trust, openness, respect and collaboration to learn effectively.

- The previous experience of the learner has to be implicit in the learning process (it is too significant to ignore).

- The adult learner needs to accept the need to learn.

- They are biased towards problem-solving as a learning activity.

- Practical relevance is a significant factor in gaining commitment.

- They only internalize learning if motivated by intrinsic factors.

It is interesting to reflect on how many of these characteristics are found in most educational organizations.

Eileen Carnell, as part of research conducted over six years, found that teachers said that effective learning experiences:

- are linked inextricably with teachers' day to day work contexts, for example, in the classroom or working with groups of colleagues in their school;

- are challenging, developmental and take place over an extended period of time;

- arise when teachers feel in control, have ownership, develop shared aims and reciprocity – supporting and being supported by respected colleagues;

- are participatory; the more teachers are engaged in activities and the more interaction with colleagues, the more effective the activities are seen;

- are practical and relevant with opportunities for reflection, learning and change;

- happen in a trusting, non-hierarchical environment;

- include pupil and peer learning dialogue;

- occur when teachers work together in social exchange, reflecting, planning and developing actions for change;

- focus explicitly on their own learning. (2001: 44)

The most appropriate model for thinking about teachers' professional development is one based on experiential learning. This stresses the importance of workplace learning and learning by doing, sharing, reviewing and applying. Dennison and Kirk (1990) talk about a learning cycle of 'do, review, learn and apply' that is illustrated in Figure 2.1. So, someone who wants to get better at taking assembly, for instance, might usefully go through the cycle in this way:

Do	Observe someone that I admire take assembly.
Review	Think about it and discuss it with them afterwards.
Learn	Learn some key techniques for taking assembly.
Apply	Try them out when I take assembly.
Do	Get someone to observe me taking assembly and give me feedback.

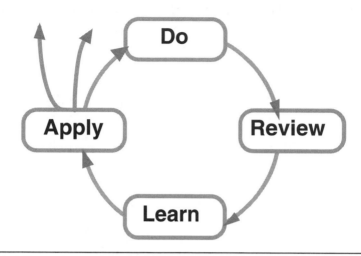

FIGURE 2.1 A LEARNING CYCLE (DENNISON AND KIRK, 1990)

LEARNING STYLES

Howard Gardner's theory of multiple intelligences and our awareness of children who are predominantly visual, auditory or kinaesthetic learners is useful in our teaching. Similarly, different adults learn in different ways and have preferred learning styles. Probably the best known analysis of this is that of Honey and Mumford (1986). They identify four types of learners who prefer to learn in different ways:

- theorists;
- pragmatists;
- activists;
- reflectors.

The theorist likes to learn using abstract conceptualization and reflective observation (lectures, papers, analogies) and ask such questions as: 'How does this relate to that?' Training approach: case studies, theory readings, thinking alone.

The pragmatist likes to learn using abstract conceptualization and active experimentation (laboratories, fieldwork, observations). Pragmatists ask: 'How can I apply this in practice?' Training approach: peer feedback and activities that apply skills.

The activist likes to learn using concrete experience and active experimentation (simulations, case studies, homework). Activists tell themselves: 'I'm game for anything.' Training approach: practising the skill, problem-solving, small group discussions, peer feedback.

The reflector likes to learn using reflective observation and concrete experience (logs, journals, brainstorming). Reflectors like time to think about the subject. Training approach: lectures with plenty of reflection time.

Honey and Mumford (2000) have a questionnaire designed to help people pinpoint their learning preferences so that they are in a better position to select learning experiences that suit them. Few people fall neatly into one category, but have a leaning towards one or two. However, it is useful for teachers to know where their preferences lie and for people organizing professional development to take this into account. For some people the form of the training activity may be a significant factor, if this is not compatible with the way an individual learns then they may be hostile to the content or message of the training.

The difference between the learning of most adults and the learning of teachers is significant because it relates so closely to their core activity at work – helping others to learn. It is analogous to the health of doctors. If individual teachers understand how they learn and can appreciate that others have different learning styles, then they will be more able to support the learning of both young people and colleagues.

People learn in different ways and have preferred learning styles but learning takes place in a variety of ways and in different settings. It can be formal or informal, within the workplace or off site. Types of informal learning for example could be:

- planned – but other things may be learned too;

- reactive and unplanned – the day-to-day learning from doing;

- implicit – learning that the individual is unaware of, but which has taken place and which others may notice (Williams, 2002).

One can also think of learning in vertical and horizontal dimensions:

- vertical – knowing more, new learning and experiences;

- horizontal – the same knowledge applied in different contexts, deeper understanding.

So teachers do not always have to learn new things to be developing professionally.

There is no easy answer to the question 'what needs to be done to help adults better learners?' but the following are worth asking:

- How open are individuals to new experiences?

- Are they seen as opportunities for learning?

- Do individuals learn from mistakes that may have been made?

- Is becoming a better learner largely a state of mind?

- Does the school help or hinder learning?

For change to occur in teachers' practices then priority must be given to the personal resources and capacity for learning of individual teachers. Responding to new demands requires a range of skills and qualities (for example, problem-solving, stress management, interpersonal skills) and effective CPD is about empowering staff so they can prepare for change. It is as much concerned with:

- the affective as the cognitive;

- process skills as with outcomes;

- personal growth as much as technical competence (West-Burnham and O'Sullivan, 1998).

■ LEARNING TEACHERS

The role of CPD in the development of learning communities has focused discussion on the ways in which teachers learn most successfully. Eileen Carnell has drawn up features of teachers who make good progress in their learning (see Table 2.1).

TABLE 2.1 CHARACTERISTICS OF LEARNING TEACHERS

Learning teachers	Explanation
... have a lifelong commitment to learning and change	This commitment is evidenced in teachers' willingness to take risks and promote new ideas. There is concern to seek out ways to improve professional growth, including evidence of a system for continuous, inquiry and complex decision-making. They keep up with professional knowledge and new conceptions; they grow personally as well as professionally.
... collaborate with young people and colleagues	Learning teachers create collaborative working relationships with pupils and colleagues. They are able to maintain collegial support groups and manage the classroom in collaboration with pupils. They are able to demonstrate reciprocity, self-disclosure and mutual respect.
... have a commitment to increasing the effectiveness of teaching and learning	This commitment is exhibited in their strong motivation to be involved in things they care about, their ways of creating more adaptive ways of teaching and learning and in their ability to reflect and understand assumptions, beliefs and values. This commitment includes understanding and respecting the diversity of their pupils.
... have a holistic, multi-perspective view of teaching, young people and relationships	Taking a holistic view of teaching and learning requires seeing pupils as whole human beings. Understanding interactions and the impact of interactions upon one's self and others is important as is self-knowledge and the ability to think critically. Teachers who take a holistic view exhibit empathy, flexibility and high levels of humane and democratic values, appreciate multiple possibilities, multiple perspectives and interdependency of relationships. They encourage complex learning.

Source: Carnell, 2001: 49

People need time after any development activity to consolidate thoughts into new and novel contexts. Small-scale action research or teacher practitioner projects undertaken after the development activity are likely to have a powerful impact on teachers, something we will discuss in Chapter 7. The Ofsted report on CPD (2002a) also draws attention to the importance of preparation time before professional development, and consolidation time afterwards.

The Hay Group's 'iceberg' model of the effective teacher (see Figure 2.2) is useful in illustrating the importance of a solid foundation of professional characteristics. Professional development that affects these will be very powerful.

A key task of managers of CPD is to encourage and develop 'learning teachers' and to facilitate planned learning and development opportunities, recognizing a variety of learning styles and approaches to learning. This can be done in a variety of ways but especially by offering:

- a structured programme of on-the-job, close-to-the-job and off-the-job opportunities;
- teacher research and enquiry;
- a culture of development within which staff feel valued in the job they do.

All of the above are likely to be found within professional learning communities.

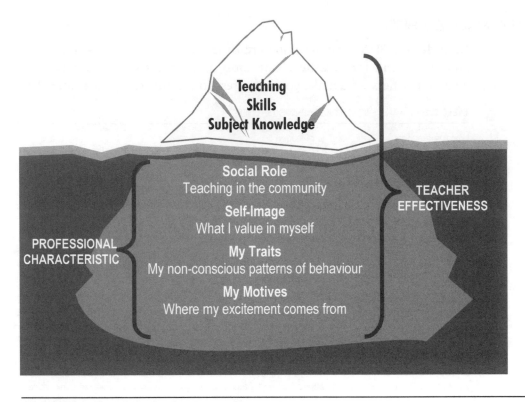

FIGURE 2.2: THE ICEBERG MODEL (AFTER HAY McBER, 2000)

PROFESSIONAL LEARNING COMMUNITIES

Training and development cultures differ; they may be quite different from one establishment to another. In some schools or departments within schools the ongoing professional development of all staff is seen as integral, given great significance and is very closely linked to the school development plan. In other places nothing could be further from the truth. In the most effective schools, the adults are learning and collaborating, as are the pupils – they are learning communities. Such schools have a positive impact on pupils' learning and benefits are usually found in teachers' work lives, classroom practice and in improvement in general across the school. The GTC believes that: 'Teachers who collaborate, learn together, share ideas and model best practice are more likely to remain in teaching. They feel valued and supported in their development and in their work' (GTCE, 2003: 3).

A learning community is constantly evolving, making use of the skills and talents of its entire people to greatest benefit. The importance of professional development cannot be overstated and a learning community would subscribe heavily to a development culture and give training and development – and its effective leadership and management – a high priority. Leaders of such communities engender an ethos that all pupils, teachers and support staff in a school are seen as learners in their own right. They also seek everyone's views and involve all in decision-making processes, supporting, developing and empowering them to feel a sense of ownership in the future direction of their organization. Teachers and others working in such communities will discuss their work openly and seek to improve and develop their pedagogy through collaborative enquiry and the sharing of good practice. Can we ensure that what may be an effective learning environment in the classroom is mirrored in the staffroom or school as a whole?

An early example of research into the nature of learning communities – although they were not labelled as such – was that of the American educational researcher Susan Rosenholz (1989). In her classic study she identified two types of school, what she referred to as 'moving' schools and 'stuck' schools. The former were 'learning enriched' and the latter 'learning impoverished' (see Table 2.2).

TABLE 2.2 TYPES OF 'LEARNING' SCHOOLS

'Learning impoverished'	'Learning enriched'
• Teacher isolation	• Collaboration and sharing
• Teachers compete with each other	• Continuous teacher talk about practice
• Lack of positive feedback	• A common focus
• Pulling in different directions	• A sense of efficacy
• Avoidance of risk-taking	• A belief in lifelong learning
• A sense of powerlessness	• Looking out as well as in
• Made to do CPD	• Focus on improving things for pupils
• Professional development treated negatively	• Feedback is welcomed
	• Safe to take risks and try out new things
	• Teachers share values

Source: adapted from Rosenholz, 1989

Rosenholtz's simple twofold classification of schools has since been developed further by those researchers interested in school effectiveness and school improvement. Using the four headings of effective and ineffective, and improving and declining, a number of categories have been defined such as 'coasting' or 'cruising', 'struggling' or 'sinking' and 'strolling' schools (see Stoll and Fink, 1996).

The importance of this classification of schools is perhaps clearer when we consider the question posed by another American educationist, Judith Warren Little. She remarked: 'Imagine that you could become a better teacher just by virtue of being on the staff of a particular school – just that fact alone' (Little, 1990). This is a key question, but how is a school transformed from one type ('learning impoverished') to another ('learning enriched)', particularly when the members of 'stuck' schools may be quite happy and not wish to move? How can a professional learning community be established? What is known about teacher or adult learning is important here.

The isolation that most teachers experience needs to be replaced with a climate that encourages observation, sharing teaching strategies, trying out new ways of teaching, getting feedback, and redesigning curriculum and methods of instruction (Bezzina, 2002). People in such groups become a 'community of practice' (Wenger, 1998).

There are five key characteristics of effective professional learning communities:

1 Shared values and vision directed towards the learning of all pupils, and greater reliance on the collectivity to reinforce objectives, rather than on individual autonomy.

2 Collective responsibility for pupil learning, helping to sustain staff

commitment, putting peer pressure on those who do not do their fair share and holding them to account, and easing teachers' sense of isolation.

3 Reflective professional inquiry as an integral part of work, including ongoing conversations about educational issues, frequent examining of practice with colleagues, mutual observation, joint planning and curriculum development. Through frequently interacting, staff convert individual unspoken, or tacit, knowledge into shared knowledge, applying new ideas and information to problem-solving to meet pupils' needs.

4 Collaboration in developmental activities directed towards achieving a shared purpose which generates mutual professional learning, reaching beyond superficial exchanges of help, support, or assistance.

5 Group, as well as individual, learning is promoted in that professional learning is more frequently communal rather than solitary, and all teachers are learners with their colleagues (Stoll et al., 2003: 3).

The following play an important role:

- school-based formal professional development opportunities – a solid basis of expert knowledge and skills and practical tools for implementing CPD (for example, professional development profiles, coaching and mentoring);

- work-based and incidental learning opportunities, based on theories of adult learning (for example, experimenting with and reflecting on pedagogical practices, experiential learning, problem-based learning and meta-learning);

- teamwork at both group and whole-school level (for example, problem-solving and creative activities within departments, key stage and pastoral groups, strategic leadership groups, teams developing whole-school policies or leading school improvement activities);

- self-evaluation and inquiry, action research, and using evidence to inform practice (for example, autumn package, Ofsted reports, pupil and teacher surveys, assessment of pupils' progress, eliciting feedback from parents);

- partnerships with people from LEAs, higher education, local businesses, and so on, involving a rethinking of the way each institution operates as well as how staff might work as part of this partnership;

- external professional development opportunities, including LEA- and other-run courses, higher degrees, membership of local working parties;

- networking through teachers and other members of school communities linking up with each other to share ideas, disseminate good practice, discuss and resolve problems, challenge each other's thinking and create new knowledge;

- critical friendships involving external agents who play a role in promoting inquiry-mindedness in school communities by helping those in schools to interpret and use data, bringing an outsider's eye to school activities and supportively challenging assumptions;

- leadership, management and co-ordination of professional activities (for example, vision-building and school development planning, performance management, orchestrating CPD, and literacy and numeracy across the curriculum) (Stoll et al., 2003: 5–6).

Effective leaders help shape the culture of a school by their behaviour. They lead the learning. This might be by constantly questioning the status quo to find better ways of achieving goals, creating environments where positive results and credits are celebrated; evaluating and affirming people; or by thinking positively and realizing that every problem presents a learning opportunity. Groups of teachers who correspond outside of school, either electronically or in face-to-face groups or meetings or networks show great potential as sites for focused, ongoing and self-directed inquiry.

NETWORKED LEARNING COMMUNITIES

In England the National College for School Leadership (NCSL), set up in November 2000, is encouraging networked learning communities to promote change through learning at multiple levels of the education system. The networks are made up of at least six schools and a higher education institution, and the underpinning notion is that the learning is from each other, with each other and on behalf of each other. (A useful account is given by Jackson, 2003, and other information is on www.ncsl.org.uk.) There are already over 80 networks collaborating across the country, including approximately 1,000 schools, 20,000 staff and around 500,000 pupils. The second cohort began in September 2003 with a further 26 networks forming a part of this cohort.

Networks are becoming very popular around the world, as they seem to provide:

- opportunities for teachers to both gain and generate knowledge;
- a variety of collaborative structures;
- flexibility and informality;
- discussion of problems that have no agreed-upon solutions;
- ideas that challenge teachers rather than merely prescribing generic solutions;
- an organizational structure that can be independent of, yet attached to, schools or universities;
- a chance to work across schools and district/local authority lines;
- a vision of reform that excites and encourages risk-taking in a supportive environment;
- a community that respects teachers' knowledge as well as knowledge from research and reform (Lieberman, 1999).

There are six interconnected levels of learning, which are the foundations for each network:

- *pupil learning* – pupils tell us about themselves as learners;

- *adult learning* – through joint work, adults teach each other the art and craft of teaching;

- *leadership for learning and leadership development* – leaders coach and facilitate others to lead;

- *school-wide learning* – adults become better every year at supporting pupil learning, just because they work in this school and network;

- *school-to-school learning* – our schools learn more because they are learning together;

- *network-to-network learning* – we feel part of a learning profession.

An example of a networked learning community is offered by Kellow (2003) who describes the origins of the Primary Schools Learning Network (PSLN) in Milton Keynes.

WHAT IS EFFECTIVE CPD?

Any discussion of what constitutes effective professional development needs to begin by asking effective for whom – the individual teacher, the school and its pupils, or the education system as a whole? And for what? The beneficiaries of CPD may not always overlap, although in many cases they will; what is helpful in enhancing teachers' professionalism is also likely to be of benefit both for pupils and their schools. On the other hand, training to meet the latest government initiative may be effective for implementing a particular strategy but not necessarily for the overall long-term development of teachers as professionals. Effective CPD is likely to consist of that which first and foremost enhances pupil outcomes, but which also helps to bring about changes in practice and improves teachers' and others' teaching, management and leadership skills and qualities. It should be 'fit for purpose' and add something to the school's overall capacity to develop; the school should be able to build upon the collective learning of its people. Exposure to and participation in a wide range of professional development opportunities is likely to bring about change to individuals' beliefs, values, attitudes and behaviours, and these may well lead to changes in classroom and school practices. Any change should, however, lead to improvement; we are not talking about change for change's sake!

Ultimately, effective CPD has to lead to improvements in pupil learning outcomes, but these outcomes must surely move beyond improved examination or test results. Attitudes, well-being and behaviour are important too.

Much has been written about what constitutes effective CPD but it should be remembered that the characteristics influencing effectiveness are multiple and highly complex. We should therefore begin with an important caveat: the technical and methodological problems of measuring the direct effects or impact of CPD especially on classroom performance – of both teachers and pupils – are considerable. This is, amongst other reasons, because the term embraces a wide variety of modes and methods, and includes professional training, education and support. The number of variables to be taken into account is considerable. Figure 6.1 in Chapter 6, for example, shows how the 'impact' of a course or a piece of training may be mediated through a number of factors. Continuing professional development can only have an indirect impact on pupil learn-

CASE STUDY 2.1: PRIMARY SCHOOLS LEARNING NETWORK

(ADAPTED FROM KELLOW, 2003)

The Milton Keynes network has developed as a partnership between 11 primary schools, the LEA and a university department of education. At its heart is the notion of teachers as researchers and active learners. The PSLN has been founded upon ten professional learning precepts:

1 Successful schools are learning communities for adults as well as children.
2 Teachers learn best when they participate actively in decisions about the content, processes and outcomes of their learning.
3 Successful learning requires time for reflection.
4 Learning alone through one's own experience will ultimately limit learning.
5 Successful learning requires collaboration with others from inside and outside the workplace.
6 Teacher learning and development should contribute to school improvement.
7 School leaders play a significant influencing role in teacher learning and development.
8 At its best, learning will have personal and professional significance for teachers.
9 Supported, sustained learning over time is likely to be more beneficial to the individual and school than short-term learning.
10 If schools are to operate effectively in devolved systems, much reliance has to be placed on trust in professional judgement at school level (Day et al., 2003).

Based on these precepts the PSLN has five key objectives:

1 To build and sustain capacity in schools for growth and improvement and for PSLN schools to develop into learning schools.
2 To seek innovative practices in teaching and learning that result in improved pupil learning and raised standards.
3 To develop leadership for learning, giving staff opportunities to lead and to develop their leadership potential.
4 To work with other schools to share and develop knowledge and practice.
5 Through staff development, to increase motivation that will improve retention.

It is too early to know how successful the learning network has been or what impact it will have on pupil learning and attainment but the early signs are promising. Teachers are beginning to regain some of their lost professional confidence and are getting opportunities to engage in activities that were previously denied them. The network is going to link with a group of primary schools in Derby and they plan to work together on joint projects. Interestingly, this initiative has not been led by headteachers and a deliberate decision was made that the leadership of the 'school improvement groups' should lie elsewhere.

The project has created an excitement within the LEA – as one headteacher put it: 'It's the most exciting thing to have happened here for years!'

ing and outcomes. Very few research studies have considered the relationship between the characteristics of professional development and any change in teachers' classroom teaching practice or the gains in pupil achievement or learning outcomes more broadly. Despite this, there is a growing body of research evidence and informed professional judgement that gives a broad indication of the essential characteristics of effective CPD.

An early National Foundation for Educational Research (NFER) study conducted by one of us found effective CPD could take a variety of forms but had a number of key characteristics. These included the clear identification of aims and objectives, along with an analysis of training needs to ensure training and development activities matched existing levels of expertise. Training needs were identified at school level following appraisal (performance management) and/or the drawing up of the school development plan. Opportunities for reflection were also important, as were action research, ongoing evaluation and follow-up work. Effective training was seen to form part of a coherent programme and was not a 'one-off' activity. The optimum use of existing resources and facilities was most likely when CPD activities were well planned, helping to promote targeted and tailor-made training, avoiding overload and minimizing disruption (Brown and Earley, 1990).

More recently, Lee (2002) reports the findings from another NFER study, a survey of teachers, who saw the key factors in the success of CPD as targeted objectives, clear structure, planning, learner involvement, and a high level of expertise on part of the deliverer.

Her Majesty's Inspectors have also recently reported on CPD (Ofsted, 2002a). In most schools, teachers attending courses continued to be the main form of professional development, although they did report a growing awareness of the value of other forms of professional development, such as sharing the expertise of teachers and using consultants to deliver training programmes addressing specific school needs. The inspectors also found that:

> Teachers, line managers and CPD co-ordinators rarely assembled an array of CPD activities to form a coherent individual training plan, designed to bring about specific improvement in a teacher's knowledge and skills. More often teachers worked on a range of loosely related activities that did not always provide good value or achieve the intended outcome. (Ofsted, 2002a: 3)

The report concluded that: 'schools on the whole failed to allow enough time to support effective professional development and to ensure that acquired knowledge and skills were consolidated, implemented and shared with other teachers' (Ofsted, 2002a: 3).

Professional development appears still to be characterized for many by fragmented 'one-shot' workshops and conferences at which they listen passively to 'experts' and learn about topics not always essential to teaching. As Boyle and colleagues point out, these traditional approaches to professional development 'appear insufficient to foster learning which fundamentally alters what teachers teach or how they teach (2003: 3). They draw upon international research evidence which suggests certain types of professional development activities are more likely than others to offer such sustained learning opportunities. These include:

- study groups in which teachers are engaged on regular, structured and collaborative interactions around topics identified by the group;
- coaching or mentoring arrangements, where teachers work one-on-one with an equally or more experienced teacher;
- networks, which link teachers or groups, either in person or electronically, to explore and discuss topics of interest, pursue common goals, share information and address common concerns;
- immersion in inquiry, in which teachers engage in the kinds of

learning that they are expected to practice with their students (Boyle et al., 2003: 3).

We now know a lot from research about the characteristics of effective induction for newly qualified teachers in England (see Bubb et al., 2002; Earley and Kinder, 1994). For example:

- It is flexible and negotiated, not imposed or predetermined.
- It meets teachers' needs (training, development, social and psychological).
- It is part of a school-wide approach to supporting all staff (a climate of mutual support and development).
- It is systematic and planned, and includes:
    - links to specific individual(s);
    - programmes of classroom observation and feedback;
    - opportunities for regular contact with other new teachers (within and outside school).
- It encourages reflection on practice (usually with a mentor).
- It enables staff to become active and valued members who can contribute to the school and its development.
- It lays the foundation for a lifelong professional career (Earley and Kinder, 1994).

Clearly teachers, newly appointed or otherwise, need specialized knowledge and a repertoire of pedagogical skills, but they need to be reflective.

Involvement in development activities by teachers and other staff is, to a large extent, voluntary but there are a number of factors that will encourage participation. Bolam and McMahon identified the following factors affecting workers in general:

- perceptions of the working environment;
- perceptions and beliefs about the benefits of development;
- judgement of senior management support;
- personality factors like identification with work;
- personal concept of career;
- sense of self-efficacy, particularly how confident the individual is about learning new skills (2003: 14).

This is a useful list. Boring, repetitive and dependent work discourages professional development and growth, whereas challenging, variable and independent work encourages it – certainly there are parallels with the classroom here. Equally personal factors and life changes can cause individuals to reconsider career priorities and goals. Professional development can help enhance performance through improved self-esteem – this along with personal well-being and a sense of professional control are all essential components of job satisfaction.

THE STANDARDS FRAMEWORK

The Dreyfus brothers (1986) see skill acquisition in terms of five levels:

> Level 1 – Novice
>
> Level 2 – Advanced beginner
>
> Level 3 – Competent
>
> Level 4 – Proficient
>
> Level 5 – Expert

However, such linear models of development are simplistic. In reality, teacher development is more like a roller-coaster with peaks and troughs: as one gets better at controlling a class one has to begin learning something new for a management role. From a developmental perspective, individual learning needs will also be shaped by factors such as length of experience, level of responsibility and, perhaps, by gender and ethnicity. The *Teachers' Standards Framework* (DfES, 2001a) sets out the standards that teachers should expect to demonstrate at particular points in their career as shown in Table 2.3. The framework summarizes the main elements in each of the standards under ten dimensions of teaching and leadership within a school. These are:

> 1 knowledge and understanding;
>
> 2 planning and setting expectations;
>
> 3 teaching and managing pupil learning;
>
> 4 assessment and evaluation;
>
> 5 pupil achievement;
>
> 6 relations with parents and the wider community;
>
> 7 managing own performance and development;
>
> 8 managing and developing staff and other adults;
>
> 9 managing resources;
>
> 10 strategic leadership.

TABLE 2.3 STANDARDS COVERED IN THE FRAMEWORK

Title	Advisory/statutory	Developed by
Qualified teacher status (QTS)	S	Teacher Training Agency (TTA)
Induction	S	TTA
Threshold	S	DfES
Advanced skills teacher (AST)	S	DfES
Subject leader	A	TTA
Special educational needs co-ordinator (SENCO)	A	DfES
Headteacher	A	TTA (updated by DfES)

Source: DfES, 2001a

The framework shows at a glance how the expectations of teachers can grow and change at different stages of a career as they take on different roles within a school. It should help people to recognize existing expertise and achievements as well as any development needs. It may also help to develop a clearer and more relevant job description or career path. Teachers' careers can and do follow a huge variety of different routes. Some teachers never want to take on management responsibilities and make extremely valuable contributions to their pupils and their schools by the quality of their teaching in the classroom. Some move through different leadership roles and eventually become headteachers. In between there are many different combinations and sequences of roles – including moves into and out of other areas of education, or other areas of employment more generally. Effective CPD needs to meet all these needs.

PROFESSIONAL DEVELOPMENT PORTFOLIOS

Teachers need a receptacle for all professional development and performance management related paperwork. A professional development portfolio is useful in chronicling where one has been and planning where one wants to go. It is not a requirement but many teachers are now keeping such a folder. Many new teachers start them in training. There are many models around such as the professional development portfolio (PDP) that one of us uses with Lambeth teachers (Figure 2.3). This embodies the wider idea of the responsible and reflective professional and is used as an ongoing record of professional development. It is a receptacle for all objectives, action plans, reflections and assessments that can stay with the teacher for their whole career and be used for induction, performance management, threshold and job applications. Some portfolios are kept electronically.

Teachers who keep PDPs say how useful they are. Here are some soundbites from teachers in a Norfolk school:

> The portfolio does make you think differently about yourself. You recognise the things that you do and it makes you feel good about the things that you do. It's very easy to become frustrated by what you are not achieving rather than by what you are achieving. And, it's so easy to forget. The portfolio is one of those ways to look at what you have achieved. I think parents should see the teacher's portfolio. It would blow their mind.

> I love doing my portfolio! I find it *really* satisfying, especially to look back at. (Berrill and Whalen, 2003: p 5)

COLLABORATION

'Learning from each other, learning from what works' is the motto of the government's CPD strategy (DfEE, 2001a). Collaboration is key and is explored in more detail in Chapter 8. The government, especially through Beacon schools and the Leadership Incentive Grant (LiG), has promoted collaboration between schools for professional development purposes. At their peak there were around 1,100 or so primary, secondary and special Beacon schools but they have not been as successful as hoped and their funding has recently ceased. Since the summer of 2003 some secondary schools (most of them former Beacon schools) have become known as 'leading-edge' schools. It is planned to have about 300 of them operating by 2006. There are no plans for primary or special schools to be awarded such status although they are able to apply to become 'training schools' (see Chapter 9).

It is also very important to give due consideration to collaboration within schools. The variation of teaching practice within a single school is likely to be as great as or greater than the variation between schools. The same is the case for pupil outcomes. For example, in the USA analyses of student learning data typically show that greater variation exists between classrooms within a school than between schools or between districts (LEAs). As Guskey (2002: 8) notes 'in other words, within the unique context of nearly every school there are teachers who have found ways to help students learn excellently'. He goes on to say that 'identifying and finding ways to share the practices and strategies of those teachers among their colleagues might provide a basis for highly effective professional development within that context' (ibid.).

Contents

1. Introduction

2. Career history
    a. CV and qualifications
    b. References
    c. Job descriptions

3. Objectives
    a. The career entry and development profile
    b. Objectives
    c. Action plans
    d. Reviews of progress

4. Professional development
    a. Induction programme at LEA and school
    b. Professional development activities and meetings
    c. Notes from professional development meetings, e.g. with induction tutor or team leader
    d. List of and certificates from courses attended
    e. List of other teachers observed and observation notes
    f.   Articles read and websites visited

5. Evidence of growing effectiveness
    a. A list of observations and monitoring of my teaching
    b. Feedback sheets following observations and monitoring
    c. The three termly assessment reports for induction
    d. Performance management statements
    e. Evidence of:
        i.   knowledge and understanding
        ii.   teaching and assessment
        iii. pupil progress
        iv. wider professional effectiveness
        v.   professional characteristics

6. Other information
    a. Policies for induction and performance management
    b. Information about the LEA, Beacon schools, advanced skills teachers and lead teachers

FIGURE 2.3 THE LAMBETH PROFESSIONAL DEVELOPMENT PORTFOLIO (BUBB, 2003b: 27)

ADVANCED SKILLS TEACHERS

Some very effective teachers gain advanced skills teacher (AST) status. The main duty of ASTs is to be an excellent teacher in their own school for four days a week. For one day a week they have to share their good practice with other teachers and help other people's professional development – not only in their own schools but also in others.

As such they are a great resource for CPD. They do things like:

- advising other teachers;
- modelling lessons;
- spreading good practice based on educational research;
- producing high quality-teaching materials;
- advising on professional development;
- establishing and leading professional learning groups;
- helping to support the performance management of other teachers;
- supporting teachers experiencing difficulties;
- helping with the induction and mentoring of NQTs;
- helping train teachers;
- working in specialist subject areas, for example, music;
- disseminating good practice within a school.

How can we disseminate good practice within school? Recognizing its existence and its importance is a good start. We also need to remind ourselves of the finding from school effectiveness research that individual teachers in their classrooms matter three or four times more than headteachers or schools themselves. So focusing on best practice at classroom level is essential. David Reynolds (2003) states that we need to rid ourselves of the notion that the way to improve the system is through school-to-school transfer of good practice – the belief which underlies Beacon and 'leading-edge' and specialist schools, for example. It is, he argues, much more sensible for schools not to be dependent on others helping them out but from learning from their own best practice. He claims that 'every school, no matter how well it is doing overall, has practitioners relatively better than others, many schools will have excellent teachers defined in national terms, and a significant proportion of schools will have world-class people' (ibid.: 23). Helping people learn from others in their schools is so much easier (and cheaper) than learning from someone 20 miles away. 'When you are "buddied" with a colleague who is doing better than you with the same children in the same school, that is when the alibis stop' (ibid.: 23).

We need to get people from the same department or school working closely together, talking and sharing experiences. But we also need to be aware of the limitations of such an approach if it is taken up to the exclusion of all else. Good schools welcome the contribution of outsiders – critical friends from the local university and the local authority, for example – and there is a real danger of schools 'recycling their own inadequacies' without it. Pachler and Field state that:

> CPD is dependent upon debate, discussion, sharing and joint learning and therefore we must be prepared to use our work context and the people therein as a resource for our learning, but also be prepared to assist in the 'generation' of sharable examples to enable the transferral and adaptation of good ideas to others. (2004: 6)

Nevertheless, Reynolds's plea for a new emphasis on internal good practice is a valid one and planned in conjunction with ASTs' in- and out-reach work could lead to improved practices. It is also a central feature of a professional learning community.

CONCLUSION

The role of CPD managers and school leaders in all this is crucial as they encourage staff to think about their own learning. Continuing professional development managers and school leaders themselves need to be up to date and demonstrate a commitment to CPD, to be 'lead learners' promoting a learning climate or culture and monitoring and evaluating the progress of teachers' and other staff's professional development. It is difficult not to be a learning teacher in a learning school! But such schools have to be managed and it is to the management and leadership of CPD that is the focus of the next chapter.

CHAPTER THREE

Leading and Managing CPD

- The professional development co-ordinator role
- The training and development cycle
- Investors in People
- Balancing needs with the budget
- Procedures to help CPD coordinators
- Case study

Professional development does not just happen – it has to be managed and led, and done so effectively ensuring it has a positive impact and represents good value for money. Research (Hustler et al., 2003) on teachers' attitudes to CPD found that the status, knowledge and approach of the CPD co-ordinator (and the leadership team or senior management team [SMT] more generally) could radically affect, positively or negatively, teachers' attitudes towards and understandings of professional development. The Office for Standards in Education found that:

> Teachers, line managers and CPD coordinators rarely assembled an array of CPD activities to form a coherent individual training plan, designed to bring about specific improve in a teacher's knowledge and skills. More often teachers worked on a range of loosely related activities that did not always provide good value or achieve the intended outcome. (Ofsted, 2002a: 3).

The CPD co-ordinator role is both crucial and often underdeveloped – many could benefit from professional development in order to do their job better. If one of the keys to effective CPD is to ensure it is effectively led and managed, then the role of CPD co-ordinator needs to be given the kudos and time it requires to be done well. We need to move from an administrative role to that of facilitator and staff supporter.

Schools often link CPD to objectives or targets as identified in both school development and personal development plans, and these in turn are related to a system of performance management or staff appraisal. In this way it is likely that an appropriate balance will be retained between school (and group) needs and the personal and professional needs of the individual – between what has been referred to, more generally, as 'hard' and 'soft' aspects of human resource management. Teachers and other staff will always feel the need to be valued and this should not be forgotten when considering the balance between identifying and meeting individual and school needs.

The effective management of CPD should ensure that support is available and conditions created which enable staff to work together and to develop and improve their workplace performance. Through headteachers, CPD co-ordinators and other staff helping to create a climate or culture which is conducive to learning – of both staff and pupils – schools and colleges are well on the road to becoming learning communities where investment in people is given the priority it deserves. Student learning is a key goal of all educational organizations, whereas the ongoing learning of teachers, support staff and other paid employees is not always prioritized or adequately resourced.

Creating a culture of learning is crucial and this is going to be shaped by the attitude and approach of educational leaders towards CPD. What messages are headteachers, principals and other educational leaders giving about the importance of professional development? Are they participating in training themselves, particularly in school-based events, are they 'leading the learning'?

If it is true that 'children learn more from adults' deeds than their words' and that 'in order to develop a love of learning in students, teachers must first be learners themselves' (Jallongo, 1991: 48), then this is equally true of teachers and others working in the organization.

This chapter considers how schools and educational systems are approaching the management of CPD. It draws upon existing research and inspection findings to illuminate some of the key issues that need to be given consideration by educational leaders. It commences with an examination of the role of the professional development co-ordinator.

THE PROFESSIONAL DEVELOPMENT CO-ORDINATOR ROLE

It could be argued that leading and managing professional development to help bring about a learning community, for all that work or study within it, is everybody's responsibility. However, formally the responsibility is most likely to belong to the professional development or CPD co-ordinator. The person undertaking this responsibility is usually a senior member of staff, often a deputy or assistant head, or in primary schools (especially small ones) the headteacher. The responsibility for managing CPD may be part of the post holder's wider 'human resources' or personnel function, but it will always be one of several other management responsibilities held.

Baxter and Chambers (1998a) have drawn upon the national standards developed by the training and development lead body (TDLB) to examine systematically the role of the CPD co-ordinator in schools. They argue that the role is so important that it should have its own set of standards and qualifications structure. They note that as national standards are being developed across the teaching profession from NQTs to headteachers and for support staff then there is a case to be argued for a set for CPD co-ordinators, especially as the TDLB standards already exist.

On the basis of these standards Baxter and Chambers have drawn up a job description, identifying key tasks across the five areas of competence (see Figure 3.1). Continuing professional development co-ordinators can assess their own performance against these key tasks so that 'they can begin to identify their own professional development targets, and perhaps to work towards an NVQ (national vocational qualification) in human resource development' (Baxter and Chambers, 1998a: 82–3). Taking the management of professional development seriously in this way 'gives reality to the concept of staff as models of lifelong learners and schools as the seed beds of a learning society' (ibid.: 83).

Job title: Professional Development Co-ordinator

Job purpose: to manage the school's staff development processes in accordance with the staff development policy. To ensure these processes contribute to the school's learning culture and the performance of pupils.

Objectives:

- To ensure that all staff have opportunities to gain the skills and attributes needed for the school to achieve its development goals;
- To ensure staff development benefits both individuals and the school;
- To ensure that all training and development resources are used efficiently and effectively;
- To ensure the principles of effective adult learning are incorporated into all staff development processes, systems and procedures.

Major responsibility areas:

A. Identify training and development needs;
B. Plan and design training and development;
C. Deliver training and development;
D. Review progress and assess achievement;
E. Continuously improve the effectiveness of training and development.

Key tasks:

A1 to identify school training and development needs in the context of the school development plan;
A2 to assure the identification of individual development needs in accordance with the staff development policy and procedures;
B1 to compile the school's training and development plan. To determine resource needs and allocate resources in accordance with the staff development policy;
B2 to design training programmes in accordance with effective learning principles and to assist others in this task;
C1 to co-ordinate the provision of training in accordance with the school's training plan. To monitor resource expenditure on staff development and to ensure expenditure stays within budget;
C2 to support and advise other managers in their staff development role;
D1 to promote the monitoring and assessment of staff learning and performance, ensuring that such activities are used to steer development and enhance performance;
D2 to collect information on performance and to assist other managers in this task, so as to contribute to evaluation;
E1 to evaluate and improve the school's training and development programmes;
E2 to evaluate and improve the school's training and development processes;
E3 to evaluate and seek to improve your own practice as professional development co-ordinator.

FIGURE 3.1 PROFESSIONAL DEVELOPMENT CO-ORDINATOR'S JOB DESCRIPTION (FROM BAXTER AND CHAMBERS, 1998a)

■ INSPECTION

It is also useful to be aware of inspection criteria. The Ofsted framework distinguishes between leadership and management. As a leader of CPD, inspectors will be looking at what you do in relation to CPD:

- Leadership shows clear vision, a sense of purpose and high aspirations for the school, with a relentless focus on pupils' achievement.

- Strategic planning reflects and promotes the school's ambitions and goals.

- Leaders inspire, motivate and influence staff and pupils.

- Leaders create effective teams.

- There is knowledgeable and innovative leadership of teaching and the curriculum.

- Leaders are committed to running an equitable and inclusive school, in which each individual matters.

- Leaders provide good role models for other staff and pupils.

In judging the effectiveness of the school's management of CPD, inspectors will assess the extent to which:

- the school undertakes rigorous self-evaluation and uses the findings effectively;

- the school monitors performance data, reviews patterns and takes appropriate action;

- the performance management of staff, including support staff, is thorough and effective in bringing about improvement;

- a commitment to staff development is reflected in effective induction and professional development strategies and, where possible, the school's contribution to initial teacher training;

- the recruitment, retention, deployment and workload of staff are well managed, and support staff are well deployed to make teachers' work more effective;

- approaches to financial and resource management help the school to achieve its educational priorities;

- the principles of best value are central to the school's management and use of resources (Ofsted, 2003a).

Inspectors are required to consider how committed the school is to staff development, as reflected in effective induction and professional development strategies and, where possible, the school's contribution to initial teacher training. They will consider the investment the school makes in its teaching and support staff. There are many indicators, such as the school's commitment to the induction of newly qualified, incoming and supply teachers; its interest in contributing to initial teacher training; the interest in contributing to training of support staff; the extent to which coherent professional development strategies are linked with improvement planning and performance management (Ofsted, 2003a).

Understanding the training and development cycle is key to the CPD co-ordinator role.

THE TRAINING AND DEVELOPMENT CYCLE

Managing CPD in any organization, be it a small or medium-sized primary school or a large multi-purpose college, requires an understanding and knowledge of many things. These include the processes by which adults best learn and the devising of plans and policies to underpin effective practice. It is also crucially important to understand the training and development cycle illustrated in Figure 3.2. This model consists of six stages, all of which are broadly subsumed within the CPD co-ordinator's job description outlined above. Each of the stages will be examined in the next three chapters. The stages are:

- identifying and analysing training needs – Chapter 4;

- planning and designing programmes, their implementation or delivery – Chapter 5;

- monitoring and evaluation: the impact of CPD – Chapter 6.

This is complex, but we hope that the next three chapters will help.

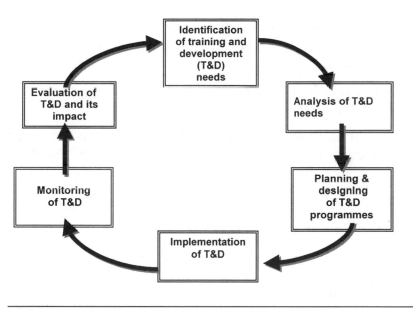

FIGURE 3.2 TRAINING AND DEVELOPMENT CYCLE

INVESTORS IN PEOPLE

Many schools have instituted a major review of continuing professional development under the impetus of applying for Investors in People recognition. This is a national quality standard that sets a level of good practice for improving an organization's performance through its people. By the end of 2002 over a quarter (26 per cent) of schools were recognized as Investors in People and a further one-sixth (15.5 per cent) were committed to achieving it. This national standard for training and development is at the forefront in helping schools to embrace a development culture and become professional learning communities and learning organizations capable of developing themselves and their workforce. Most importantly, there is plenty of evidence to show that it has helped to ensure that a culture of training and development is embedded within a school's CPD structures and processes.

The national standard is made up of four underlying principles which are underpinned by these four questions:

- Do all staff understand the vision, core values, aims and objectives of their school?

- Do all staff understand and accept their role in the success of the school?

- Do all staff have the skills, knowledge and capability to fulfil their roles?

- Are there planning and review processes to ensure that the above criteria are continuously met?

The four underlying principles are:

- *Commitment*: an Investor in People is fully committed to developing its people in order to achieve its aims and objectives.

- *Planning*: an Investor in People is clear about its aims and its objectives and what its people need to do to achieve them.

- *Action*: an Investor in People develops its people effectively in order to improve its performance.

- *Evaluation*: an Investor in People understands the impact of its investment in people on its performance.

Within these four principles there are 12 indicators and schools have to provide evidence that demonstrate that all are met. An extract is shown in Table 3.1 (and the indicators for measuring impact are in Table 6.1 in Chapter 6).

TABLE 3.1 INVESTORS IN PEOPLE – PLANNING

Principles	Indicators	Evidence
Planning An Investor in People is clear about its aims and its objectives and what its people need to do to achieve them	5. The organization has a plan with clear aims and objectives which are understood by everyone	The organization has a plan with clear aims and objectives People can consistently explain the aims and objectives of the organization at a level appropriate to their role Representative groups are consulted about the organization's aims and objectives
	6. The development of people is in line with the organization's aims and objectives	The organization has clear priorities which link the development of people to its aims and objectives at organization, team and individual level People clearly understand what their development activities should achieve, both for them and the organization
	7. People understand how they contribute to achieving the organization's aims and objectives	People can explain how they contribute to achieving the organization's aims and objectives

There are many examples of accounts of schools and colleges that have achieved recognition as Investors in People. For example in late 2002 the DfES published a CD of its conference report 'Achieving excellence through partnership' and this includes case study accounts from a college and a school. The CD is available from the DfES. Further information about Investors in People can also be found on their website and at the website of Investors in People UK.

Investors in People has presented schools with a number of challenges especially as far as the last principle, evaluating the impact of its investment in people on its performance, is concerned (see Chapter 6). Research into Investors in People in the education sector has also demonstrated three other factors of significance, namely:

- the need to address the training and development requirements of support staff as well as teachers;

- for all those staff with management responsibilities to see this as including the need to take responsibility for the development of other people (their staff development role);

- that there is not necessarily a conflict between the needs of the school and that of individual working within them (Earley, 1996).

It is the latter, which the next section addresses.

BALANCING NEEDS WITH THE BUDGET

Continuing professional development co-ordinators – like everyone else – have to work within budgetary constraints, and sometimes one finds oneself awash with money and at other times there are massive cuts. A CPD co-ordinator in a secondary school told us in July 2003, 'Rarely have I had to refuse someone but now it's going to be like rationing in war-time'. Some people survive by being creative with their interpretation of budget headings within the Standards Fund (the main source of CPD monies).

The DfES intends to move away from ring fenced grants and centrally run programmes so that by 2005–06 all the funding for CPD will be channelled through the Education Standard Spending (ESS) arrangements – in effect devolving the vast majority to schools. Funding for induction will be incorporated in ESS from 2003–04 and for teacher sabbaticals from 2004–05. When the ESS is reduced or has to cover a host of people's professional development there are hard decisions to be made, and the potential for individuals to feel hard done by is great. Consider this teacher's point of view made on the *Times Educational Supplement* (*TES*) Website Professional Development Forum:

> Is attending a headteachers' conference really more important than four training days for staff? Which adds more to raising standards? Which would have more impact: a very stressed teacher who is enduring appalling behavioural problems attending training aimed at supporting teachers in that situation or a headteacher attending the same course and cascading useful information in a five minute soundbite at a staff meeting?

Managing CPD is a complex affair in which many priorities compete for attention. Procedures followed can often come to reflect custom and habit rather than a considered response to changing circumstances. It is important, to step back and ask such questions as:

- Why are we doing this?
- What do we need to achieve?
- Is this method the most economical, efficient and effective?
- What is in the best interests of our pupils?
- What is the evidence about levels of need?
- Are there better ways of achieving the desired results?
- Could another organization do this for us more effectively and economically?
- Are our procedures competitive compared with possible alternatives?

BEST VALUE

It is valuable to consider the principles of best value known familiarly as the four Cs:

Challenge – is the professional development pitched at the right level for all participants?

Compare – how does your school's CPD compare with other schools and between parts of the school? Are you getting good value for money from your spending of the CPD budget?

Consult – listen to the views of staff especially over the use of CPD funding; ask around for the best forms of CPD, the best providers, consultants, etc.

Compete – as a means of securing efficient and effective CPD.

PROCEDURES TO HELP CPD CO-ORDINATORS

Continuing professional development co-ordinators need systems to help them do their job and raise the status of professional development in the school. One of the ways that Ashmanor School in Surrey does this is to have a professional development committee. This consists of:

- professional development co-ordinator, the deputy head;
- headteacher;
- a support staff representative;
- a department head;
- main pay scale teacher;
- one other member of staff.

The committee decides the school's annual professional development targets, which fit in with the SDP. For instance in one year these were:

1 To apply to become a Training School.
2 To monitor the effectiveness of the training course booking and evaluation form.
3 To achieve re-recognition of Investors in People status.

4 To implement the revised annual reviews of support staff.

5 To give all staff copies of the Infofax file.

6 To apply for Designated Recommending Body status.

7 To set up performance coaching training courses.

8 To review the staff development policy.

It is helpful to be able to discuss CPD issues with others – things like how to spend money efficiently, choosing from the bewildering array of consultants and courses, how not to add to teacher workload and how to meet the needs of a very disparate group of people. Continuing professional development policies are useful in making clear expectations and entitlements. The headteacher of Columbia Primary School in Tower Hamlets says,

> Our professional development policy starts with a statement that says that we believe that our school should be a community of learners, working together for the development of all, that the school staff are its most important asset, and that all of them need to feel valued and motivated in order to work well. Improving the quality of teaching and learning is a key ingredient in improving our school. We also have a need to increase our knowledge and expertise, not just within the stated aims of the school but to fulfil personal goals and aspirations. (Bentley, 2002/03: 59)

At Worth Primary School procedures and processes were not coherent and integrated but fragmented, having weak or no linkage between school development planning, appraisal, target-setting, data analysis, lesson observation and professional development. The headteacher set up a process that has the gathering and analysis of pupil progress information and lesson observation at its heart. This core and objective information and data now informs the appraisal interview, which in turn informs the professional development, coaching and support of individuals and teams; all this, in turn, informs the development plan. As skills and capabilities became more proficient the process has moved from being a once a year event, to being the key process in understanding the organization, co-ordinating and maximizing the talents and aspirations of staff, impacting powerfully on the school's climate, culture and results.

This is how it works. A specific and confidential 'training and development action plan' is created by the personnel team leader in consultation with the senior management team. This operational action plan contains training needs applicable to both individual members of staff and/or groups of staff. The plan identifies estimated course fees, cover and leave/costs. Generally needs identified are designed to improve the performance of an individual or group so as to improve expertise and effectiveness. Training also takes place to equip individuals and groups to meet new requirements/policy or demands. Individual needs are normally identified by the individual and their team leader through performance management interviews. Group needs can be identified by performance management interviews, staff/quality assurance meetings, assessment and review procedures which bring to light areas in need of development.

Only the broad costing of the confidential and operational action plan are added to the strategic and public 'personnel development plan', which usually makes up a third of the whole-school development plan. The 'personnel development plan' is created by the team leader after consultation with the personnel team which contains governor and staff members. Only CPD that is not linked to school needs or is expensive, such as long degree courses or secondments, are discussed by the personnel team and submitted for the express permission of the governing body.

Once the strategic personnel development plan has been set and agreed by the personnel team it is included as part of the draft SDP which is approved finally at a joint meeting of the curriculum, personnel and resource and finance teams. The finance team is then charged with building a budget to meet the demands of the curriculum and personnel teams. The various plans are prioritized and the finance team can trim demands subject to budget limitations. The confidential training and development action plan is never discussed by the finance team as it does not have the mandate to select from or edit the key elements of the whole SDP.

Occasionally training and briefings need to be arranged for individuals and groups to meet immediate and unforeseen needs; the personnel team leader arranges such events if possible. If such unforeseen and ad hoc events prove essential (briefings related to changes in the law, assessment, national curriculum, etc.) staff may attend these events, but they are not generally regarded as part of the school's training plan and do not count towards the individual's development as identified through performance management. Attendance at such events is recorded in the CPD file but is not related to the needs of the individual or team for coaching purposes (Taylor, 2004).

CASE STUDY

There are few accounts written by professional development co-ordinators themselves that give a sense of what the job entails and how it can be successfully carried out. Dan Connor discusses the challenge of becoming a professional development co-ordinator of a high school in Luton (Connor, 1997). He describes how the school had become involved in school-centred initial teacher training (SCITT) and how the lessons learned from that encouraged a move out of a 'training day/off-site courses' model of provision to a mentoring approach. He writes of the difficulty that all CPD co-ordinators face – that of, 'taking the management of professional development a stage further than administration, beyond the bounds of matching courses to development plans and post-Ofsted action plans and into the realms of a fundamental rethink about what constitutes real professional development and looking at how we realize an aspiration to realize it' (Connor, 1997: 47).

The case study below shows how Columbia Primary School in Tower Hamlets manages professional development of its staff. It is based on an article published in *Professional Development Today* by Penny Bentley, the headteacher and CPD co-ordinator (Bentley, 2003).

CONCLUSION

Perhaps the single most important feature of leading and managing CPD is to encourage and promote a commitment on the part of the individual and the school to professional and personal growth. Leading and managing people's development – making

CASE STUDY 3.1

Penny Bentley is headteacher of Columbia Primary School, located in a socially disadvantaged part of east London. In the article she reflects on how her school manages CPD and gives a number of insights into the role of leadership in the process. She shows how Columbia school is able to give professional development a high priority despite a number of competing priorities, and how CPD fits in with the school's performance management system.

Against a context of social disadvantage and high pupil mobility a culture of learning is found which no doubt the head has helped to shape through her leadership style and the importance she attaches to people management. She provides a good account of how CPD has to be managed as well as led. The different needs of staff are given high priority and attempts made to provide a programme that reflects this. This is achieved by dividing the staff into groups or categories (for example, NQTs, senior managers, support staff) and identifying their needs by a range of methods (for example, performance management interviews, priorities of the school development plan, demands of central government initiatives). It is also achieved by ensuring staff development funds are spent wisely and cost-effectively. Continuing professional development is provided largely through the school's in-service training programme, most of which reflects the targets stated in the SDP, although other development opportunities found include mentoring and coaching, performance management meetings, planning consultations, monitoring of teaching and learning, working party membership, observation and feedback. Staff also attend training courses and conferences, but these are seen as only part of a much wider 'menu' of training and development opportunities. Lastly, although Penny Bentley says little about evaluation, she does note that what really matters is how CPD impacts on teaching and learning. This is the final part of the training and development cycle.

Here is the professional development that different people at Columbia have recently had as Penny Bentley describes:

An NQT

This NQT would have had the school induction programme, the short one at the start of the year and then his NQT induction programme throughout the year. We buy into the LEA induction programme that is offered on alternate Wednesdays. The Wednesdays in school are led by co-ordinators and organized by the school and staff development co-ordinator. The NQT is also supported by his parallel teacher, and he also has a mentor. Also he has been on the national literacy strategy, 'Grammar for writing' course. He went to a conference on refugee children because he has a refugee in his class and was particularly eager to support him better. He has been to circle time training with Jenny Mosely because he identified that he was not leading circle time well and wanted to do that better. He has also had extra observations as an NQT, so he has had three observations a term with individual feedback, and has done three observations a term of other people teaching.

A middle manager

He has been on the 'Grammar for writing' course. He went to Year 6 mathematics booster training. He went to booster English training and on a course on RE [religious education] assessment at the professional development centre [PDC]. As the humanities co-ordinator he went on a course at the Museum of London about teaching 'Victorians' and he went to some agreed RE syllabus planning courses again at our local PDC.

A senior manager

She is head of the early years unit. Her courses are obviously at a much more senior level. She has attended lots of conferences and workshops on the general area of effectiveness and improvement in the early years, including a seminar on what are children learning in the early years. So in her career she has reached a much more reflective stage, she is not really learning skills any more. She has also done NPQH [National Professional Qualification for Headship] training this year.

The overseas supply teacher
She has done all the school things and especially the induction at the beginning of the year. We sent her to the introduction to numeracy hour and literacy hour, run by the LEA. She has had extra observations and feedback because she is so unfamiliar with the English system. As is the case for NQTs, she has three observations a term with individual feedback.

The headteacher
I try to provide a good model for professional development of course, as all good heads should. It's important for me to keep up to date with good classroom practice through the school CPD programme. I go to the LEA Heads Consultative regularly. I attended an Excellence in Cities day conference about learning support units. I went to the Tower Hamlets LEA two day headteachers' conference. I did the Leadership Programme for Serving Headteachers (LPSH), which I found extremely useful and rewarding. I went to an exclusions training session which was really boring and useless, but that happens occasionally doesn't it? I have been to several conversations at the London Leadership Centre, and to a 'Leading and Learning' conference run by the *Guardian* and the Hay Group. I have started doing executive mentor training, which I am finding really useful and interesting. Finally, I got my ICT [information and communications technology] co-ordinator to teach me how to use PowerPoint!

CPD work – therefore means providing structures and procedures to co-ordinate developmental opportunities so as to promote such growth and help staff develop and improve their workplace performance. An understanding of how adults learn and the training and development cycle can help here, but it also means creating a culture where learning is seen as central to everything that is done, where there is a community of learners or a professional learning community.

Ongoing professional development should be fully integrated into the life of the school, not seen as something brought in from the outside by 'experts', and there should be clear and consistent means of identifying the needs for CPD and assessing its effectiveness. Continuing professional development co-ordinators need to balance the development needs of the individual and the institution, and promote a positive and participative attitude to CPD from all educational managers. It is also important, as discussed in the previous chapter, that there is an understanding of how adults learn and what constitutes effective learning.

CHAPTER FOUR

Identifying training and development needs

- Individual or school needs
- Taking account of workload and well-being
- Finding out what CPD staff want and need
- Catering for a range of people and learning styles
- Performance management
- Setting objectives

The first two stages of the staff development cycle are concerned with the identification of staff needs and their analysis. The measurable discrepancy between the present state of affairs and the desired state of affairs is the first and pivotal issue of CPD or staff development management. No CPD should be undertaken without taking into account what teachers and other staff already know and can do. It is therefore important to identify individuals' needs along with those of the school and the education system. Needs identification is about discovering individuals' needs for training and in which particular areas it might be most effective.

INDIVIDUAL OR SCHOOL NEEDS

Continuing professional development co-ordinators and other educational leaders have to ensure that training and development programmes meet the needs of both individual staff and their schools, minimizing any tensions that may exist between system needs and priorities (the school development plan) and those of individuals (the individual development plan). Continuing professional development has to meet several, sometimes competing, needs:

- the school's agenda in the form of its development plan;
- government initiatives;
- LEA initiatives;
- individuals' needs – which can be broken down into the professional, personal and propersonal, as we outlined in previous chapters.

To make best use of time and money, there needs to be 'joined up' thinking across all these areas. This is not easy: Her Majesty's Inspectorate (HMI) (Ofsted, 2002b) found, for instance, that the link between performance management and the school's other planning cycles and procedures was weak in around three-fifths of the schools they visited.

One of the key issues that CPD co-ordinators have to consider is managing the tension between the demands of the school (as reflected in school development plans), the latest government or local initiatives and the needs of individuals. In the past, professional development has been much better at addressing school needs than individuals' needs. However, CPD can only be effective if it is rooted in a commitment to evaluate and move forward individuals' basic teaching competence. Without this, school development is unlikely to occur and certainly not at the speed required to ensure continuing improvement. Individual and school needs have to be brought together. This has to be managed within a finite budget.

The different approaches to the management of people (or HRM) that schools take will make a difference here. Is the human resource approach one of 'hard' economic utilitarianism or more of a 'soft' developmental humanism where staff are valued, morale is high and they are likely to be well motivated? Interestingly, the Ofsted handbook tells inspectors that 'professional development should reflect the professional and career needs of the individual, as well as the needs of the school' (2003a). It is important to remember that professional development can serve both individual *and* system needs – it is not always a case of serving one or the other. Fortunately, to make matters easier, the two often go together – individuals' needs very often overlap with those of the school. Also, it is important to remember that development cannot be forced – it is the person who develops (active) and not the person who is developed (passive). People who are excited and motivated by the experience of their own learning are likely to communicate that excitement to pupils.

One of the issues to consider is the degree to which training provision, particularly off-site courses, can effectively meet individual professional development needs. Balancing the needs of individuals with those of the school, especially with limited CPD budgets, has already been alluded to. School development and other plans will clearly show priorities but Connor argues that 'without a clear analysis of individual need, strategies for corporate development can fall on barren ground' (1997: 49). He gives the example of a department in a secondary school:

> Let us assume the English department has identified the need to strengthen its teaching of media. The second in department is sent on a course run by an external provider. An adviser is brought to a team meeting and does a splendid job of outlining a creative, activity based approach to the teaching of the subject centred on the concept of pupils doing things: making newspapers, editing TV news bulletins, writing comment columns and the like. So far, so good. But what of the two newly qualified members of the department who struggle to achieve purposeful order with group work? What of the teacher of 30 years' experience who does not perceive the need at his time of life to master the skills of desktop publishing and what has that got to do with English teaching anyway, thank you very much? (Ibid.: 49)

■ PERSONAL DEVELOPMENT

But what about *personal* development? Managers and leaders of CPD need to ensure that personal development is not marginalized as it is crucial to teacher effectiveness and school success. Research makes a compelling case for personal development as a key component of teacher development. In the introductory chapter professional development was defined as the knowledge and skills relating to 'occupational role development' and personal development as the development of 'the person, often the "whole person"' (Waters, 1998: 30), and that personal development was 'often necessary to complement and "complete" professional development' (ibid.: 35).

Also personal development can have wider benefits. As Davey suggests: 'An individual's personal development may not be used immediately within an institution but often constitutes a resource which can be drawn upon in the future to the benefit of the wider education service' (2000: 34).

The more common approach to personal development adopted by schools is best described by Waters's term 'propersonal development'. This is development that is not genuinely 'personal' in its focus but is personal development for professional development purposes (Waters, 1998: 35). Teachers and educational leaders are increasingly being asked to acquire and develop their emotional intelligence as well as their knowledge and skills. Research, especially into highly effective leaders is pointing to the importance of this and it reinforces Waters's exhortation for teacher development which links improved personal management with increased professional efficacy. Do most schools' CPD policies and practices recognize fully that professional and personal spheres are mutually supportive and beneficial?

As we have seen, the stance of individual schools to staff development and the management of their people resource is crucially important, and it may be, as Carol Adams of the GTC has suggested, that we need 'human resources policies fit for the 21st century', in which employers 'see them as valuable assets to be nurtured and developed' (Woodward, 2003). Continuing professional development co-ordinators should ensure that this nurturing includes elements of personal development. This has been recognized by another government initiative, the *Staff Health and Wellbeing* project which states its preferred school HRM policy as one that clarifies the personal developmental needs of teachers in the same way as in other professions:

> The business world is recognizing that there is a link between health and wellbeing of employees and the productivity of an organization. There is a compelling business case to be made for investing in the wellbeing of employees. Similarly it could be argued that the health of a school community and its capacity to be effective is, in part, a product of the health of the staff who work there. (DfES, 2002b: 7)

However, meeting the needs of individuals makes the CPD co-ordinator's role yet harder. There are many different people taking many different roles in schools. Each person will have different needs, different learning styles and will be at a different stage of development. Table 4.1 illustrates five stages that new teachers typically go through. Clearly there is no point in planning professional development requiring someone to think deeply about assessment for instance, when they are in the 'Survival' stage battling for control. Equally, teachers at the 'Moving On' stage will want more than quick tips.

TABLE 4.1 FIVE STAGES THAT TEACHERS GO THROUGH

Stage	Characteristics
Early idealism	Feeling that everything is possible and having a strong picture of how you want to teach ('I'll never shout'). This is a fantasy stage where you imagine pupils hanging on your every word.
Survival	Reality strikes. You live from day to day, needing quick fixes and tips. You find it hard to solve problems because there are so many of them. Behaviour management is of particular concern – you have nightmares about losing control. You are too stressed and busy to reflect. Colds and sore throats seem permanent.
Recognizing difficulties	You can see problems more clearly. You can identify difficulties and think of solutions because there is some space in your life. You move forward.
Hitting the plateau	Key problems, such as behaviour management and organization, have been solved so you feel things are going well. You feel you are mastering teaching. You begin to enjoy it and do not find it too hard, but you do not want to tackle anything different or take on any radical new initiatives. If forced you will pay lip service to new developments. Some teachers spend the rest of their career at this stage.
Moving on	You are ready for further challenges. You want to try out different styles of teaching, new age groups, take more responsibilities.

Source: Bubb, 2003a: 63

Hustler et al. have drawn pen portraits of types of teacher saying, 'It is clear that the "person" a teacher is, makes a difference, revealed from the somewhat differing learning styles, personality characteristics, and social situations reflected' (2003: 220).

TAKING ACCOUNT OF WORKLOAD AND WELL-BEING

Staff well-being is important to consider in relation to professional development. We all remember how a course became a beacon to look forward to and how we returned from it with a spring in our step. To a degree, CPD co-ordinators need to look at the potential of CPD to motivate, refresh and reward. There may be teachers for whom some inspiring CPD will really help keep them in the job and being effective.

For instance, some schools, mainly in the independent sector, give a term's sabbatical for teachers with more than 20 years' service. Teachers have to plan what they are going to do with the time, but they are encouraged to follow personal interests not things to do with their job. So they spend a term not working but travelling or reading all the works of William Shakespeare or walking the length of the Thames in chunks of a day or two. The school expects nothing from this other than a refreshed teacher – a reward for those rare people who stay in the same school for 20 years.

Many teachers work over 60 hours per week in term time and simply do not feel that they have the time for professional development, that it will be another thing to do – a burden. Training during the day causes extra work in preparing lessons for others to teach, having to deal with problems afterwards and not getting the curriculum taught and course work done to a good standard. Continuing professional development in twilight sessions is hard because people are tired. The venue for professional development is important to consider. Courses are held in a range of rooms and buildings, not all of which are conducive to professional development. They can be judged in terms of the quality of the food rather than the learning, which is not to dismiss the importance of feel-good factors. Training in hotels tends to offer a pampering touch, which might be worth the extra expense but may not. Some courses are held in places that are hard to get to, especially on public transport. All these things need to be considered so that the professional development meets individual needs and circumstances.

Some schools offer teachers flexibility in how they spend their CPD time. Many CPD opportunities are arranged for after school either within the school or nearby at the LEA professional development centre. Teachers agree to attend at least 15 hours of CPD outside of the school day, and they log this. In recompense the school allows those teachers to do what they like on three of the five statutory INSET days. Staff like this flexibility in meeting their specific needs when they want. It is seen as preferable to a 'one size fits all' approach to school training days. Other schools pay staff for professional development activities that take place at weekends or holidays. This is explained in clause 16.2.5 of the *School Teachers' Pay and Conditions* (DfES, 2002a).

FINDING OUT WHAT CPD STAFF WANT AND NEED

So how are the training and development needs of individuals gleaned? Typical methods for the former are management reviews and discussions. Connor describes what is a common school pattern around placing CPD within the context of team and school development or improvement plans:

> Much of this is based around the most important management set piece in the school, a series of formal review meetings between team leaders, the headteacher and a linked deputy. At these meetings development priorities are discussed and agreed within the structure of the whole school needs and action is formulated. This then provides the context for team leaders and the school to plan their professional development activities for the year. (1997: 48)

The most used methods for assessing the training and development needs of individuals are interviews and questionnaires. Performance management reviews can be extremely useful to elicit participants' views of their needs, but are not always helpful because it is often difficult for teachers to think about those areas of their own practice where they feel least knowledgeable, skilled and competent.

Effective needs assessment is an important factor in contributing to the success of training programmes. This cannot always be derived from interviews and questionnaires – some people do not know what they need. Monitoring of teaching, such as observation, is useful in such cases. The time and effort put into identifying needs accurately is well worthwhile.

The role of individuals in the identification of their needs has often been a minor one. Indeed, there is evidence that where they do choose the professional development they undertake, it can be in a random and ad hoc way:

> It involved them glancing through a list or booklet of advertised professional development courses prepared by their employing schools or professional association. They selected a course to attend based on criteria such as their interest in the topic, when and where it was to be held, and/or its cost, and whether or not the school or employer will meet these costs. The linking of the course to their actual professional development needs appeared to be of minor significance. (Harris, B., 2000: 26)

Professional development portfolios are useful in chronicling where one has been and planning where one wants to go (see Chapter 2) and helping individuals to be greater advocates for their own learning needs. Some people draw up individual professional development plans (IPDPs).

CATERING FOR A RANGE OF PEOPLE AND LEARNING STYLES

Any school will have a range of people working within it. If one looks just at teachers, there will be people with a range of experience and needs, and who vary in how effective their teaching is. Kathryn Riley (2003) distinguishes two broad groups of teachers, which she calls the 'glow-worms' and 'skylarks'.

THE GLOW-WORMS

Many of the 'glow-worms' find it difficult to think beyond the confines of their classroom. Locked into a dependency culture by prescriptive reforms, they are cautious and lack spontaneity, caught up in a 'painting by numbers approach to teaching'. They find it difficult to see how they can take responsibility for their own professionalism. Nevertheless, the 'glow' of teaching is still there, however dimly lit and however intermittent. They occasionally get excited about new things such as interactive whiteboards that they see having a direct impact on pupils. To 'glow' again, this group will need to be fanned and nurtured.

THE SKYLARKS

The 'skylarks' recognize some of the difficulties created by the centralized reform process. However, they seem less constrained and less likely to see themselves as prisoners of the government's agenda than the glow-worms. Skylarks talk about the need to put the 'sparkle' back into teaching. They are keen on sharing good practice with colleagues in other schools, having sabbaticals and secondments; participating in international and professional exchange programmes. They want 'professional learning' that is distinctively different from the 'professional development through courses' model typically available to teachers. The skylarks want time and space to develop.

LEARNING STYLES

One must also remember that people will have varying preferred learning styles (see Chapter 2). It would also be useful for CPD co-ordinators to audit the range of learning styles amongst their staff. Importantly, such an audit may help to explain teachers' and support staffs' perceptions and expectations of the training they receive, and to support schools in recognizing and facilitating different ways to support individuals' learning.

The challenge for CPD co-ordinators is to ensure that all groups and types of people get the professional development that will move them on. In any size school this is difficult, but in a large one there will be more people to liaise with. Do you ask people what they want or wait for them to ask? You will find yourself torn between government and local initiatives, where the school wants to go and individual needs. Having a professional development committee with whom to discuss these issues is useful (see Chapter 3).

PERFORMANCE MANAGEMENT

Participation in CPD is an essential part of any performance management (PM) cycle and it certainly is a central feature of the scheme introduced in English schools in September 2000 (DfEE, 2000a; 2000b). The positive role of PM in CPD has recently been reiterated by the government (Miliband, 2003), which sees performance management as:

- a way to recognize and promote excellence and professionalism;
- improving the quality of teaching;
- focusing on pupil achievement;
- having the annual appraisal interview as 'just one moment in a continuous process of review and improvement';
- teachers learning from each other on the basis of structured observation and hard evidence;
- identifying professional needs and meeting those needs individually and as part of a team;
- promoting transparent relationships with no hidden agendas and recognizing a teacher's right to respond to feedback;
- reassuring parents and taxpayers that education is idealistic but also hard-headed in promoting high standards.

The linkage between performance management and professional development is crucial and the DfES wants 'every teacher to work in a vibrant professional learning community in which they recognise the importance of CPD in improving their teaching and their pupils' learning' (Miliband, 2003: 6). This needs to start during initial training, with teachers seeing 'performance management as their right and continuing professional development as their duty'. As the Minister notes:

> As teachers make their way through their careers, we then need to honour that principle, by ensuring that performance management provides opportunities for regular reflection on a teacher's needs and leads to informed judgements about the appropriate action that should follow in terms of setting development objectives, providing access to relevant development opportunities and reviewing progress.

Effective performance management arrangements provide schools with a route to better reconciliation between the individual's and the school's priorities for development. They allow individual, departmental or section and whole-school developmental priorities to be identified and enable individuals to see how their own development fits into and contributes to the wider school or departmental developmental agenda.

The notion of managing performance is controversial, however. In unsound hands performance management can be used to control, to ensure uniformity and to de-professionalize; in sound hands it can be used to support, coach and validate good practice, whilst respecting and promoting proper autonomy, creativity and variety. Used with flair the process can be used to support the school's vision and help develop pupils and staff alike; it is an effective instrument but it is only as effective as the person who uses it. Individuals whose team leader does not get round to holding individual meetings or does not carry them out well will suffer. One secondary deputy, in charge of performance management and CPD, gets frustrated: 'You have to chase, chase, chase and don't take no for an answer. It's worse than getting the kids to get their course work in.' He now sets a training day aside for the interviews to make sure that they happen.

Worth Primary School in Cheshire (see Case study 4.1) has made great efforts to give professional development the high priority it deserves and to link it closely with performance management and other planning processes. It has also endeavoured to ensure that value for money linked to effective CPD and pupil outcomes is paramount.

CASE STUDY 4.1: WORTH PRIMARY SCHOOL

The senior management team, governors and all staff of Worth Primary School are highly committed to, and greatly value, training and development, and fund it appropriately. The school believes that receiving and providing high-quality, effective training and development enables the organization and individuals continuously to improve and develop. Well-trained, well-motivated and effective staff, governors and trainees are a valuable resource that can be used to provide a first-class education for all pupils.

The school unashamedly puts performance management at the heart of professional development, it sees performance management as a structured, professional dialogue that reviews and enhances organizational effectiveness, staff motivation and professional development. Team leaders at Worth see PM as a key tool in moving an organization from being a series of processes, structures and separate groups of individuals to an effective, flexible and focused learning organization. There is a direct linkage between pupil progress targets, professional development targets, action plans and the school development plan; one informs the other in a cycle of growth and development.

Training is consciously reduced in quantity but enhanced in terms of quality, impact and monitoring. For professional development to be regarded as effective it must impact on the individual member of staff, change a behaviour or process and be seen to impact on pupils and colleagues. Virtually all professional development is organized within set training days or a few twilight sessions; ad hoc training and meetings are unpopular and are strongly discouraged. This ruthless focus on that which is needed saves precious time, goodwill and funds that are so often wasted in so many organizations. Every event and development has an 'opportunity cost'; these must be reviewed and all resources placed where and when they are most effective.

Source: Taylor, 2004

Performance management is an ideal forum for discussing individuals' needs but schools vary in how well it works. Clearly it should be a forum to discuss professional development, but some schools and teachers do not take it very seriously, as illustrated in this posting from a teacher on the *TES* website: 'Ninety per cent of the time it is toothless ticky-box bollocks. I was appraised a year ago and got a good report, which highlighted some training needs about which I have asked about at three monthly intervals since but without result. What nonsense it all is!' (Bubb, 2003c).

Her Majesty's Inspectorate's report into PM found that there was scope for improvement in objectives related to teachers' professional development in at least half of the schools they visited (Ofsted, 2002b). There was a tendency for objectives to be activities or tasks, such as 'produce a report', 'attend a training course'. They often did not detail the strategies or the support needed, including resources and training, to help progress. Training plans are one of the weakest features of performance management practice.

Making the performance management or professional development interviews more useful for all concerned is key. Money and time are precious resources that need to be spent well. These sorts of questions, based on *The Career Entry and Development Profile* (TTA, 2003a), may structure people's thinking:

- What aspects of your job would you like more experience in – strengths or interests, weaknesses or areas of limited experience?

- What do you find most interesting and rewarding about your job? Why? How do you want to develop these?

- What are your main strengths and achievements? What brought them about? What's helped your learning?

- Do you have any new roles that you need help with?

- Is there anything that you planned to achieve in the recent past that you didn't? Why not? Can you learn anything from this?

- How do you see your career panning out? What's the next step to get you there?

USING COACHING/MENTORING SKILLS IN DISCUSSING PROFESSIONAL DEVELOPMENT

It is generally agreed that adults learn best when they determine their own focus and that they learn through being asked questions and being given time to reflect. Coaching is a development tool that helps people move forward in their work, and can be used by line managers or people who help others decide their professional development priorities. Moss and Silk (2003) recommend that those acting as coaches/mentors ask searching questions to help staff find their own professional development needs. The power of the coaching model comes from the use of questions, rather than advice. The coach's expertise is in active listening on a number of levels, asking powerful questions and holding the member of staff accountable for the actions agreed.

Some of the tools used in a coaching conversation are:

- active listening (contextual to elicit meaning);
- rephrasing concisely;
- clarifying questions;
- asking permission;
- acknowledgement;
- accountability.

It is important that people feel ownership of their objectives. They should be jointly negotiated or at least the result of talking to someone, with the individual being proactive about identifying areas to develop, and how they can be achieved.

SETTING OBJECTIVES

The benefit of objective-setting as a way to manage steady improvement by children and adults is well recognized. Objectives provide a framework for teachers doing a complex job at a very fast pace. They encourage people to prioritize tasks and make best use of time and other resources, and feel a sense of achievement when objectives are met. However, one teacher said: 'What is the point of setting objectives? I have to be able to do *everything* to be able to teach at all. If my planning, control, assessment, teaching strategies or whatever are not right everything falls apart' (Bubb, 2001: 27 original emphasis). She has a point. To be effective, all areas have to be met. However, if the processes of reflection, setting an objective, drawing up an action plan and evaluating the impact of the learning do not take place, professional development may be reduced to the level of ad hoc activities. The very act of writing things down causes people to consider whether they are the real priorities and gives them something to focus on.

These steps are useful in the identifying and analysing of needs:

1 Examine evidence about your teaching – test results, observation feedback, letters from parents, and so on.

2 Summarize key points.

3 Reflect on professional development needs, ideally with another person.

4 Identify goals/objectives.

5 Draw up an action plan.

A frequent problem with objectives is that they are not made specific enough, which can lead to failure. Bubb's research on NQTs (2001) found that many objectives were too large so that they had to be repeated. For instance, one induction tutor wanted her NQT 'to teach the National Literacy and National Numeracy Strategies effectively'. Wherever possible, individuals' objectives need to link in with other developments in the school such as those in the SDP. For instance, in a school where a priority was 'Improve the quality of teaching in AT1 mathematics at Key Stage 2 through a comprehensive staff training programme', an individual teacher's professional development objective was: 'Participate in training in the teaching of AT1 mathematics through school-based courses, self study and observation of other teachers.'

Objectives should be SMART: **S**pecific, **M**easurable, **A**chievable, **R**ealistic and **R**elevant and **T**ime-bound. This is, of course, also true of learning objectives in lesson plans or targets on individual education plans (IEPs). Unfortunately this is easier said than done. Consider an objective such as 'Improve control'. This may be too large, and could take a long time to achieve. It is better to be more specific about what needs most urgent attention. Always remember that objectives should be able to be met, while containing a degree of challenge.

DIAGNOSING A PROBLEM AREA

Some teachers and other staff have suffered from not having areas for development accurately diagnosed. It is very hard to decide what to work on when things are not going right because each problem has a huge knock-on effect. Always remember that objectives should be able to be met, while containing a degree of challenge, but setting ones which will be useful and that contain the right amount of challenge is not easy. Particularly when someone has a problem, it needs to be reflected upon and diagnosed accurately in order to draw up the most useful objectives and plan of action. Brainstorm its features and results. For instance, Rachel's control problems include the following:

- Her voice is thin and becomes screechy when raised.
- Sometimes she comes down hard on the pupils and at other times she lets them get away with things.
- She takes a long time to get attention.
- She runs out of time so plenaries are missed, the class is late to assembly, and so on.
- Pupils call out.
- Pupils are too noisy.
- A small group of pupils is behaving badly.
- Even the usually well-behaved pupils are being naughty.

Look at your list. Does it seem a fair picture? It is easy to be too hard or too generous. Then list some positive features, relating to the problem area. For instance, Rachel:

- really likes and cares for the pupils;
- speaks to them with respect;
- plans interesting work for them;
- is very effective when working with individuals or small groups;
- has better control in the early part of the day, and works hard.

Think about why things go well. Reflection on successes is very powerful. The process of analysing strengths is very helpful and this positive thinking can now be used to reflect on problems. Try to tease out the reasons for the problem. Think of actions to remedy situations – they can be surprisingly easy. It is often the small things that make a difference.

Rachel completed a very detailed action plan (see Figure 4.1) because she had such problems. Such detail is not always necessary, although it illustrates how breaking a problem into manageable chunks helps.

CONCLUSION

Identifying and analysing needs can be time-consuming but, like any in-depth look at pupils' learning needs, the effort is worthwhile. The next challenge is to find the best way to meet needs – the topic of the next chapter.

Name: Rachel   Date: 1 Nov   Date objective to be met: 16 Dec

Objective: To improve control, particularly after playtimes, in independent literacy activities, at tidying-
               up time, and home-time

Success criteria	Actions	When	Progress
Gets attention more quickly	Brainstorm attention-getting devices with other teachers Use triangle, etc. to get attention	4.11	7.11 Triangle made children more noisy – try cymbal
Rarely shouts	Voice management course Project the voice Don't talk over children	19.11	23.11 Using more range in voice – working!
Plans for behaviour management	Glean ideas from other teachers through discussion and observation Watch videos on behaviour management strategies Write notes for behaviour management on plans	4.11	12.11 Improvement through lots of tips, staying calm and being more positive. Not perfect and exhausting but better
Successful procedures for sorting out disputes after playtimes	Glean ideas from other teachers Ask playground supervisors to note serious incidents Children to post messages in incident box	11.11	18.11 Incident box really working for those who can write and I can now tell when there's a serious problem
Successful procedures for tidying	Discuss what other teachers do Start tidying earlier and time it with reward for beating record. Sanctions for the lazy	8.11	25.11 Sandtimer for tidying working well though still a few children not helping. Might try minutes off playtime
Successful procedures for home-time	Discuss ideas with other teachers Monitors to organize things to take home Start home-time procedures earlier and time them (with rewards?)	25.11	2.12 Changed routine so tidy earlier. Some Y6 children helping give out things to take home
Children succeed in independent literacy activities	Ideas from literacy co-ordinator Change seating for groups Differentiate work Discuss with additional adults	2.12	9.12 All class doing same independent activity working better Mrs H helping

FIGURE 4.1 AN ACTION PLAN TO MEET AN OBJECTIVE (BUBB et al., 2002: 111)

CHAPTER FIVE

Meeting CPD needs

- Collating CPD needs
- Finding what the CPD options are
- Action plans

COLLATING CPD NEEDS

Meeting professional development needs is a key task. Collating everyone's CPD needs is important so that you can identify areas of commonality and get the whole picture. The data gathered about training needs, at both individual and school level, will need to be analysed and, most likely, a report written and presented to the headteacher and governing body. Table 5.1 is an extract from a secondary school co-ordinator's logging system. This relates to courses attended, the twilight INSET training that the school runs and the informal ways that relate specifically to identified performance management needs.

FINDING WHAT THE CPD OPTIONS ARE

The range of professional development activities is huge and offers on-the-job, off-the-job, and close-to-the-job opportunities. Developing a culture of development and enquiry has been the key to many schools' success, and this is explored further in Chapters 2 and 7. People often think only of courses but here are some ideas for self-study, observations, extending your professional practice and developing your pastoral experience.

SELF-STUDY

1 Reflecting on progress so far.
2 Reading the educational press.
3 Learning more about strategies for teaching the pupils with special needs.
4 Learning more about strategies for teaching pupils with English as an additional language (EAL).

TABLE 5.1 PROFESSIONAL DEVELOPMENT NEEDS IDENTIFIED THROUGH PERFORMANCE MANAGEMENT

Teacher	Professional development need	External CPD	Internal CPD	Informal
A	Leadership development for middle managers NQT mentoring	LftM Induction tutor course	Observation skills	Books on induction, etc.
B	Public examination officer Connect 3 Network Manager	Course		Discussion with previous exam officer
C	AS Drama Unit 3 PGCE mentoring	PGCE mentor training		HoD; other schools
D	See Career Entry Profile		NQT Induction	
E	Connexions training	Visit other schools		
F	AS/A2 PE Sports Leadership Award Sports Co-ordinator Learning styles	Exam board course LEA meetings	Learning styles	Reading
G	CAD/CAM GCSE Electronic Products, Systems & Control	Course	HoD	
H	SEN Code of Practice Co-ordination of work of outside agencies	SEN meetings; network with Sencos	Ed Psych session	
I	KS3 National Strategy Performance Management for non-teaching staff	LEA courses		Coaching from deputy
J	GNVQ Computer-generated report writing Liaison with outside agencies Use of PowerPoint Citizenship	Course	Report session	Self-study on PP
K	Getting QTS	OTT course		Develop portfolio
L	Intranet	Visit schools with intranets	Science Dept	
M	AS/A2 German Interactive whiteboard	IoE course		Self-study
N	KS3 NLS Target-setting	LEA courses	Eng Dept	

5 Learning more about strategies for teaching very able pupils.

6 Visiting local education centres, museums and venues for outings.

7 Looking at the educational possibilities of the local environment.

8 Working with the SENCO on writing individual education plans.

9 Improving subject knowledge through reading, observation, discussion, and so on.

10 Analysing planning systems in order to improve your own.

11 Analysing marking and record-keeping systems to improve your own.

■ OBSERVING OTHER PRACTITIONERS

    1 Observing other teachers teaching.

    2 Observing teachers in other schools – similar and different to yours.

    3 Observing someone teach your class(es).

    4 Observing someone teach a lesson that you have planned.

    5 Observing how pupils of different ages learn.

    6 Discussing lesson observations.

    7 Tracking a pupil for a day to see teaching through their eyes.

    8 Watching a colleague take an assembly.

    9 Observing a visiting expert.

   10 Shadowing a colleague.

   11 Visiting and seeing other schools in action.

   12 Observing and working with an artist in residence.

■ EXTENDING PROFESSIONAL EXPERIENCE

    1 Leading school-based INSET.

    2 Rotating roles/jobs.

    3 Developing your professional profile.

    4 Taking part in developing a learning community.

    5 Posting comments to an online staffroom such as the *TES* staffroom.

    6 Co-ordinating/managing a subject.

    7 Assuming the role of leader for a special initiative in school.

    8 Carrying out action research in the classroom/school.

    9 Contributing to a professional publication.

   10 Gaining experience of interviewing.

   11 Acting as a performance reviewer.

   12 Serving as a governor.

   13 Contributing to courses.

   14 Serving on professional committees/working parties and so on.

   15 Becoming a union representative.

   16 Leading/supervising non-professionals who work in the classroom.

   17 Working on extracurricular activities.

   18 Taking part in staff conferences on individual pupils.

   19 Working with other professionals such as education psychologists.

   20 Working with an exam board or marking examination papers.

   21 Networking and sharing with a group of colleagues from another school.

22 Team teaching.

23 Learning through professional practice with others.

24 Developing use of ICT.

25 Counselling parents.

26 Collaborating with peripatetic teachers.

27 Mentoring a trainee or NQT.

28 Organizing a display.

▮▮ WORKING WITH PUPILS

1 Taking responsibility for a group of pupils on an off-site visit.

2 Developing teaching skills across a wide age and ability range.

3 Working with pupils on school councils.

4 Working with pupils to present an assembly, play, performance events.

5 Working with pupils preparing a school year book.

6 Integrating the use of pupil websites and online communities into teaching.

7 Using email/video conferencing between pupils.

8 Negotiating targets and evaluating work alongside pupils.

9 Mentoring and counselling pupils.

10 Helping pupils with peer mentoring.

There is a big movement towards school-based professional development. As someone on the *TES* staffroom says: 'Teachers are the most valuable resource we have for INSET. If more teachers exchanged ideas and shared good practice (cliché) on a regular informal basis, we would all be better off.' Some schools' staff are better at this sort of dialogue than others. You will really benefit if you are part of a networked learning community, as some schools are (see Chapter 2).

▮▮ OBSERVATION

Whatever role people have and whatever stage they are at in the profession, they will learn a great deal about their job from watching others doing it. Similarly, the more people watch children learning, and think about the problems that they have, the better their teaching will be. Newly qualified teachers find this the most useful of all induction activities (Totterdell et al., 2002).

Effective teachers make the most of any opportunities to observe others, formally or just informally around the school. They watch a range of people. It is very cheering to see that everyone has similar problems and fascinating to study the different ways people manage them. Peer observation is stressful, so in a sense things get worse before they get better, but it is worth getting over initial discomfort or reluctance and shyness about being observed and sharing problems with colleagues.

However, observing so that one gets something out of it is not easy. People need to have a focus for observation because there is so much to see that they can end up getting overwhelmed. Observations need to be linked to something that people want to develop. For instance, someone who wants to improve pace in introductions, needs to notice the speed of the exposition, how many pupils answer questions and how the teacher manages to move them on, how instructions are given, resources distributed, and how off-task behaviour is dealt with.

It is essential to look at teaching in relation to learning. Always think about cause and effect. Why are the pupils behaving as they are? The cause is usually related to teaching. People should be encouraged to jot down things of interest, certain phrases that teachers use to get attention, ways they organize tidying-up time, and so on. Forms with prompts (Figures 5.1 and 5.2) can help observers focus by writing a few bullet points about what they have learned, and the ideas that could be implemented. It is valuable for staff to log who they have observed using a form such as Figure 5.3.

CASE STUDY 5.1: TEACHERS' OBSERVATIONS FOR PROFESSIONAL DEVELOPMENT

Julian was interested in developing his explanations of mathematical concepts so that he could make things clearer and not get thrown by pupils' questions. With this clearly in mind, he chose to observe mathematics lessons where new topics were being started. He learned the benefits of rock-solid subject knowledge and scaffolding information. He also gained a broader repertoire of questioning techniques that he was able to try out in his own teaching.

Diana had problems with behaviour management, so observed a teacher with a good reputation for control. She gained some ideas, but found that much of this experienced teacher's control was 'invisible' – he just cleared his throat and the class became quiet. So, she observed a supply teacher, and someone with only a little more experience than herself. It was hard to persuade them to let her observe, but when they realized how fruitful the experience and the discussions afterwards would be, they accepted. These lessons, though not so perfectly controlled, gave Diana much more to think about and she learned lots of useful strategies. Both teachers found it useful to have Diana's views on the lesson, as a non-threatening observer, so they too gained from the experience.

Miranda wanted to improve how she shared learning intentions with pupils so she observed a teacher who was known to be good at this. She not only listened well to the teacher's explanation of what he wanted the pupils to achieve but saw that he wrote different lesson outcomes for each group under the headings 'What I'm looking for'. As well as focusing on the teacher, she watched the pupils carefully and spoke to them about their understanding of what they were doing and why. This gave her insight into children's learning and areas of confusion.

■ COURSES

Although it is important to get away from sole reliance on courses, there are clearly some great benefits to attending external input. The trouble is that there is so much to choose from. Penny Bentley, the head of Columbia Primary School says, 'I am sometimes amazed that I can go through a huge pile of post and most of it will be advertising for courses. Most of it I put straight in the bin' (Bentley, 2002/2003: 59). Some CPD

LESSON OBSERVATION SHEET

Teacher
Subject
Learning objective

Date and time
Additional adults

Prompts:	OK	Comments. What has the teacher done to get this response?
Pay attention		
Behave well		
Relate well to adults and pupils		
Are interested		
Understand what to do		
Understand why they're doing an activity		
Gain new knowledge, skills		
Speak and listen well		
Have errors corrected		
Work hard		
Act responsibly		
Understand how well they have done		
Understand how they can improve		
Enjoy the lesson		

FIGURE 5.1 LESSON OBSERVATION SHEET – HOW WELL PUPILS LEARN (BUBB, 2001: 90)

Observing other teachers – what have you learned? What could you implement in your classroom?

Teacher   Year Group   Subject   Date and time

Arrangement of the room	What and when implemented
Resources	
Behaviour management	
Teaching strategies	

FIGURE 5.2 FORMAT FOR RECORDING IDEAS FROM OBSERVATIONS

A Record of Observations of Other Teachers

Date	Time	Class	Teacher & school	Subject & Focus

FIGURE 5.3 RECORD OF OBSERVATIONS (BUBB, 2003a: 148)

co-ordinators collate all courses in an INSET bulletin and give it to all staff, but this is very time-consuming and may encourage demands that you simply do not have the budget to meet. Most schools build up a small bank of tried and tested providers whose courses they know will be successful. Outfits that cancel courses cause a huge problem especially if supply cover has been booked, money paid and expectations raised. You also need to consider the timings, prices and environment – some LEAs use poor quality venues, whereas others are based in swanky hotels.

One of us (Sara Bubb) runs the same day-long induction tutor courses for various organizations. Her rate of pay is fixed, but participants have to pay vastly different amounts. At one extreme these courses are free to teachers, in that the LEA or TTA subsidizes them from central funds. Universities and LEAs charge about £90 (or less if there is some sort of service-level agreement) but at the other extreme, courses held in hotels and organized by private consultancies cost around £220 per person. All that people in the hotel are getting extra is a pleasant venue and good food – and perhaps handouts in a folder rather than simply stapled. You will have to decide whether the extra money is worth the feel-good factor.

Course descriptions and target audience are very important to look at to ensure that training will meet needs. Schools are becoming more used to complaining when the course does not deliver what it promises, as in this case:

> Really the course was absolutely awful. It was advertised as a course for classroom practitioners and Sencos but basically it was an optician telling us about machines that can meas-

ure a child's perception ... I got nothing from the course, certainly nothing practical for my children or anything which made me think about my work. (Hustler et al., 2003: 211)

Some people love going on courses: they seem to be professional course attenders. CPD co-ordinators need to have some system, such as Figure 5.4, of making sure that courses are allocated fairly and that they relate to needs. Staff should keep a record of courses attended and their impact (see Figure 5.5) in their professional development portfolio. In this way, courses should be seen as more than 'a good day out ... a bit of fun' (Hustler et al., 2003: 213).

SABBATICALS, TRIPS ABROAD, AND SO ON

Teachers may have an opportunity to take a sabbatical or a trip abroad. The purpose of sabbaticals is to create opportunities for experienced teachers to take on a significant period of development to enhance their own learning and effectiveness, and to bring subsequent benefits to their pupils and their school. Government organizations, charities, unions and industries all have a history of supporting teacher involvement in educational research with the opportunities on offer changing from time to time.

The professional bursaries, best practice research scholarships, teachers' international professional development (TIPD) programme and the sabbaticals offered by the DfES and National College for School Leadership all offer great opportunities. Advertisements for such things are often placed in the *TES* as well as in professional association journals. Advice on European Union funded initiatives is available from the Central Bureau, which is part of the British Council.

The teachers' international professional development scheme enables people to learn

Name
Event details and costs
Why do you need to attend this professional development?
What specifically do you want to get out of it?
How is it addressing your professional development objectives?
How will this event aid your development?
What will be the benefits to the school?

FIGURE 5.4 STAFF DEVELOPMENT BOOKING FORM

Date venue	Course title	How I've implemented ideas

FIGURE 5.5 A RECORD OF COURSES ATTENDED

from and contribute to educational ideas and good practice throughout the world. One group visited four primary and four high schools located in and around Cape Town, South Africa.

◼ MA COURSES AND FURTHER STUDY

Quite a few people consider doing some further study within five years of starting work as a teacher. Teachers, almost by definition, like learning. Some will be keen to improve their tennis and are adult education groupies, and a few like some rigorous intellectual stimulation. They get fed up with one-day professional development sessions, especially when so many of them reflect the school's or the government's agenda and not theirs! They want (and deserve) something more substantial. So, for many people the logical step is to do a higher degree usually a Master's degree.

> I decided to do an MA as I was fed up with the very poor level of INSET available – nothing went deep enough into any area, and I wanted to understand teaching and learning a bit

better. I prefer to pay for the course myself, because then I am not beholden to the school – I do not have to provide feedback from my research, and am not bound to research according to the 'party line'. Yes, it takes up a lot of time, but being able to think freely, to read widely and thereby make changes in your own personal practice makes it worthwhile! (From the *TES* staffroom)

An MA usually takes one year full time or two years part time. There are many to choose from. Within each MA course you usually have some modules that are compulsory and others from which you can choose, so that you study what you like.

The costs of doing an MA in education on a part-time basis are between about £1,000 and £1,600 a year. Some schools pay for it, or make a contribution. Doing an MA is not easy but few regret doing so, and many are passionate, such as this evaluation from an MA student at the Institute of Education: 'It is difficult to write in a few lines the positive impact the course has had on my personal and professional life – I know that sounds a little melodramatic – but it is the case! It's been a thoroughly stimulating and enjoyable experience.'

USING EXTERNAL PROVIDERS OF CPD

There are many external providers of CPD: consultants, LEAs and higher education institutions (HEIs). Some schools buy in external providers to deliver training within their building or join with some other schools. 'We went to another school to see XXX, who is absolutely wonderful … you come out absolutely inspired … it's like a breath of fresh air' (Hustler et al., 2003: 208).

More typically schools send one or two people on courses and expect them to cascade information back. There are pros and cons to each approach. Courses may well not deliver in the way promised, and travel, parking and general wasting of time finding the venue reduce the effectiveness. In-house sessions usually do deliver what the staff need/want and people have less trouble with travel, parking, and so on. Some of these issues were considered in Chapter 4 under the heading 'Best value'.

To assist schools in gaining a better understanding of what they can expect from outside providers of training – still the predominant form of CPD – the Department for Education and Employment (DfEE) published a code of practice in 2001. The *Good Value CPD* document (DfEE, 2001c) sets out over four pages a code of practice delineating what schools and individuals can expect from people and organizations that are publicly funded to provide professional development. The code is based on existing good practice and the principles underpinning high-quality professional development. Good value CPD should:

- meet individual, school and national development priorities;
- be based on good practice – in development activity and in teaching and learning;
- help raise standards of pupils' achievements, including those with special educational needs;
- respect cultural diversity;
- be provided by those with the necessary experience, expertise and skills;

- be planned systematically;
- be based, where appropriate, on relevant standards (for example, subject leaders, SENCOs);
- be based on current research and inspection evidence;
- make effective use of resources, particularly including ICT;
- be provided in accommodation which is fit for purpose;
- provide value for money;
- have effective monitoring and evaluation systems, including seeking out and acting on user feedback to inform the quality of future provision (DfEE, 2001c).

It states that the planning for CPD shall begin with the identification of objectives emerging from the PM and school development processes and that from these 'it will be possible to identify needs, decide what development activity is required and how to provide it, and define the outcomes and how to measure them' (ibid.: 2). The provider of CPD, after a needs assessment analysis, should agree with the school or individual the needs to be addressed, the purposes of the development activity and the success criteria that will be deployed, including, where appropriate, the desired outcomes for pupils' learning and development. The provider should also set out clearly details of those individuals delivering the training as well as, where relevant, the research and inspection evidence that will be informing their input (ibid.: 2). Courses should indicate the target audience and giving an outline of the overall aims of the activity, details of venue, accreditation and progression routes, and so on.

The *Good Value* code of practice also expects providers to state in advance the delivery methods planned and the expectations of participants. Delivery is expected to meet a number of criteria (for example, high-quality materials, differentiation of delivery, necessary expertise, high-quality venue, and so on). In addition, providers during the planning stage must establish success criteria to see the degree to which the provision has been successful in improving opportunities for pupils to succeed. The code of practice recognizes that not all of these outcomes will be easy to measure but does expect any assessment process to include a clear framework for considering the impact on pupils' learning. Participants must be given the opportunity to offer comments on the quality of the provision, whether needs have been met and what improvements might be made. Finally, it makes reference to monitoring processes, equal opportunities and health and safety.

RUNNING TRAINING YOURSELF

Running training yourself has many advantages. It can ensure that input is tailor-made to the school context and its staff. It may be cheaper – but may be not if one adds up the many hours that you are likely to spend in planning it … and worrying about it! Teaching your colleagues is never an easy – or enviable – task. They may not listen to you as well as they would an outsider or a 'name'. Does this comment from a teacher on the *TES* virtual staffroom ring true?

> Next time you sit in a staff meeting you'll see all the behaviour present in a disruptive Year 9 class. How many teachers nail a pupil for being 'unmanageable' and then take a pride in

behaving that same way with colleagues – being stroppy, self-centred and argumentative for the sake of it.

Teachers do not always make brilliant learners, especially at the end of an exhausting day, or in an INSET session when large numbers of your audience want to finish their packing or talk about their holiday. You are bound to have some people who do not want to be there, and others who delight in finding fault with your teaching strategies. Do not panic. You just need to prepare with the cunning of a battle strategist.

It is useful to think of a course (or part of one) that went well and consider the factors that led to its success. For instance:

- The trainer was motivating, had good knowledge of the topic, knew people's needs, had credibility and was confident.
- The group was correctly targeted, receptive and wanted to be there.
- The session was well planned and paced predicting issues but flexible to needs and built in follow-up work in the school.
- The content was really useful and relevant.
- It was run at a quality time in a suitable venue.

Conversely analyse training that did not go well. For instance:

- There were too few or too many participants.
- People were tired; had unrealistic expectations; saw it as a day off; were not intellectually ready; had tunnel vision; arrived late and left early; one person dominated unhelpfully; there was an air of negativity.
- The course did not meet needs.
- The room was not big enough or was inappropriately arranged.
- There were problems with refreshments or technology.
- The tutor was tired, ill prepared, delivered training that people had done before, did not keep to time, or lacked detailed knowledge.

So, the secret is to copy elements that have worked well and avoid things that have not been successful. If only life were so easy! A good starting point is to think 'What do you want people to get out of the session?' As with any lesson, a focus on the learning objectives is key – but not very easy. You might want to refine it by asking yourself what you hope the new teacher, the deputy and the seen-it-all-before cynic will get out of it. Are your aims realistic for the time allocated? How are you going to achieve your intended outcomes? Few people like going to meetings, so how are you going make sure their time is spent well? Will they come prepared? Do you need an agenda? What snags can you foresee?

Take account of the audience's preferred learning styles and make your presentation appeal in visual, auditory and kinaesthetic ways. Think about what sort of meetings or courses you have enjoyed and got something from – the two do not necessarily go together. What were the elements? What sort of training do you not like? What has worked for your staff in the past? For instance, some people hate courses where they are expected to do an activity every five minutes. Nor do many people like hundreds of PowerPoint slides being flashed up, or speakers who recite every word of every slide.

Most people like a bit of pace, a chance to talk through issues, and a trainer with personality and a lot of humour who can keep control of the group, especially that pain who keeps asking such stupid questions.

Think about seating and groupings. Plan the session to a tight schedule. Think of what will work best at the time of day you will be doing the training. What about handouts? If you have some, what will be on them and when will you give them out? As a participant, we want them stapled together, but as trainers we do not like people to read ahead. Are not these just the sorts of dilemmas you face when teaching classes? Yes, but unfortunately you cannot tell adults off when they misbehave, as you can children. They will think it strange when you give them a sticker, too! But you can think about how you will deal with mobile phones going off and people who are late and who wander off the point. Public humiliation is tempting, but remember that you have to work with the culprits.

Expect to be nervous. Being prepared and organized will help, but also give yourself a bit of quiet time before you start so you can focus on the task ahead. Practise your opening line. If you find the thought of everyone looking at you terrifying, get them to look at a screen or a flip chart. Give the group a clear purpose and outcome for the session, and the big picture – what is going to happen.

Make sure you explain any activities clearly – and why you are asking people to do them. Give people tight time limits so they get on with the job. Be selective in the amount of feedback you ask for, because it can take a lot of time and get repetitive. Keeping to time is tricky. Finishing early is never a problem. Over-running is a big no-no, so you will need strategies for moving things on. In your plan you might want to distinguish absolute must-dos from items that can be omitted if you run out of time. No matter how well you plan, you will have to think on your feet.

One last tip: do not apologize for having no time for a certain activity – it will make that part appear highly attractive, and people will feel cheated. Pull the learning together in a slick way with a few minutes to spare and everyone will be happy.

■ SCHOOL-LED TRAINING WITH THE HELP OF A CONSULTANT

Clapton Girls' Technology College in Hackney has run two year-long CPD programmes, the 'Management Development Programme' and 'Teacher 2000'. They each took a year to plan and then ran for a year, as seminars held every three or four weeks. The 'Management Development Programme' has won several awards and was the brainchild of Anne Gold, who works at the Institute of Education. She was the consultant on the programme.

Eileen Carnell, also from the Institute of Education, worked with a small group of teachers on devising 'Teacher 2000' which they delivered to a larger group of teachers over a year.

> In those programmes we involved about 20 different teachers. The 'Management Development Programme' was very successful. One of the successes was that 50 per cent of those on the course went on to obtain a promotion within a year. Unfortunately many of them went to posts outside of the school! (Day, 2003: 52)

With 'Teacher 2000', the impact was much more on classroom practice. The head-teacher, Cheryl Day, said 'you could go into the staff room and hear people talking about ways of learning and how to deliver the curriculum, instead of talking about behaviour or something else' (ibid.).

VIDEOS, SOFTWARE AND DVDs

Videos have long been used for CPD (for a recent example see Hopkins, 2002b) but of much more recent origin is software (for example, 'Transforming learning' – see Hobby, 2001) and DVDs. The latter offer a very good alternative to leading a professional development session yourself. An organization called enabling educational excellence has made interactive DVDs and support materials on topics such as managing challenging behaviour, handling parents, and working with gifted and talented pupils (Brereton, 2001). They enable people in schools to run high-quality training without a trainer, and to use all or parts of it time and time again with individuals, groups and the whole staff. One CPD co-ordinator said:

> Facilitating this training would not be difficult for most CPD co-ordinators. If I can learn to use a DVD, I think anybody could! The preparation did not take very long, as most of it is already done for you. The paper work necessary could easily be prepared by support staff and the co-ordinator just needs to read through the training guide and run through Module 1, about 30 minutes, to understand the structure of the course. Once started the discussion flows quite easily from the on-screen prompts and all you will have to do is keep an eye on the time! (enabling educational excellence, 2002)

ACTION PLANS

When an individual is happy with the professional development objective(s) and knows all the CPD options, they need to break it down into bite-sized chunks – steps or success criteria – and think what they will have to do and what help they will need. People may like to use a SWOT (strengths, weaknesses, opportunities and threats) analysis to help them choose the most suitable activity and to make sure they get the most out of it. Thinking about their strengths and weaknesses, particularly in terms of preferred learning styles, should focus them. Considering potential opportunities and threats is also useful. If people can predict threats something can be done about them so that they don't happen. Figure 5.6 is an example of a completed SWOT analysis.

After completing a SWOT analysis, people should ask themselves:

- How can I use my strengths to enable me to take advantage of the opportunities I have identified?
- How can I use these strengths to overcome the threats identified?
- What do I need to do to overcome the identified weaknesses in order to take advantage of the opportunities?
- How will I minimize my weaknesses to overcome the identified threats?

Aim for an objective to be met within the year but with the smaller steps completed half-termly. This will encourage people to be realistic, focused and give them a well-deserved sense of achievement. There are some case studies below.

CASE STUDY 5.2: OBJECTIVES AND ACTION PLANS

Primary teacher
Professional development objective: To improve personal effectiveness in the teaching of writing.

Linked training plan:

1 Meet for one session of directed time each half-term with the literacy co-ordinator to review lesson plans and lesson evaluations in the teaching of writing.
2 Observe the literacy co-ordinator teaching writing to own class once in the academic year and to literacy co-ordinator's class once in the academic year, followed by feedback on both occasions to develop practice further.
3 Take part in all of the school's in-service training on writing.

Success criteria:
- Improved planning for writing. For example, planning includes clear and progressive learning objectives matched to pupils' abilities and a variety of strategies for writing for different purposes. Evidence from reviews of lesson plans and from the school's procedures for curriculum monitoring and evaluation.
- Improvement in the quality of teaching and learning in writing lessons. Evidence from two focused lesson observations and from scrutiny of pupils' work.

Secondary geography teacher
A geography teacher in a large secondary school wanted to be involved in his school's work on Key Stage 2/3 transition. He agreed, for his professional development objective, to become better informed about Key Stage 2 geography in the partner primary schools, apply his new understanding to his teaching in Year 7, and use it to help the geography department ensure better cross-phase continuity and progression. The evidence of success included the documentation that would result from his work. The strategies for achieving this objective were detailed in his personal development and improvement plan. He would:

- visit two partner primary schools, to discuss their work in geography with the co-ordinator and the pupils and observe some of the teaching;
- interview some Year 7 pupils about their views on geography;
- attend the planned LEA course on Key Stage 2/3 transition.

He would report on the outcomes of these events to his team leader by an agreed date. He would then prepare a paper for the whole department proposing changes to the Year 7 geography curriculum, which would be discussed one afternoon in the summer term when the whole department was off timetable. All of these events were carefully timetabled. During the year, the teacher learned much about what pupils had learned in Key Stage 2 geography and what they liked and disliked in the subject. Several improvements to the department's scheme of work were made as a consequence.

Proposed activity: *A course on observation and feedback skills*
What do you want to get out of it? *Greater confidence and knowledge of how to observe someone and discuss the lesson sensitively but usefully.*
Factors within you that might affect your ability to carry out this activity? Strengths *Enjoy courses; take an active part; really want to do it.*
Weaknesses *May be too shy to do the role-play activity; may not have the chance to carry out an observation soon after the course.*
External factors that might impact on this activity? Opportunities *Someone who comes recommended is running the course; I've got funding for the course; may meet someone really nice; may learn things that I didn't expect.*
Threats *May not be allowed to attend if there's nobody who can cover my lessons; would rather not be out of school at this end of term; may get paired up with someone I don't like; course may get cancelled; people may not want me to observe them.*
What needs to be strengthened in order to carry out this activity? *Cover – emphasize its importance.* *Book an observation and let the head know – then it'll happen.*

FIGURE 5.6 A SWOT ANALYSIS

Action plans can be written in the easiest way, according to individual styles. There is a range of formats but Figures 4.1 (in Chapter 4) and Table 5.2 are useful examples of a working document.

CONCLUSION

Meeting needs in the most effective and cost-effective way is not easy. Staff will need to be encouraged constantly to evaluate whether the professional development activities are meeting needs appropriately and to change them if necessary. The impact of professional development is paramount, and it is to this that we now turn.

TABLE 5.2 ACTION PLAN

What do you want to achieve?	Why?	How?	When	Cost	Progress
Better management and greater understanding of my induction tutor role	I'm the induction tutor for 4 NQTs and need to do the job better and more efficiently. The skills I'll develop will help with my PM role	Induction tutor training course at the university – 4 days accredited which will be the start of my MA	Oct 17+	£390	
		Read newspaper articles, TTA documents and books recommended by the course	Sept+	0	Set up indiv induction progs
		Network with other induction tutors	Oct+	0	
Start an MA Ed	Get my brain working; want to think more deeply about educational issues; prepare for leadership role	Enrol on MA after induction tutor training course is completed, which will give me the first 20 credits	July	?	

CHAPTER SIX

Monitoring and Evaluation: the Impact of CPD

■ Monitoring

■ Evaluating impact

■ Models of evaluating impact

■ Spreading the impact

■ How schools have evaluated impact

The final stages in the staff development cycle are concerned with monitoring and evaluating the impact of professional development and training. Both are neglected areas. Monitoring activities are essentially about ensuring that things are going according to plan and, if they are not, taking appropriate action to ensure they are. Gauging the impact of CPD or evaluating its effectiveness – the sixth and last stage in the staff development cycle – is much more difficult. Few evaluation studies concerning CPD make any reference to its impact on teacher behaviour or pupil learning outcomes. However, evaluation is necessary to provide a sound basis for improving and upgrading programmes and processes but it needs to be relatively easy and inexpensive, otherwise it may be seen as diverting scarce resources away from other more important activities. Evaluation of training and development should be attended to but it often gets marginalized or forgotten.

MONITORING

The monitoring of professional development at the most basic level importantly consists of checking that what has been planned has happened. This can be carried out in a wide range of ways: reminding people, asking for progress reports, and so on. The difficulty lies in finding a system that is manageable, efficient and that works. Writing progress notes on an action plan (see Figure 4.1), on what has been learned through observing colleagues (see Figure 5.3) or going on courses (Figure 5.5) are all valuable. However, measuring someone does not make them grow: it is simply the check that proper nourishment has had its natural effect. Time to talk with colleagues, for the exchange of expertise and the development of professional understanding, will have far greater and more beneficial effects.

EVALUATING IMPACT

Evaluating staff development for its impact is challenging as 'it involves checking the links of a long chain between a training programme for individual staff and beneficial results for the school' (Baxter and Chambers, 1998b: 31). Investors in People has made schools much more aware of the need for systematic evaluation measures. A school's understanding of the impact of its investment in people on its performance is a fundamental aspect of the standard as shown in Table 6.1. The three indicators are central to professional development so, clearly, there are advantages to CPD co-ordinators making use of this structure. Schools

> need to understand that staff development is the most powerful tool for change at their disposal. It is also the most expensive in terms of time, energy and money. It is for its contribution to ensuring that the benefits of this investment are achieved and sustained, that evaluation must now be considered an essential component of the staff development process. (Ibid.: 32)

TABLE 6.1 INVESTORS IN PEOPLE – THE PRINCIPLE OF EVALUATION

Principles	Indicators	Evidence
Evaluation An Investor in People understands the impact of its investment in people on its performance	10. The development of people improves the performance of the organization, teams and individuals	The organization can show that the development of people has improved the performance of the organization, teams and individuals
	11. People understand the impact of the development of people on the performance of the organization, teams and individuals	Top management understands the overall costs and benefits of the development of people and its impact on performance
		People can explain the impact of their development on their performance, and the performance of their team and the organization as a whole
	12. The organization gets better at developing its people	People can give examples of relevant and timely improvements that have been made to development activities

The most valuable and informative evidence is that obtained at first hand, from observations of the area that staff have chosen to develop. Talking to staff about their development is important. Assertions and intentions are useful but CPD co-ordinators need to have evidence of the actual impact of professional development. For instance, what do you think of Mary's professional development described in case study 6.1?

MODELS OF EVALUATING IMPACT

Over the years a number of models to evaluate the impact of training and development have been devised. One of the first and perhaps the best known is the framework for evaluating training developed by Kirkpatrick and first published in 1959 in the *Journal of the American Society of Training Directors*. This has been adapted and developed over the years but Kirkpatrick's four-step framework remains the model or framework for evaluating most training programmes in business and commerce. As Bubb and Hoare (2001: 114) explain 'this is primarily because of the simplicity of the model, how it relates to the trainee and the workplace and the way in which it can readily be applied to almost every type of work situation and learning process'.

CASE STUDY 6.1: A MUSIC TEACHER

Mary, a music teacher, got funding from the school to pay for her to learn a new instrument, but one that she was not going to teach so its contribution to her professional development was dubious. However, she asserted that she extended her knowledge about successful learning by becoming a learner herself and that this impacted on her teaching because she realized that she expected pupils to accept musical procedures without further questioning. As a learner, Mary needed to ask questions and be given specific answers; as a result, she modified her teaching methodology to include these aspects of learning. This professional development impacted directly on pupil learning and on the teacher–pupil relationship; it introduced a new paradigm of relationship that is 'learner-to-learner'.

She also spent professional development money on ICT hardware. This did not impact on her educational work in the same way as her music lessons. The new monitor and printer support Mary's desire to organize her administration efficiently, which is admirable but debatable in terms of being an educational use of *developmental* funding. Such requirements could have been noted on the department development plan.

Source: adapted from Minnis, 2003

They go on to state that the Kirkpatrick model explores the relationship between training and the workplace at four levels:

- reactions;
- learning;
- behaviour;
- results.

These are measured at suitable points during the training process. The first three are essentially trainee based, while the fourth changes emphasis and centres on the effectiveness of the training for the organization.

LEVEL 1: REACTIONS

By evaluating reactions, you find out if participants enjoyed the training, if the training environment was suitable and comfortable and if the trainers were capable and credible. In short, you are trying to learn what participants think and feel about the training.

LEVEL 2: LEARNING

By evaluating learning, you determine the extent to which trainees have done the following three things as a result of their training: changed their attitudes, improved their knowledge or increased their skills.

LEVEL 3: BEHAVIOUR

By evaluating behaviour, you determine if the trainees are using or transferring their newly learned knowledge, skills and behaviours back on the job. In other words, what behaviour changed because people took part in a training session?

CASE STUDY 6.2: THE LEVELS OF IMPACT OF JILL'S ONE-DAY INDUCTION TUTOR TRAINING COURSE

Level 1: reactions
Despite the day being well-organized and in pleasant surroundings, Jill did not enjoy the day because she had to sit next to and work with her ex-husband's second wife – the woman her husband left her for!

Level 2: learning
However, she gained much new knowledge and increased her skills. The handouts reminded her of her learning.

Level 3: behaviour
Jill used her newly learned knowledge, skills and behaviours in working with the two NQTs.

Level 4: results
The NQTs said that the school's induction was initially poor but improved after Jill attended the course. They really noticed a difference because of all the new systems and found their induction very effective. They felt well supported, and monitored and assessed fairly so that they were able to make good progress in their first year.

This impacted on their pupils who learned more and behaved better as a result of improved teaching by their inexperienced teachers.

■ LEVEL 4: RESULTS

By evaluating results, you determine if the training has affected school results or contributed to the achievement of an objective. This final evaluation which considers both personal evaluation and company benefit makes the Kirkpatrick model so suitable for so many types of training (Bubb and Hoare, 2001: 114–15).

Another American, Thomas Guskey, has developed and refined Kirkpatrick's model more specifically for education. He is clear that: 'We need to make evaluation an integral part of the professional development process … Systematically gathering and analysing evidence to inform our actions must become a central component in professional development technology' (Guskey, 2000: 92). The evaluation of CPD, in particular examining its impact and whether or not it meets individualized 'learning perspectives' so that the potential of training opportunities is realised, is very important. Professional development does not just happen – it has to be managed and led, and done so effectively ensuring it has a positive impact and represents good value for money. In Britain those schools that have sought Investors in People status have highlighted these issues and others.

Guskey talks in terms of five levels of evaluation of CPD with improved pupil outcomes being the desired result. These five levels, shown in Table 6.2, are:

- participants' reactions;
- participants' learning;

- organization support and change;
- participants' use of new knowledge and skills;
- pupil learning outcomes.

Level 3 – organization support and change – is not found in the Kirkpatrick model and refers to the key role that the school can play in supporting or sabotaging any CPD efforts. The focus needs to be on the attributes and organisational features of the school that are necessary for success. Guskey asks:

> Did the professional development activities promote changes that were aligned with the mission of the school or district (LEA)? Were changes at the individual level encouraged and supported at all levels? Were sufficient resources made available, including time for sharing and reflection? Were successes recognized and shared? (2002: 47)

These kinds of issues he concludes can play a large part in determining the success of any CPD efforts. In general terms we need to ask ourselves, in what sense are we a professional learning community (see Chapter 2)?

The other important contribution that Guskey has made is getting us to focus on 'the bottom line' and to think more broadly about what constitutes pupil outcomes (level 5). As can be seen in Table 6.2 he divides pupil (or what he prefers to call student) outcomes into:

- cognitive (performance and achievement);
- affective (attitudes, beliefs and dispositions);
- psychomotor (skills, behaviours and practices).

We might find the terms a bit off-putting but it is a most useful classification. The cognitive is the most obvious – pupil attainment (the dreaded performance tables!) or knowledge and understanding. This might include examination results, grades, test scores – but we need to look at achievement in the round and think of the education of the whole child. The affective domain is crucially important and includes such things as pupil attitudes and dispositions. For example, has their attitude to school changed, their study habits improved and are they more predisposed towards the subject? Are they attending more regularly? And what about pupils' self-concepts? Do they have greater confidence in themselves as learners and do they accept more personal responsibility for their actions and behaviours?

Psychomotor outcomes or skills and behaviours might include such things as classroom behaviour, homework completion rates, participation in school activities including attendance at lunchtime and after-school clubs, and retention and drop-out rates. For example, have pupils adopted healthier eating habits and other desired practices, are they reading more outside of school time, are they more involved or active in their learning, do they engage more in classroom discussion?

All of this information about the impact of CPD – and, of course, some of it is easier to measure than others – can be used to guide improvements in the CPD cycle, including the design and implementation of training programmes and their follow up. Guskey notes that in some cases information on pupil learning outcomes is used to

TABLE 6.2   FIVE LEVELS OF PROFESSIONAL DEVELOPMENT EVALUATION

Evaluation level	What questions are addressed?	How will information be gathered?	What is measured or assessed?	How will information be used?
Participants' reactions	Did they like it? Was their time spent well? Did the material make sense? Will it be useful? Was the leader knowledgeable and helpful? Were the refreshments fresh and tasty? Was the room the right temperature? Were the chairs comfortable?	Questionnaires administrated at the end of each session	Initial satisfaction with the experience	To improve programme design and delivery
Participants' learning	Did participants acquire the intended knowledge and skills?	Paper and pencil instruments Simulations Demonstrations Participant reflections (oral and/or written) Participant portfolios	New knowledge and skills of participants	To improve programme content, format, and organization
Organization support and change	Was implementation advocated, facilitated and supported? Was the support public and overt? Were the problems addressed quickly and efficiently? Were sufficient resources made available? What was the impact on the organization? Did it affect the organization's climate and procedures?	District (LEA) and schools records Minutes from follow up meetings Questionnaires Structured interviews with participants and district or school administrators Participant portfolios	The organization's advocacy, support, accommodation, facilitation, and recognition	To document and improve organization support To inform future change efforts
Participants' use of new knowledge and skills	Did participants effectively apply the new knowledge and skills?	Questionnaires Structured interviews with participants and their supervisors Participant reflections (oral and/or written) Participant portfolios Direct observations Video or audio tapes	Degree and quality of implementation	To document and improve implementation of programme content
Student learning outcomes	What was the impact on students? Did it affect student performance or achievement? Did it influence students' physical or emotional well-being? Are students more confident as learners? Is student attendance improving? Are dropouts decreasing?	Student records School records Questionnaires Structured interviews with students, parents, teachers and/or administrators Participant portfolios	Student learning outcomes Cognitive (performance and achievement Affective (attitudes and dispositions) Psychomotor (skills and behaviours)	To focus and improve all aspects of programme design, implementation, and follow-up. To demonstrate the overall impact of professional development

Source: Guskey, 2002: 48

estimate the cost-effectiveness of CPD, sometimes known as 'return on investment' or 'ROI evaluation' (2002: 49).

In England, David Frost and Judy Durrant (2003) have developed a framework to show how the process of development work culminates for the teacher in the transformation of professional knowledge. They argue that the outcomes of training or CPD can be seen not only in terms of professional development of individuals, but also in the extent to which there is an impact on pupils' learning, on colleagues' learning and on organizational learning. They suggest that teachers may also be able to make a contribution beyond their school.

- *Impact on pupils' learning*:
  - attainment;
  - disposition;
  - meta-cognition.
- *Impact on teachers*:
  - classroom practice;
  - personal capacity;
  - interpersonal capacity.
- *Impact on the school as an organization*:
  - structures and processes;
  - culture and capacity.
- *Impact beyond the school*:
  - critique and debate;
  - creation and transfer of professional knowledge;
  - improvements in social capital in the community.

(See Frost and Durrant, 2003 for the full framework.)

This framework enables teachers and schools to think beyond the effects of particular CPD provision or a training event and to focus more on their impact. In other words, the focus is on the actions of the teachers and not so much on the development programmes and training events themselves.

Frost and Durrant note that causality is very difficult to establish, and the impact or effects of a particular programme or activity cannot be isolated. They have designed tools and activities to enable teachers themselves to plan, track and evaluate the impact of their activity and, rather than retrospectively evaluating the impact that has already taken place, the intention is to encourage teachers to think more broadly about the influence they may have, thereby increasing impact as they adjust their planning accordingly. For example, they may be encouraged to introduce more collaborative working, they may talk to the headteacher to offer to run a staff development session in their school and they may agree to contribute to a conference or run a session for another group on their specific area of expertise.

SPREADING THE IMPACT

The impact of any professional development is increased if other people within the school can benefit from it. Figure 6.1 illustrates that one person's professional development activity can benefit others and thereby more pupils if the school has systems to enable this to happen. This is known as 'cascading' and has been one of the key methods used in the national literacy, numeracy and Key Stage 3 strategies. One person is trained at a LEA course and then delivers the training to staff at school. There are benefits to this model, particularly in terms of cost. However, much depends on the time available to cascade and the quality and confidence of the individual, and their perceived status in the school. Cascading happens at the start of new initiatives but the impact is reduced if there is no support or input later on. Her Majesty's Inspectorate found that 'schools on the whole failed to allow enough time to support effective professional development and to ensure that acquired knowledge and skills were consolidated, implemented and shared with other teachers' (Ofsted, 2002a: 3). They recommend that people should have half a day's non-contact time after each day's course to cascade and set up ways to implement new ideas.

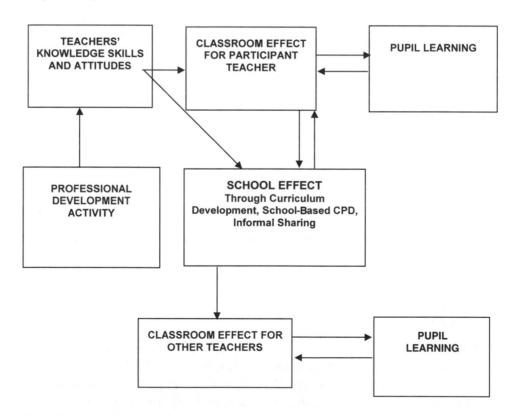

FIGURE 6.1 LOCAL EVALUATION OF INSET (ADAPTED FROM ERAUT, et al., 1988)

HOW SCHOOLS HAVE EVALUATED IMPACT

This section has examples of how two schools have evaluated staff development. In Case study 6.3, a questionnaire was devised in Cullompton Community College to see what activities had the greatest impact on the school. In Case study 6.4, Worth Primary School describes how it works out the cost-effectiveness of different professional activities.

■ VALUE FOR MONEY

Worth Primary School in Cheshire (see Case study 6.4) – itself an Investor in People – has worked hard to ensure it obtains value for money from its training and development budget, and has devised some interesting ways to measure this and link it to performance management and, ultimately, to pupil outcomes.

CASE STUDY 6.3: CULLOMPTON COMMUNITY COLLEGE'S EVALUATION OF CPD

This case study of evaluation of CPD is based on an article by Davey published in *Professional Development Today* (Davey, 2000).

John Davey, the Vice-Principal of Cullompton Community College in Devon, wanted to devise a cost-effective way of evaluating staff development that was simple to administer and analyse, and would be sustainable. He wanted to know:

- how staff perceive the impact of developmental activities on their classroom practice and school improvement;
- which activities have the greatest impact on raising standards across the institution;
- which provided the best value for money, in order to ensure that limited budgets can be used to greatest effect.

"When we started to plan we became aware that there were two particular dimensions to staff development: those activities that took individuals forward in their professional practice and those activities designed to benefit the institution. These activities would have considerable overlap and in most cases both types of activity would assist in raising standards. An individual's personal development may not be used immediately within an institution but often constitutes a resource which could be drawn upon in the future to the benefit of the wider education service". (Ibid.: 34)

Recognizing this dual aspect to staff development led him to two key questions, one about how individuals had developed and one about how the institution had benefited. The key questions were:

- In what ways am I a better teacher than this time last year (in the classroom or in other roles)?
- How has this improved the experience of the pupils I teach and helped them raise their achievement?

A questionnaire was devised to be completed by staff that we have adapted in Figure 6.2. Davey found that the staff development activities perceived to have the greatest impact on teaching were those which 'took place within the school, had direct relevance to classroom practice and which provided a forum for sharing between professionals where there was an opportunity for participants to set at least part of the agenda' (p. 38).

While initially the school was mainly concerned with issues of cost effectiveness, the exercise led the leadership team to re-evaluate the importance attached to work-based and in-house activities and realise that they can have greater impact than those organized and run externally.

EVALUATION OF STAFF DEVELOPMENT

Name:...

In order to complete this evaluation you will need to set aside approximately 30 minutes. Some of this time will be for writing but thinking through your experiences during the year is at least as important.

The aim of this evaluation is:
- to document details of all the activities staff have been involved in this year
- to identify which activities have been of value
- to assess the impact staff development activities have had on teaching and learning
- to obtain details of the training needs perceived by staff.

1a. Please list the training activities you have been involved in during the year

Non Pupil Days (completed for you)

DATE	ISSUES COVERED	*
1&2/09	Target setting and getting. Examination analysis. Year team meetings.	
02/09	ICT training and departmental time.	
16/10	Ofsted preparation. Departmental work.	
04/01	Target setting, CATs work. Year team meetings. Departmental time.	
05/02	School improvement course. ICT training. Departmental work.	

Courses or other external activities:

	DATE	TITLE	ISSUE COVERED	*
1				
2				
3				

1b. Other activities that have contributed to your professional development (e.g. being observed, observing colleagues, mentoring, meetings, personal reading, etc.).

	DATE	TITLE	ISSUE COVERED	*
1				
2				
3				
4				

Of the activities listed above which <u>three</u> have had the greatest influence on your work? Please indicate by putting an asterisk in the last column.

1c. Insights or expertise gained during the year that you can share with other staff.

	TOPIC	EXPERTISE OR INSIGHTS OFFERED
1		
2		
3		

2. *Having considered the various staff development activities you have been involved in during the year please answer these questions:*

In what ways am I a better member of staff than this time last year (in the classroom or in other roles)?

How has this improved the experience of pupils I work with and helped them raise their achievement?

3. *What are your professional development needs now?*

	Topic	Specific needs
1		
2		
3		

Thank you for taking the time to think and write. Your help will assist us in making the most effective use of the limited funds available for staff development.

FIGURE 6.2 EVALUATION OF STAFF DEVELOPMENT (ADAPTED FROM DAVEY, 2000)

CASE STUDY 6.4: WORTH PRIMARY SCHOOL'S REVIEW OF IMPACT AND COST-EFFECTIVENESS

All training and development is reviewed with regard to its effectiveness. In-house training sessions are planned and reviewed upon completion. Courses, conferences or speakers are selected as appropriate. Review of external courses will also take place with further training planned if necessary. Individual training may be provided in-house or externally. Course application forms and a brief section of the in-house CPD review sheets are completed prior to application for a course; these are submitted to the personnel team leader for approval. Upon completion of a course or development process, the review section of the CPD form is completed and discussed with the personnel team leader, the de-brief section is completed and signed by the team leader. The course advert and form are added to the individual's training and development file. The file is reviewed during appraisal and part year to ensure targets are being met and results forthcoming.

The cost-effectiveness of any training or development is broadly assessed by dividing the effectiveness rating by the cost; this gives a cost per percentage point. This has thrown up some interesting data with the cheaper, more local courses appearing inexpensive but when supply costs, food, travel and so on are added they often produce quite low cost-effectiveness ratings. The apparently more expensive consultant or specific trainer, who is asked to come to school to address a specific need, often proves more cost-effective per person, per percentage point (see the example in Figure 6.3).

Source: Taylor, 2004

Cost-effective		Not cost-effective	
INSET ½ day for 10 teachers		INSET course for 1 teacher	
Staff satisfaction rating: 90%		Individual satisfaction rating: 60%	
Travel time	0 hrs	Travel time	2 hrs
Trainer fee	£200 (1/2 day)	Course fee	£90 (1/2 day)
Staff travel	£00 (in house)	Staff travel	£16
Food	£50 (sandwiches)	Food	£00
Cover	£1200*	Cover	£120**
Total	£1450	Total	£226
Cost per person	£145	Cost per person	£226
Cost-effectiveness rating		Cost-effectiveness rating	
£145/90%= £1.61/percentage point		£226/60%= £3.76/percentage point	

Notes:

* As this was an INSET day there was no actual cost to school, a nominal supply cost per person is included so the comparison can be made, also if we attempt to be proper in our accounting there is an opportunity cost as school is paying staff to be at this event.

**A full day cover is needed to cover the travel time unless the course is so close to school staff can return for the afternoon session.

FIGURE 6.3   AN EXAMPLE OF CALCULATING COST EFFECTIVENESS OF CPD ACTIVITY (TAYLOR, 2004)

CHAPTER SEVEN

Collaboration and Enquiry: Sharing Practice

Graham Handscomb

- Collaboration
- Research – teachers doing it themselves
- The research-engaged school

The road towards increased collaboration amongst teachers and between schools in which they work has been long and tortuous, but the signs are that the collaboration movement is beginning to gather pace and credibility. Recognition of the benefits of teacher collaboration and sharing of practice, combined with growing commitment to developing teachers as researchers of their own practice, has started to transform our understanding of what constitutes effective continuing professional development.

This chapter examines the dynamic relationship between collaboration, enquiry and CPD, along with the challenges involved in sharing expertise. Examples of effective approaches are offered for consideration.

COLLABORATION

Together the two ingredients of teacher collaboration and enquiry make a potent brew. In the context of the movement towards all schools becoming self-managing they have contributed to a reconceptualization of CPD in terms of processes owned and developed by teachers, with the school perceived as a reservoir of expertise and experience to be used. Thus a modern CPD agenda emerges which has the following features:

- tapping school expertise, not importing it;
- CPD focus on pedagogy and the 'craft of the classroom';
- the teacher is best placed to conduct classroom enquiry;
- developing, seeking out and sharing practice;
- developing communities of practice within and beyond the school;
- LEAs, government and others adopting a partnership role.

This emphasis on collaboration whilst specifying the school as the locus of CPD, reflects national drivers for change and poses certain challenges. The arrival of the era of collaboration, ironically, has occurred when there is a continuing commitment to school autonomy and diversity. Perhaps one of the greatest educational challenges facing government, LEAs and schools alike over the next few years is how to move forward on each of these three priorities.

This tension is also reflected in the *Code of Practice on LEA/Schools Relations* (DfEE, 2000f), which establishes:

- the principle of school autonomy;
- the responsibility for school performance and improvement rest, in the first instance with schools themselves;
- within this context advocates the sharing of good practice within schools.

Therefore, placed alongside the LEA's core role to monitor, challenge and intervene in inverse proportion to success, is the role of promoting and facilitating the sharing of good practice. Effective schools are thus seen as those that manage autonomously but also share and seek out good practice within the wider educational community.

So the modernized school is not portrayed as ploughing its own furrow, perhaps to the detriment of others. True the diversity agenda is as strong as ever, and fears of divisiveness still persist. But the *Code of Practice on LEA/School Relations* makes it clear that 'autonomy does not mean isolation' (DfEE, 2000f). Improvement, including the contribution of CPD, is now seen as essentially a collaborative exercise.

COLLABORATION AND PROFESSIONAL LEARNING

There is now a growing and authoritative consensus that the most effective professional learning is focused on teachers' classroom practice and is collaborative. The government's professional development strategy stresses the importance of 'learning together, learning from the best, and learning from what works' (DfEE, 2001a). Similarly the General Teaching Council's (England) *Teachers' Professional Learning Framework* (GTC, 2003b) states that teaching has often been experienced as an isolated activity and that teacher development has consequently suffered from this. It claims that an increasing body of professional development work demonstrates 'the value of moving collegial learning from the margins of professional practice to the heart of it'. The GTC sees classroom teachers 'not only as classroom experts in a single school but also as members of the broader education community' (GTC, 2003b).

So learning together is advocated because it tends to focus development on classroom practice. As Harris (2002) puts it: 'improvements in teaching are most likely to occur where there are opportunities to work together and to learn from each other'. She also identifies gains in terms of teachers' professionalism and well-being stating 'collaboration is important because it creates a collective professional confidence that allows teachers to interact more confidently and assertively' (ibid.). The NCSL's 'Networked Learning Communities' initiative (outlined in Chapter 2) strikes a similar note.

WHAT DOES COLLABORATION LOOK LIKE?

So given that there is now a considerable momentum towards collaborative professional learning in schools, what does this look like in practice and how is it achieved? The benefits of consortia working are:

- identifying joint problems and issues, and more effectively tackling them together;
- networking wide experience and expertise;
- economies of scale – effective and efficient joint training and sharing of resources;
- 'commissioning power' to secure CPD providers, LEA facilitators and higher education partnerships;
- establishing and developing research communities;
- keying into local, regional and national opportunities;
- building a body of new professional knowledge within the consortium.

Fostering effective collaboration, however, is not plain sailing and, as noted in Chapter 2, establishing the right culture is key. It is unlikely to develop or to be replenished without seeking out and sharing practice beyond the school. Here are some key things to think about when setting up a consortium:

- Be clear about why your schools want to consort; common features/agendas/developments.
- Get started on a specific project together; this will help to build relationships and explore consortium potential.
- Make arrangements for some monitoring of early work and development so that organizational issues are identified and logged.
- Then look at ways you need to organize yourselves to make the best use of time and have the most impact.
- Consider producing a consortium development plan, containing limited, ambitious but attainable priorities in a specified time.
- Check that your consortium is focused on improving classroom practice.
- Ensure the consortium is founded on practical opportunities for shared professional learning.

Case study 7.1 describes an established consortium of small rural primary schools.

A CONTINUUM OF PRACTICE

Despite, or perhaps because of, the increased momentum towards collaborative professional learning, there has been insufficient attention given to what is entailed in the identification and sharing of practice between teachers and between schools. On the one hand, it will involve promoting the sharing and exchange of *interesting* and *innovative practice*, whilst on the other, also helping to build a body of knowledge about *effective* and *best practice*. The big issue here is the casual ease with which people often talk of sharing *best* practice when actually what is being disseminated is untried, untested *interesting* practice. Schools and organizations that support them, like LEAs, have a role in both these areas. So there is a need to promote a dynamic environment that fosters practitioner creativity, whilst also ensuring clarity about what works, and whether practice is of a high standard and stands the test of time.

CASE STUDY 7.1: A PRIMARY SCHOOL CONSORTIUM

Four small rural schools within a primary schools consortium worked in partnership with the University of Cambridge Department for Education on a school improvement research initiative. The group of schools had established themselves into a consortium for some time. The success of the consortium was reflected in the investment each school made in terms of:

- consortium management – regular management meetings attended by all headteachers, robust consortium management procedures;
- development planning – all schools committed to specific actions to implement in the consortium development plan;
- finance – each school investing £1 per pupil into the consortium finances;
- professional development – common non-pupil days and common weekly staff meetings agreed across the consortium to enable joint professional development linked to the consortium development plan.

This research project arose out of several years' experience of working together for professional development purposes, including work with Cambridge University. At consortium management meetings the schools' headteachers consider the individual needs of schools and identify areas for shared INSET provision and school improvement projects.

The project focused on school-based enquiry. It was decided that three non-pupil days involving all (40) teaching staff at the above schools would be devoted to this project and two twilight sessions per term for staff. An accreditation outcome was the award of the Cambridge Certificate of Further Professional Study. Teachers would pursue some school-based enquiry using research methods to study aspects of 'Teaching and learning linked to monitoring and evaluation'. Theoretical aspects of teaching and learning and monitoring and evaluation linked to management (subject leader roles) and school-based enquiry were introduced on the two non-pupil days. Following practice in research techniques – carrying out interviews, questionnaires, observations – each school chose to focus on enquiries, which were relevant to their own school development. These were:

- the effectiveness of the ICT suite in supporting children's learning;
- improving writing (linking writing to motor skills at Key Stage 1 and strategies to improve spelling at Key Stage 2);
- investigating ways to improve children's ability to read and write for information;
- investigating the development of listening skills;
- developing thinking skills.

Whilst each school pursued its own lines of enquiry it used schools in the consortium to help with planning and testing out ideas and development. Assistance from the university staff with theory and research methodology enabled some rigour to the investigations.

The project involved staff from all schools engaging in research-based improvement. Originally a range of staff from each school participated. However, as the popularity of the project grew, many more took part and in some schools all the staff, including support staff, conducted a research project. This meant that there was a critical mass of research development in each school. Children and staff in each school have benefited from the research and that progress has been made in the development of the schools as learning communities. It is hoped that further developments will occur between schools so that the learning community is extended within the consortium. The LEA has worked actively with the consortium to facilitate opportunities to disseminate outcomes within Essex and on national conferences. It has also assisted the schools in making Networked Learning Community and Best Practice Research Scholarship applications.

In his analysis of the role of the LEA in the promotion and analysis of school practice David Woods makes the following helpful distinctions:

> In the literature on school improvement the terms 'best', 'good' and 'innovative' practice are used in a variety of ways. Good practice is generally used to mean practice which is professionally judged to be effective, but may require further evidence and validation; best practice is used to mean practice which is proven over time, backed by supporting evidence; innovative practice may highlight new and interesting ways of doing things, with early indications of success. (Woods, 2000)

This is perhaps most helpfully illustrated as a continuum (see Figure 7.1) ranging from creative practice, to good practice, to best practice. So, for example, a teacher who has developed a set of practices in her classroom that works well with her group of learners, might be characterized as being at the left-hand side of the continuum. As this is shared with other school colleagues, who adapt and apply it in their different settings, it gets tested against a range of teacher professionalism and might then be termed 'good practice'. Eventually it might be developed into school-wide approaches, shared in other school settings, benchmarked and validated by supporting evidence and proven over time – and thus merit the accolade 'best practice'. Clearly calibration and judgements made about such distinctions should be part and parcel of the professional discussion, debate and agreement amongst teachers, schools and other parties like HEIs and LEAs, and all of these types of practice have a part to play in the quest for continuous professional development and school improvement.

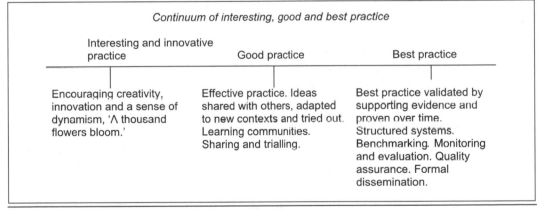

FIGURE 7.1 A CONTINUUM OF PRACTICE (HANDSCOMB, 2002/3)

■ TO NETWORK OR NOT TO NETWORK?

Even with such clarity about the nature of best practice, the process of actually sharing expertise between practitioners is in itself problematic. In McIntyre's research on 'expert teachers' he concludes that it is often difficult to disseminate the practice of good teachers because, by their very nature they tend to be intuitive, and use tacit expertise and knowledge, and their work is usually particular to themselves and their immediate context (McIntyre, 2001). Hargreaves has given considerable thought to this problem of how to 'bottle' and share teacher practitioner knowledge:

> If one teacher tells another about a practice that he finds effective, the second teacher has merely acquired information, not personal knowledge. Transfer occurs only when the knowledge of the first becomes information for the second, who then works on that information

in such a way that it becomes part of his or her context of meaning and purpose and pre-existing knowledge and then is applied in action ... Transfer is the conversion of information about one person's practice into another's know-how. (Hargreaves, 1998)

So ensuring the effective transference and application of practice to other classrooms as part of collaborative professional development is far from easy. The report of the sub-group of the National Education Research Forum (NERF), chaired by Hargreaves, showed this to be a highly complex process (NERF, 2001). Referring to the application of research to policy and practice, the report distinguishes between the key elements of knowledge production, dissemination and use, each of which in turn have specific processes that need to be addressed. Robust sharing of practice involves a process of producing, disseminating and using new knowledge.

Some would argue that the process is so difficult that it casts doubt on the feasibility of transference of practice between different schools. David Reynolds (2003) is adamant that there is little evidence of collaboration working or of transference of good practice between schools sticking. He advocates schools 'learning from their own best practice' (ibid.: 23). By contrast David Hopkins (2002a) strongly endorses the effectiveness of networks. He acknowledges that collaborative networks need to guard against cosiness and be committed to 'quality, rigour and a focus on outcomes', but insists on their transforming power. For schools addressing the issues of sharing practice and networking it would be useful to consider where they stand regarding these two contrasting views.

RESEARCH – TEACHERS DOING IT THEMSELVES

The concern about 'soft' unproductive collaboration is resolved in Alma Harris's view if a strategic link is made with teacher enquiry and research: 'For teacher development ... to occur, commitment to certain kinds of collaboration is centrally important. However, collaboration without reflection and enquiry is little more than working collegially. For collaboration to influence personal growth and development it has to be premised upon mutual enquiry and sharing' (Harris, 2002).

The image of educational research for many teachers is something done by others in academic institutions – complex, difficult to access, and of limited relevance. Unfortunately, some developments in educational research have suffered from these features. However, this is changing. Increasingly, classroom practitioners have discovered the merits of investigating an aspect of their work that directly contributes to improved practice and benefits the children they teach. For instance Case study 7.2 is about one school's action research in art and emotional literacy and Case study 7.3 is a collaborative project funded by the DfES Best Practice Research Scholarship scheme.

A number of LEAs are involved in leading school-focused research activities. Here is a selection of research projects that schools in Wiltshire are involved in:

- identification of pupils with poorly developed emotional literacy in order to provide opportunities for remediation;
- implementing an 'enrichment' curriculum for all pupils;
- improving student critical faculties in making judgements;
- exploring the impact of the mentoring system for gifted and talented pupils to further strengthen the scheme;

CASE STUDY 7.2: A SCHOOL PROJECT TO RAISE THE STATUS OF VISUAL ART AND DEVELOP EMOTIONAL LITERACY

Alderbury and West Grimstead School set up a project to raise the status of visual art and develop emotional literacy through creative approaches. Their aims were very specific:

- to raise the status of visual arts in school;
- to further develop emotional literacy through creative approaches to raise levels of attainment and behaviour;
- to encourage young professional artists to work in schools;
- to contribute to an LEA and national model;
- to create new community links;
- to address gender issues related to boys' attitudes and skills in the visual arts;
- to link with LEA Out of School Hours Learning Initiative (OSHLI) bid with which the school is intending to be associated;
- to link with the LEA seminars on Creativity – 21st Century Learning Initiative.

The project included three artists working with different age groups. One worked at weekends and holidays with pupils, to create tiles for the school pond area. This involved a group of children ranging in ability from those with special educational needs, including behavioural difficulties, to children with particular talents.

We particularly aimed at including a group of boys who would otherwise not take part in such creative work as well as a group of girls whose self-esteem needed to be boosted. The aims of raising self-esteem were fully realised and a bonus has been sowing the seeds of future creative work amongst these children.

The work undertaken raised the self-esteem of all the children involved, and had a visible effect on their behaviour. Attainment was raised through achieving success in Art, which then had a knock-on effect on effort and achievement in other subjects. The involvement of a variety of professional artists proved inspirational for both children and staff. Work done with the 21st Century Learning Initiative has been fed back to staff and governors, and many of the initiative's recommendations have been implemented. The teachers now have more confidence to block-teach work in many subjects, instead of trying to fit each subject in the crowded curriculum into each week. They now feel that they have the freedom and support to 'think outside the box' when it comes to setting homework, to encourage far more wide ranging talents and activities than purely academic skills.

Research underpinning the project included carrying out activities with pupils, evaluating pupil responses, attending LEA creativity sessions, associated reading and disseminating information to staff and governors.

The headteacher, Jennifer Pitcher, spoke of the benefits of being engaged in research and development: 'The creative work that we were already doing helped us to make a strong case for applying for OSHLI funding, and this in turn has strengthened our links with the community' (Pitcher, 2003).

- improving attainment in Year 7 by stimulating pupils to become independent learners;
- investigating websites useful to those new as heads to devise an easy guide for suggested use (*Wiltshire Journal of Education*, 2003, available on www.wiltshire.gov.uk).

TEACHERS TAKING HOLD OF RESEARCH

Most teachers would not readily engage with the notion of being a 'teacher-researcher'. A more helpful term, which describes the skills that are part of good teaching, is the teacher as enquirer. This alludes to teachers who are keen to reflect upon and critique their practices. They make good use of research and evidence to stimulate new ways of

---

CASE STUDY 7.3: PRIMARY MODERN LANGUAGES PROJECT

A group of ten teachers were each awarded grants of around £2,500 to investigate and develop aspects of the teaching and learning of modern foreign languages (MFL) in primary schools. A university tutor leads the collaborative research group that meets centrally at the university and provides ongoing support to individuals by visiting their schools to advise and guide the research.

Each teacher is focusing on one of ten strands of the research, for example 'special educational needs', 'assessment', 'information and communications technology', and so on. The group supports one another through paired visits to observe and discuss approaches. They also use some of their funding to employ a part-time researcher to conduct interviews with teachers, pupils and parents, and to collect and process additional data from the ten schools taking part. The programme of meetings includes inputs on issues surrounding the teaching of MFL and generic issues such as the management of change.

The teachers are disseminating their 'work in progress' and the outcomes of the project to local and national audiences, for example, at subject and research conferences and through professional journals. One teacher has become an advanced skills teacher allowing her to visit local primary schools to provide training and support based on her research. Others have formed a working group to improve primary–secondary transition in collaboration with the LEA.

Source: Frost and Durrant, 2003

---

thinking and to try out new ideas, and then systematically to evaluate the impact of any subsequent change they have brought about.

Teachers have long been involved in examining their practice in this way to make further improvements. But when does such activity 'count' as research? What is the relationship between large-scale research conducted by a university department and a piece of evidence-informed practice carried out by a teacher within the classroom? And how is such evidence-informed practice any different from what good teachers do anyway in refining and honing their craft in day-to-day lesson preparation and evaluation?

One view is that evidence-informed practice typically involves the individual teacher, reflecting on her own classroom practice and sharing this with colleagues, whilst in contrast 'research' is seen as involving a larger-scale more systematic enquiry. Another view is that these two characterizations are not different in kind, but rather two ends of a continuum of practice in which 'evidence-informed practice' merges into 'research'. However, many have found this a difficult debate and would be uncomfortable about making too sharp a distinction between evidenced-informed practice and research. There are tensions between the world of academic research and teachers pursuing research as part of their professional learning and practice, but many have become convinced of the great potential of practitioner research to transform both the classroom and the teacher.

Schools in the modern age are required to be self-evaluating, open to scrutiny, evidence-based and data rich. Yet teachers and schools may not be empowered effectively to use the data in which they 'swim':

> schools are at the same time, often 'information poor'. This is, in part, because teachers feel no ownership of the data they are expected to use, nor is it necessarily data that they value. It is, nonetheless, high stakes, so teachers find themselves busy in 'implementation' rather than inquiry, lacking in self-confidence to convert what they know or believe into a form that

provides robust counter-evidence, that speaks with conviction from teachers' own context and experiences. (Handscomb and MacBeath, 2003)

The increasing engagement of teachers in both using research and carrying out research is helping to instil new confidence and ownership, and empower the teacher to effect evidence-based change – but further progress is still needed. Over recent years the majority of schools have become self-evaluating; the challenge now is for these to develop as *self-researching* institutions.

THE RESEARCH-ENGAGED SCHOOL

'As things stand, it is difficult for researchers and teachers to find an area in which they can negotiate the agenda for research on teaching and learning. Teachers are in danger of being the passive objects of research rather than active partners who contribute to the creation and dissemination of new knowledge' (Hargreaves, 1998). There has been some positive movement since Hargreaves wrote these words and stimulated the helpful debate that followed, but more needs to be done to enable teachers to lay claim to the research agenda, as part of their professional development and practice. Cordingley (2003) reports a growing awareness of the power of teachers researching their own work in terms both of better classroom practice and professional learning. However, to be effective, teachers need to gain some understanding of what is already known in the area of practice they wish to investigate. Unfortunately, school-based consumers of research have considerable obstacles put in their way; research abstract summaries do little to aid practitioner access and at worst actually get in the way or mislead! Developments like the GTC 'Research of the Month' website are endeavouring to improve teacher access and skill development. These are some of the projects that have been written about:

- Making research accessible to teachers;
- Researching effective pedagogy in the early years;
- Effective pedagogy using ICT for literacy and numeracy;
- An investigation into gender differences in achievement;
- Inside the literacy hour – a study of classroom practice.

In such a 'research-engaged school', research and enquiry would permeate all aspects of its life, including teaching and learning, professional development, and school planning and decision-making. There is a gathering interest in exploring the extent to which schools are becoming research-engaged – are they 'emergent', 'established' or 'established embedded' (Ebbut, 2003)?

At local level some LEAs are forming research forums of practitioners, officers and higher education representatives. The Essex Forum for Learning and Research Enquiry (FLARE) has identified and explored four dimensions of the research-engaged school:

- It has a 'research' rich pedagogy.
- It has a research orientation.
- It promotes research communities.
- It puts research at the heart of school policy and practice (Handscomb and MacBeath, 2003).

Implications for schools are posed in each of these dimensions, including some basic audit questions by which schools can begin to examine their outlook and practice (see Figure 7.2).

■ THE NEW CPD?

The case for collaboration and for empowering teachers to research their own practice is convincing. As Harris (2002) observes:

> there is sufficient evaluation evidence to show that when teachers are engaged in dialogue with each other about their practice then meaningful reflection and teacher and learning occur ... and ... there is now a growing literature that demonstrates and endorses the importance of evidence-based research as the basis for improving teaching.

As a consequence, a new perspective on CPD can be fashioned, focused on school-based processes, interschool collaboration and teacher enquiry. The ingredients of this *new* CPD are:

- school determined and led;
- focused on pedagogy and 'the craft of the classroom';
- tapping expertise already present, enriched by partnerships beyond the school;
- effective teacher learning is collaborative – within and beyond the school;
- teachers as leaders of learning in the broader educational community;
- schools sharing and seeking out good/best practice;
- the teacher as enquirer and researcher of their own practice;
- just as schools have become self-evaluating they now need to become self-researching;
- the growing and developing school is a research-engaged school.

However, although consortia working, collaboration and development of an enquiring research culture are becoming established features of the professional development and school improvement agendas, ensuring effective sharing of validated practice remains problematic. If schools are really to put collaboration to work then they need to give much more robust thought and analysis to processes involved in creating genuine communities of practice. Conversely, teachers and schools need to be supported and equipped to access and conduct research investigations that will help to transform their practice.

Do people have access to tools that help them challenge their practice?

100%	75%	50%	25%
Yes, the development of research and enquiry skills is built into the school's professional development planning and practice	Major projects are supported by the development of research and enquiry skills	Some individuals have taken an interest in using research and enquiry to challenge and improve their practice	There is little evidence of people having access to opportunities to develop research and enquiry skills apart from isolated cases
☐	☐	☐	☐

Please tick the appropriate box

FIGURE 7.2 THE RESEARCH-ENGAGED SCHOOL (HANDSCOMB and MacBEATH, 2003)

PART II: LEADING AND MANAGING THE CPD OF SPECIFIC GROUPS

Introduction

In this second part of the book we move from the broader picture of managing and leading professional development to look at the specific needs of particular groups in the school community. It examines the implications of the training and development cycle for all those who work in schools. We look at specific categories of people in schools – support staff, trainee teachers, newly qualified teachers, those in their second to fifth years, supply teachers, middle managers, school leaders and governors – and their training and development needs. Each group will contain people of varying degrees of effectiveness and enthusiasm, and all will have had different experiences. Drawing on research, we consider the key issues that need to be addressed for each group and suggest ways in which their professional development might be met.

The framework of national standards, developed by the TTA and the DfES (DfES, 2001b) in a colourful wallchart, is useful in describing key features of people's work at different stages. The wallchart combines the standards for QTS, induction, threshold, subject leaders, SENCOs, advanced skills teachers and headteachers. The standards are organized under ten headings or dimensions:

- Professional knowledge and understanding;
- Planning and setting expectations;
- Teaching and managing pupil learning;
- Assessment and evaluation;
- Pupil achievement;
- Relations with parents and the wider community;
- Managing own performance and development;
- Managing and developing staff and other adults;
- Managing resources;
- Strategic leadership.

Within each element or dimension there are clear expectations of people whether they are trainees, NQTs, applying to cross the threshold or headteachers. These are useful to consider in terms of professional development and help people see CPD as ongoing and on a continuum – *continuing* professional development and training – from the cradle to the grave! Too often professional development has not met the needs of groups in the middle of the career structure. The notion of lifelong learning is epitomized by the phrase 'we never stop learning'. Continuing professional development co-ordinators in schools therefore need to ensure that those providing training are clear about what knowledge, skills and attributes are to be developed, and at what stage in a teacher's or school leader's career.

A key task of leaders and managers of CPD is to encourage and develop 'learning staff' and to facilitate planned learning and development opportunities, recognizing a variety of learning styles and approaches to learning. We have shown in Part I of the book how this might be achieved by, for example, offering:

- a structured programme of on-the-job and off-the-job opportunities;

- practitioner or group research and enquiry;

- a culture of development within which staff feel valued in the job they do.

Continuing professional development co-ordinators must also be aware of the 'bigger picture' and address staff needs in common where possible, whilst fitting in with the school's needs and addressing national priorities. This can be a delicate balancing act. They have to ensure that training and development programmes meet the needs of both members of staff and their schools, minimizing any tensions that may exist between system needs and priorities (the school development plan) and those of individuals (the individual development plans).

The DfES baseline CPD study (Hustler et al., 2003), published in the summer of 2003, found that the principal drivers for CPD activity over the past five years have been school development needs and national priorities, and that these had taken precedence over individual needs. Teachers feel that personal/individual interests now need more emphasis. In Part I we argued that effective performance management arrangements provide the means to better reconciliation between the individual's and the school's priorities for development.

We wholeheartedly support the baseline CPD's study recommendation for ring-fenced funding for individual professional development: 'More resources need to be ring-fenced by government for personal/individual CPD and for those activities where school needs and individual needs can be clearly interrelated' (Hustler et al., 2003: xii). We support this because individual professional development – the growth and learning of all staff – is crucial to school improvement. As we argued in Part I, we need to move to an entitlement model of CPD or lifelong learning. Managers and leaders of CPD need to ensure that individual or personal development is not marginalized as it is crucial to staff effectiveness and institutional success.

Individuals also must be encouraged to be proactive in taking responsibility for their professional development. Some staff seem ignorant of or blinded to CPD opportunities, thinking that CPD is something that is done to them, which they passively receive whether they like it or not. Every group that we discuss in the following chapters needs to have a clear idea of outcomes and be able to judge the impact of professional development.

CHAPTER EIGHT

Support Staff

- Types and range of support staff
- Analysing and meeting needs
- Progression routes and accreditation options
- Teachers working with support staff
- Looking ahead

Greater flexibility in school budgets and local management of schools (LMS) have meant the number and range of support staff working in schools has increased considerably over the last decade and, in the light of the government's remodelling agenda, is likely to increase further in the near future (DfES, 2002d; 2003a). Table 8.1 shows that the total number of support staff rose by 8,300 to reach 225,300 in January 2003; the number of teaching assistants rose by 15,900 to reach 122,300; the number of administrative staff rose by 800 to reach 50,600; the number of 'other' support staff went down by 9,900 to 34,400 (DfES, 2003a). Increases have occurred in both the number and type of responsibility and, with their different roles, support staff now make up greater numbers than teachers in many schools. But what of their training and development needs? What are these, how are they identified and how can they best be met? What are the main challenges for teachers and their CPD needs as they are increasingly working with a group of what are sometimes referred to as associate staff or 'paraprofessionals'? We begin by looking at the various types of support staff increasingly found in schools.

TYPES AND RANGE OF SUPPORT STAFF

Traditionally, teachers and support staff have been treated differently within schools; for example, access to appraisal and performance management, training and development, and involvement in school decision-making processes have usually been the right of professional staff but not other paid employees. Other adults working in schools were often taken for granted, marginalized or, in some cases, totally ignored! Investors in People (see Chapter 3) has helped to rectify such a situation by insisting that organizations give due consideration to the training and development needs of *all* staff – that 'the organisation is committed to ensuring equality of opportunity in the development of its people' (IiPUK, 2000: 6).

TABLE 8.1 NUMBERS OF SUPPORT STAFF (thousands)

	1997	1998	1999	2000	2001	2002	2003 (p)
Teaching assistants [2]							
Teaching assistants	35.5	38.8	39.3	45.3	55.6	57.3	73.1
Special needs support staff	24.5	26.0	29.5	32.4	37.7	46.7	46.8
Minority ethnic pupil support staff	1.2	1.5	1.5	2.1	2.5	2.5	2.5
Total	61.3	66.3	70.3	79.8	95.8	106.4	122.3
Administrative staff							
Secretaries	27.6	28.5	29.1	30.2	30.6	25.6	24.7
Bursars	4.1	4.2	4.4	4.7	5.0	4.9	5.1
Other admin/clerical staff	7.5	7.3	7.7	8.3	10.7	19.3	20.8
Total	39.2	40.1	41.2	43.2	46.3	49.8	50.6
Technicians							
Total	12.7	13.1	13.5	14.2	15.0	16.6	18.0
Other support staff							
Matrons/nurses/medical staff [3]	1.2	1.2	1.2	1.2	1.2	1.8	1.7
Child care staff (boarding schools) [4]	3.4	3.4	3.1	3.3	3.2	3.2	0.4
Other [5]	18.7	19.7	22.1	23.1	27.4	39.3	32.3
Total	23.3	24.4	26.5	27.5	31.8	44.2	34.4
Total support staff	136.5	143.8	151.5	164.7	189.0	217.0	225.3
Total excluding nursery schools	134.1	141.5	149.0	162.1	186.3	214.2	222.4

Notes:
Support staff in maintained nursery, primary, middle and secondary schools, special schools and pupil referral units in England.[1] Full-time equivalents: January of each year.
(p) provisional.
1. Includes non-maintained special (and special and general hospital schools).
2. Includes nursery assistants in nursery schools.
3. Included with 'other' in nursery schools.
4. Due to a reporting problem at source, the number of child-care staff has not been recorded accurately by schools, resulting in child-care staff being distributed across other support staff categories.
5. Includes: librarians, welfare assistants, learning mentors and any other support staff regularly employed in schools; matrons, nurses, other medical staff in nursery schools.

Source: DfES, 2003b: table 13

The label 'non-teaching' staff is less frequently used in schools today as we have come to realize that defining a person's job in terms of what they do not do is no longer acceptable, whilst 'paraprofessional' is beginning to gain popularity in usage. Support staff is the term we have chosen to use in this chapter and it includes all those people who undertake paid employment in schools other than teachers and heads. Examples would therefore include: learning support assistants, special needs assistants, bilingual or ethnic minority achievement assistants, welfare assistants, nursery nurses, learning mentors, financial, administrative and secretarial or office staff; meals staff, midday and playground supervisors, grounds staff (including the site manager or caretaker), cleaners, crossing patrol personnel, learning resource and library staff, technicians and ICT support staff. With so many paid employees in schools performing a myriad of roles, it is helpful to group such activities into broader categories and to give brief consideration to each.

■ ASSISTANTS WITHIN THE CLASSROOM

Within the classroom, support can be given to teachers and children generally in the form of teaching assistants (TAs) or to support specific children with learning difficulties, as learning support assistants (LSAs) or special needs assistants (SNAs) do. Learning mentors work with pupils at risk of underachievement and others work with those for whom English is not their first language. Nursery nurses have an essential role in early years' settings. Volunteers and parents also play a large part in some classes.

■ FINANCIAL AND ADMINISTRATIVE ASSISTANTS

Bursars, finance officers, administration officers, secretaries and assistants usually undertake administrative duties within schools. Administrative assistants (such as the school secretary) are often the first port of call for parents and other visitors to the school.

■ MIDDAY SUPERVISORY ASSISTANTS

Midday supervisory assistants oversee the children during lunch and play times. Some are also TAs or LSAs.

■ ASSISTANTS WITHIN THE SCHOOL

This includes people with school-wide responsibilities such as learning resource managers, library staff, technicians and ICT support personnel. Site managers, premises staff and cleaners could also be included under this fourth category of support staff.

ANALYSING AND MEETING NEEDS
■

We know very little about the training and development needs of the various categories of support staff. It is an underresearched area, although there is a growing knowledge base; for example, Trevor Kerry (2001) has written about working with support staff, Ann Watkinson (2003) on teaching assistants and David Naylor (1999) on midday assistants.

The DfES wishes to encourage the development of three broad career progression routes for support staff, described as the 'pedagogical', 'behaviour and guidance', and 'administration and organization' (2002a: 8). The pedagogical route would serve those supporting pupils and teachers in the learning process and would include a new (and contentious) higher-level teaching assistant role. The behaviour and guidance route would involve all those helping schools with pastoral, attendance and discipline issues, including learning mentors who support individual pupils. The administration and organization route covers school administration and could lead to a higher-level bursar role.

The DfES has produced lots of support materials for teaching assistants and provides a regional induction programme, which they plan to extend to all support staff (DfES, 2002d). Materials produced by the DfES have been distributed to schools – an induction training file for newly appointed assistants and a 'good practice guide' for their management (DfEE, 2000d; 2000e). This material recommends schools provide TAs with a mentor, whether an SMT member or SENCO. New TAs are provided with four days of training, to which they must be accompanied by their mentor for one and half days. (For further information see the DfES website.)

Watkinson (2003) argues that TAs must be included in relevant school-based INSET and meetings, and must plan with teachers and feedback to them. It is important such staff are paid for the time spent in such activities, including travel and child-care costs of attending off-site training. Also as Watkinson notes:

> They also need time, resources and facilities to prepare just like teachers, which may well include access to ICT. They can have hidden skills and talents which need cherishing, they need training to do a job properly, they should be monitored and evaluated. They should have job security and career prospects and be a visible part of the whole school staff team with all the facilities and socialising that go with such membership, such as use of the staffroom and car park and inclusion in the end of term 'dos'. They should have similar access to and assistance with course attendance and expenses as are given to teachers. Pupils, governors and parents need to be aware of their role. They need a voice, recognition and valuing. (2003: 30)

For most support staff opportunities to develop their skills are broadening and becoming formalized and Watkinson suggests most now attend whole-school INSET, which was a rarity until recently. It is good practice to include all staff in whole-school training.

According to the DfES consultation paper, *Developing the Role of Support Staff* (DfES, 2002g), all support staff would benefit from basic training in behaviour management, child protection, special education needs (SEN) and disabilities, and working with pupils who have English as a second language. Training in behaviour management helps prepare TAs to maintain classroom discipline, cover for absent teachers and supervise larger groups during assemblies, school trips or sports. Managing discipline is often acknowledged as a key issue where joint training is especially valuable. Training together can lead to a shared perspective, helps to reduce anxiety and it demonstrates that those in authority are showing an interest in the work that TAs do (Mortimore and Mortimore, 1993). Other research (for example, Swann and Loxley, 1998) has shown that training TAs on their own is unlikely to have much of an impact or be successful because of their relatively powerless status as a group. Frustration can result if TAs feel that teachers are not listening to them or making full use of their experience and expertise. The most successful training is that which includes teachers for at least some parts (Watkinson, 1999). The pairing of teachers and TAs enables them to support each other in their learning whilst giving them an opportunity to develop consistent and co-ordinated approaches to such matters as behaviour management (Lorenz, 1998).

It is important to ask the question with TAs – indeed with all staff – is training targeted at their needs? If it is not then it can be a missed opportunity and perceived as 'a waste of time'. Are mechanisms in place in school to enable this to happen? Training must be supported by the SMT and the support staff member's line manager and, whenever possible, followed up. Some schools include support staff in whole-school staff meetings on a rota system, when they are given an opportunity to feedback on successful training or practice. This is to be recommended but care should be taken as it can be quite daunting for some TAs and may damage their confidence and self-esteem. As has been found with other staff, relevant CPD often improved perceptions of self-worth and generated a feeling of being valued by the school. It also improves confidence in TAs' relationships with teaching staff and with the pupils (Dixon, 2002).

Involving support staff in school-based CPD helps them to see themselves more clearly as part of the team, colleagues will value them more highly and their confidence and self-esteem will be enhanced. Also there is likely to be a narrowing of any 'them' and 'us' feelings and the boundary between professional and paraprofessional groups of staff is likely to become blurred. Giving support staff opportunities to take part in whole-school meetings and INSET training has been shown to lead to greater confidence in the performance of their roles in school (Kendall et al., 2000: 31).

An example of how one school successfully works with its teacher assistants is briefly outlined in Case study 8.1.

CASE STUDY 8.1: HOW CASTLEFIELDS INFANTS SCHOOL WORKS WITH TEACHING ASSISTANTS AND OTHER SUPPORT STAFF

This 155-pupil school for infants in Yorkshire is highly committed to the training and development of its 14 support staff. They have:

- pinpointed key areas where the school needed to expand provision;
- consulted TAs about areas of expertise they wished to develop;
- matched TAs' aspirations with the needs of the school;
- involved TAs in all curriculum planning meetings;
- introduced a clearly defined, incremental career path for TAs;
- encouraged TAs and other support staff to develop professionally by attending courses and undertaking study for qualifications with school support.

Teachers and TAs at Castlefields hold joint planning meetings, go on courses together and even occasionally spend residential weekends together. Teaching assistants are consulted on how they wish to develop professionally. They have attended courses on counselling, behaviour management, reading progression in phonics, planning for Ofsted, dyslexia-friendly schools, child protection, Internet use and first aid.

The governing body has established a career structure and appraisal system for support staff, offering a means of moving up the local authority pay scales. All support staff are encouraged to develop skills, to become more confident and to use their expertise. In this way they are seen as playing a fundamental role in raising pupil achievement.

Source: adapted from Williams, 2002.

Little is known about *midday supervisors* and their training needs. We do know, however, that they are infrequently offered training opportunities and rarely trained in what might be described as a core skill – group and behaviour management. As the Elton Report (1989) noted many years ago many midday supervisors rely entirely on their status as adults as a source of authority. Naylor (1999), one of very few to have investigated (and provided for) their training needs, makes reference to such things as games organization and encouraging appropriate social behaviour in pupils. He found midday supervisors rarely talked about behaviour management in terms of school behaviour policy, suggesting a real need for training to link to the school's expectations of their pupils. Also how can midday supervisors help children to develop friendships at break times? Several guides are available (for example, Mosley, 1996) to help schools with the training and support of midday supervisors. How many schools have considered such guides? Has yours? Henry Maynard Infants School in Walthamstow has given their midday assistants ICT and behaviour management training, and six have enrolled on an accredited national vocational qualification (NVQ level 2) course with the school in partnership with a local sixth form college (Kabra, 2002).

Bursars and business managers can play a significant part in school management, bringing their expertise to bear on the planning and management of resources, as well as taking some of the management load off headteachers. Recent research has found that in addition to financial duties, management and leadership roles are increasing in importance. The DfES sees bursars as playing a key role in helping to implement the government's remodelling agenda (DfES, 2002f). Bursars are taking on more diverse functions and need greater degrees of support and training.

The DfES's guidance document about bursars is intended to assist heads, governors and others involved in running schools, who may be thinking of taking on a bursar or developing the contribution of someone already employed by the school. It considers bursar tasks and responsibilities at three levels: 'basic', 'intermediate' and 'advanced'. These descriptors are used to help explain the potential span and range of the role of bursars (DfES, 2002f). Linked with all this are plans to offer more support and training to bursars, including a course and qualification offered by the National College for School Leadership (see next section).

PROGRESSION ROUTES AND ACCREDITATION OPTIONS

With the growth of support staff in schools attempts have been made to raise their profile by introducing more opportunities for accreditation and consideration given to possible career progression routes. There are now nationally recognized qualifications developed specifically for teaching assistants, which provide clear progression routes into and within employment. The DfES has provided materials encouraging TAs to take part in accredited courses. For those TAs interested in their own professional development and who wish to progress, a co-ordinated and accredited programme of NVQs and vocationally relevant qualifications (VRQs) was approved in 2001. The Local Government National Training organization has developed a suite of national occupational standards for TAs which include NVQs at levels 2 and 3. There are two NVQs specifically developed for teaching assistants on the national qualifications framework – one at level 2 (suitable for people new to the role or whose responsibilities at work are limited in scope) and one at level 3 (suitable for experienced teaching assistants whose working role calls for competence across a varied range of responsibilities).

There are also specialist courses now available to classroom assistants to work towards qualified teacher status. Teaching assistants who have successfully completed a specialist teacher assistant (STA) course can use these for credit towards a higher-level qualification such as a Certificate of Higher Education, a Diploma of Higher Education or a foundation degree. A pioneering diploma course which allows teaching assistants to spend four days a week at work and one day training to teach in a special centre is outlined in the box below.

COLLEGE CONNECTIONS

Headteacher Richard Parker designed the diploma course with University College, Northampton, after spotting a need for training that spanned the gap between assistant and teacher.

'I was under the impression assistants deal with paint pots, when really they do sophisticated curriculum support work,' he says. 'This is about maximizing potential. The teaching assistants have become so much more proactive. The benefits for morale are enormous. They are saying: "At last people believe in us. At last we have a career progression".'

A two-year foundation degree gives associate teacher status, so staff can teach up to Key Stage 3. A third year is being developed to give qualified teacher status, and a fourth year a subject specialism.

Designing the course was 'a massive undertaking', but of 51 teaching assistants who enrolled in September 2001, 48 are on course for a foundation degree this summer – a low dropout rate by most universities' standards.

'We now have four people who will graduate in July and join the staff,' says Parker. 'These are people who know the school and will probably stay with us rather than moving on after a couple of years. Any school with a university within touching distance could set this up. You need a supportive local authority, and assistants need the support of their schools.'

Source: from *Guardian* special report, 'A load off your mind', 13 May 2003

Further guidance on the relationship between the DfES induction training materials and the national occupational standards for teaching assistants, including how the induction programme can be used to support achievement of the NVQs, is available by accessing the DfES website at www.teachernet.gov.uk and typing 'teaching assistants' into the search engine.

Nationally, there is a wide range of training available for TAs but the main opportunities for qualifications are:

- DfES induction training (basic training available to all TAs after starting the job);
- national literacy and numeracy strategy training;
- Key Stage 3 strategy training;
- NVQs level 2 and 3;
- Higher level – foundation degrees;
- The Graduate and Registered Teacher Programme for those who want to qualify as teachers;
- The Early Years sector-endorsed Foundation degree, allowing an employment-based route to becoming a teacher (see Haughton, 2002).

Knowledge about training and accreditation options and availability is important as the lack of such information makes career progression and development planning for support staff difficult.

The DfES guidance document (DfES, 2002e) notes that although qualifications for teaching assistants are not mandatory, ensuring they have access to relevant training and qualifications will:

> help LEAs and schools to maintain high quality support for teaching and learning in the classroom. It also demonstrates to teachers, parents and Ofsted, as well as teaching assistants themselves, that teaching assistants are recognized and supported as valued members of the school staff team. Gaining a nationally recognized qualification is good for self esteem and confidence as well the ability to do a good job, all of which contribute to job satisfaction, staff retention and raising standards in schools. (DfES, 2002e)

Watkinson (2003), who has been involved in these national developments, has analysed the work of TAs in terms of a number of levels, delineating the skills and competences, and knowledge and understanding expected at each level. She suggests four levels and possible titles for each, with the fifth level leading to qualified teacher status. This is shown in Table 8.2, which can also be used as a basis for drawing up job descriptions for different types of TAs. Some LEAs are tackling the career structure issue by making use of these different categories – entry level, intermediate, advanced and senior (see Haughton, 2002).

The other area where significant developments in accreditation have recently taken place concerns *bursars*, financial administrators or school business managers. Bursar training leading to a Certificate of School Business Management is now available from the National College for School Leadership. This training covers the functions associated with the bursar (see below), and is open to everyone who is already working in a maintained school in England, or intends to do so. The emphasis is on enabling participants to make a greater practical input to schools. As with other NCSL programmes it makes use of a combination of face-to-face and online learning, and the evaluations to date have been positive. The programme aims to develop the role of the business manager as part of the school's leadership team with the aim of helping to reduce the heads' workload – or at least enable them to focus more on learning-centred matters. The NCSL has now made the bursar programme available nationally with 750 places made available in 2003. A higher-level diploma programme was piloted during 2003 with 100 places.

TEACHERS WORKING WITH SUPPORT STAFF

Support staff, like any other staff members within the school, have to be managed. Appointment and management procedures will create extra work for school leaders and managers, but teaching assistants will also increase the workload of *all* teachers as they have to plan for and recognize the effects of additional adults in classrooms. The standards for qualified teacher status (TTA, 2002a) and induction (TTA, 2003b) acknowledge this. As Watkinson notes:

> The appointment and induction of TAs can be time consuming as with teaching staff. Just as with any other member of staff this involves the appointment processes of interviewing, induction training and probationary periods. TAs need important documentation relating to their job before they start, and managers must ensure TAs know all the emergency, health and safety, confidentiality and child protection procedures at the very earliest opportunity. SEN, relevant curriculum and behaviour policies should be part of that early package. A mentor, and clear line management needs to be established, the former particularly if there is any external course involvement such as the DfES Induction training. (2003: 30)

TABLE 8.2 POSSIBLE LEVELS OF EXPECTATIONS AND COMPETENCIES FOR TAs

Level	Competencies expected (supporting the teacher[s] and personal development)	Experiences typical in school (supporting the school)	Knowledge and understanding (supporting the pupil and the curriculum, teaching and learning)	Possible title	Pay scale
1	Carry out instructions Show common sense Follow school policies Relate appropriately to pupils and adults	Domestic chores Basic child care In class: Follow and repeat instructions of teacher	Understand how the school community works and how to be part of a team Take responsibility for own actions; use equipment safely	Welfare/care assistant	Entry levels on single status scale
2	Able to work under the direction of teacher, with selected children Assist in classroom task set by teacher Take charge of their own professional development	Facilitate curriculum delivery; carry out practical tasks Work and interact with groups, in sight of teacher Aware of resource provision See individuals are different; facilitate independence	Has a framework of understanding of learning theory and child development Needs intended learning objectives with activities Support pupils with SEN and facilitate their learning Attend IEP reviews Carry out NLNS responsibilities after training	Competent teaching assistant	?
3	Able to use initiative appropriately tasks, especially in private nursery situations, but not take responsibility for children's learning in school Evaluate routines, provide welfare, guidance and support to children	Under direction of teacher: devise resources and activities to support learning; take groups outside classroom; participate in planning and assessment; provide reports and records; perform teaching activities Understand education system and code of practice	To have an awareness of parts of the NC, for example, literacy and numeracy, or Early Learning Goals Know about physical, emotional, intellectual, spiritual cultural development Support children with particular needs and develop expertise Contribute to IEP reviews Relate to parents	Advanced or specialist teaching assistant	?
4	Work in partnership with teachers Share in planning and assessment Contribute to decision making Training and management responsibilities	Can take responsibility, under direction of teacher, for a particular aspect of curriculum development, resource management, or equipment maintenance Able to lead a team of other TAs/adults Take a class in an emergency, using planning directed by teacher and reporting back to teacher	Able to undertake study with reflection and assignments Understand some of the requirements of the NC Know about learning objectives and aspects of the NC; Have some understanding of teaching and learning theory Able to contribute to the formulation of IEPs	Lead teaching assistant	?
QTS	Undertake responsibility for teaching and learning of pupils; manage additional adults, and so on		Teacher requirements	Qualified teacher	Teachers' pay scales

Source: Watkinson, 2003: 31

THE CERTIFICATE IN SCHOOL BURSAR MANAGEMENT

The certificate helps to enable all bursars, school business managers and senior administrators to:

- manage resources more efficiently, effectively and sensitively;
- enhance and renew their understanding of administration and management;
- evaluate the efficiency and effectiveness of educational institutions;
- evaluate and analyse management strategies that support effective curriculum and learning development;
- develop management decision-making skills;
- understand the nature of effective schooling in the twenty-first century;
- understand the environment within which education is delivered.

The course is made up of seven modules:

1 The Educational Enterprise;
2 Financial Management;
3 Human Resource Management;
4 Information and Communication Technology, Management Information Systems;
5 Facilities Management;
6 Risk Management;
7 Administrative and Support Services Management.

For more information see the NCSL website at http://www.ncsl.org.uk/bursar or email bursar@ncsl.org.uk.

Source: adapted from DfES, 2002f

Teachers may well have to be trained in the management of additional adults. Also attitudes may need to change if support staff are to be considered as equal members of the school community and their contribution valued. Teachers' perception of support staff remains questionable and is sometimes negative (Kerry, 2003). Table 8.3 gives an indication of some of the issues and possible solutions that may need consideration in any training aimed at teachers working with support staff and particularly teaching assistants (Bubb, 2003b).

It might be helpful to ask support staff if they can devise a similar list from their own perspective. Similarly, Kerry (2003) who has researched support staff's needs, suggests we ask two key questions:

1 What do you do in your school to ensure that teachers are trained to manage the work of support staff effectively?

2 What do these teachers do that marks them out as successful managers of support staff?

He suggests that teachers need to be made aware of how to manage support staff, and to be trained in the skills of management. There is no shortage of literature offering advice and guidance and practical strategies for effective classroom support (for example, see Balshaw and Farrell, 2002; Kay, 2002; Watkinson, 2002) and these would be useful additions to any school's staff development library.

TABLE 8.3 ISSUES AROUND SUPPORT ASSISTANTS (BUBB 2003c)

Issue	Ideas/solutions
Being unsure of the additional adult's role	Find out exactly what they are paid to do. For instance, some special needs assistants are funded to work with individual SEN pupils
Not sure when they are going to be in the class	Find out exactly when they are coming and make sure they know that you're expecting them
Not wanting to ask them to do menial tasks	Again, look at their job description. Most are happy to help out
Some do too much for the children and encourage over-dependence	Model the sort of teaching you want. Do not be afraid to mention concerns – they have not benefited from training like you and so are usually more than pleased to be given advice
Some have little control over the children	Again, model how to manage behaviour. Speak to their line manager if it is a big problem
Some can take over the class	This is very tricky. Speak to them about the need to establish yourself as the teacher, but otherwise get advice on how to deal with this
Some talk when the teacher has asked for everyone's attention	Theatrically or humorously emphasize that you need *everyone's* attention
Some don't do quite what you have asked them to	Explain, model, write instructions; speak to them about your concern
Some are stuck in their ways and do not like new ideas and practices	Tricky. Try to get them on your side by asking for their advice, their patience in trying things out
Planning for them, but they do not turn up	Make sure they and others know how much you depend on and value them. Make a fuss if they are taken away too often

LOOKING AHEAD

Creating the right school climate where teachers and support staff work in partnership, and feel part of a team is going to be facilitated by staff development for professional and paraprofessional staff, both individually and, at times, together. The CPD needs of both groups of staff need to be recognized, including those relating to working effectively with each other. A whole-school approach to CPD with joint planning and, where appropriate, joint training is to be recommended.

This is going to be even more important in the future given the government's remodelling agenda (DfES, 2002d) and the fact that many more support staff will be working in schools undertaking an increasing range of responsibilities. Since September 2003 teachers should no longer undertake 24 clerical and administrative tasks, such as bulk photocopying or stocktaking. Personal assistants have been recruited to give teachers and subject departments the administrative back-up they need, and from September 2005 it is proposed that invigilating external exams will be taken over by adults other than teachers. Suitably qualified adults will also undertake tasks not expected of a trained teacher, such as supervising detention periods or even taking assemblies (DfES, 2002d). In the classroom there will be more adults, including a new category of higher-level teaching assistants.

In its consultation document, *Developing the Role of School Support Staff* (DfES, 2002g: 8), the government proposes a number of things:

- to extend induction training for all support staff, building on the success of the DfES induction training for TAs;

- to encourage the development of the three career progression routes;

- to develop standards for higher level TA roles, and smoother progression routes for support staff to QTS;

- training for behaviour and guidance roles;

- extend customized training for school bursars and business managers;

- map existing qualifications to fit within the proposed career progression framework; and,

- to provide new training provision.

Much is happening or proposed but research by a support staff union has shown that the quality of training varies considerably and support staff pay is often poor. Four in ten schools do not pay teaching assistants during school holidays and many work extra hours for no additional pay, and one in five teaching assistants needs a second job to make ends meet (*Guardian*, 13 May 2003). Obviously, many of these issues are beyond the control of schools and CPD co-ordinators. Some, however, are not and this chapter has highlighted the importance of attending to the training and development needs of support staff. The training and development of support staff has improved and in the light of the government's objectives is likely to continue to improve. Schools with Investors in People status have been shown to have managed support staff more effectively than those without this status (Ofsted, 2002c). Some schools lack confidence in managing, deploying and developing this particular people resource and need training (PwC, 2001). Support staff have much to contribute to schools, and those heads and CPD co-ordinators who ignore them, either through ignorance or lack of training, are doing their pupils a grave disservice.

CHAPTER NINE

Initial Teacher Training – the CPD Needs and Benefits

- Different ways to be involved
- ITT partnership – pros and cons
- CPD needs of mentors

There are many benefits to be gained by schools and their staff from engaging in initial teacher training, particularly its effect as a catalyst for continuing professional development. Under the new Ofsted inspection framework, schools' ITT involvement is formally commented on. It can help the development of reflective learning communities with wider links to higher education and other schools.

DIFFERENT WAYS TO BE INVOLVED

Many schools are involved in initial teacher training in a variety of different ways. There are three main routes to qualified teacher status, which are compared in Figure 9.1:

- The undergraduate route – people combine subject studies with professional training over three or four years and are awarded a BA (QTS) or a BEd.
- The postgraduate route – which is offered full time for one year, part time or through a flexible programme and gives a post-graduate certificate in education (PGCE) with QTS, unless the PGCE is for the post-compulsory sector.
- Employment-based routes (England and Wales) – the Graduate Teacher Programme which is for people with a degree, and the Registered Teacher Programme, for people without a degree but with two years' higher education such as an HND. Both courses give qualified teacher status, but trainees have to be over 24 years old.

Many changes have happened in ITT in the past couple of years and acronyms abound, which may leave people confused. The BA (QTS) or a BEd is a teaching qualification and a degree, and normally takes three years. Just under half of all primary school trainees are on undergraduate courses, whereas the PGCE outnumbers the BA QTS/BEd in secondary by about 12:1 as can be seen in Figure 9.1.

	BEd, BA (QTS)	PGCE	GTP
Entry requirements	Eng & maths GCSE C, science C for primary people born after 1.9.79	Eng & maths GCSE C, science C for primary people born after 1.9.79; degree	Eng & maths GCSE C, science C for primary people born after 1.9.79; degree; 24+ years old
Apply through	UCAS	GTTR	A DRB
Time spent in school	32 weeks for 4 year courses and 24 weeks for 3 year courses	24 weeks for secondary and 18 weeks for primary	Almost all
Funding for trainee	None	£6,000 bursary	Possible £13,000 salary £4,000 training grant
£4,000 Golden Hello	No	Secondary maths, science, ICT, MFL, DT, English	No
Loans repaid	If teaching maths, science, ICT, MFL, DT or English for half the week	If teaching maths, science, ICT, MFL, DT or English for half the week	If teaching maths, science, ICT, MFL, DT or English for half the week
Secondary numbers 2002	1,313	15,472	3,400 sec & primary
Primary numbers 2002	6,488	7,988	Ditto

FIGURE 9.1 COMPARING ROUTES INTO TEACHING

Most people do a PGCE based at an ITT provider. Post-graduate certificate in education courses last for about 38 weeks but involve a great deal of time in school, usually in six-week blocks starting with observing teaching and learning, then working with small groups, then team teaching and finally taking whole classes independently. Primary PGCEs spend at least 18 weeks in school, and secondary PGCEs at least 24 weeks – over half of the course. When at college, learning takes place in lectures, seminars, workshops and tutorials. The PGCE combines theory and practice and trainees will have written assignments to do as well as planning for school experience. There are 'flexible routes' for people who cannot do a full-time PGCE.

The Fast Track programme is for a very small number of people who do a PGCE at specified institutions. It is an accelerated development programme towards leadership positions. The entry requirements are high. People need a strong academic record and they have a half-day computer-based assessment, an interview for a place on a PGCE course and then a two-day residential assessment. There is a system of job brokering so that they only work in schools that have advertised a fast-track position. When working they get one extra point on their salary each year, which is funded by the DfES, so that they may reach M6 on the mainscale and be able to apply to cross the threshold after about three years.

School-centred initial teacher training (SCITT) is run by groups of schools, with some input from outside. All courses lead to qualified teacher status and may also lead to a PGCE validated by a higher education institution.

The Graduate Teacher Programme (GTP) is growing fast and is for people with a first degree who want to train on the job in England or Wales. It suits people who have already got a good amount of school experience. Entry to what are called Designated Recommending Bodies (DRB) is competitive, with places going to the best applications in priority funding categories, which are (in this order):

1   Secondary shortage subjects – mathematics, science, modern foreign languages, ICT, DT and English.

2   High-quality primary applications.

3   Applications in any subject or phase that make the teaching force more representative of society, for example increasing men in primary teaching, teachers from minority ethnic groups and teachers with disabilities.

4   High-quality secondary applications in any subject.

5   Applications to train people currently working as teaching assistants.

The Teacher Training Agency pays a grant of up to £4,000 to cover the cost of training and for the strongest candidates may pay up to £13,000 to the school as a contribution to the trainee's salary.

The snag with the GTP is that schools have to employ an unqualified teacher before they know that the person will have a place on the programme. Places are very competitive and experiences have been mixed, with a fair number of people getting turned down or, if accepted, feeling that they were left to sink or swim. School-based training via the GTP route can be isolating for both trainees and mentors. It was originally thought that people on the GTP would be supernumerary but in most cases they have full responsibility from the start. To obtain QTS people have to have teaching experience in two schools and at two consecutive key stages – clearly this is a problem for a school that is actually employing one as a class teacher. The GTP requires a big commitment from schools because most learning is on the job:

> GTP trainees are in school full time apart from occasional central training days. This has implications for their training and our professional development in that we have been able to develop a programme of in-house training customized to the needs of the individual and working to the strengths of our staff. We have also been able to organize some of the training to coincide with the PGCE block practices and in some instances we have opened up the invitation to GTP trainees in other schools in the borough. (Kabra, 2002: 33)

Teach First started in 2003. This is the business and government-backed organization that provides teacher and business training to attract talented graduates to schools facing teacher shortages. After a short but intensive training at an ITT institution, Teach First places participants in London secondary schools that have at least one-third of pupils eligible for free school meals, are not in Special Measures, and can provide the necessary support.

Many schools have trainees on teaching practice but a small number are designated as training schools. The difference between being a school that mentors beginning teachers and being a training school is an increase in funding so that roles and responsibilities within a HEI partnership are expanded. There are also Partnership Promotion Schools, which are dedicated to encouraging more active school involvement and to developing innovative ways of working within ITT partnerships.

ITT PARTNERSHIP – PROS AND CONS

As the outline above indicates, the TTA is shifting responsibility for training teachers away from ITT providers, into a 'partnership' with schools. This means that for the GTP schools are practically on their own and even on PGCEs have nearly 50 per cent of the responsibility for making sure that the trainee is successful. So ITT partnership has mixed blessings.

NEGATIVE ASPECTS

Training someone for the new generation of teachers is a great responsibility. How do you know that you will do it right? It is a complex skill and one in which ITT providers are very experienced. At least one person on your staff will need to have the specialist skills to train beginning teachers and to share their knowledge with others involved. They will need specific CPD and support in handling tricky situations. They will need to understand the QTS standards fully (TTA, 2002a) and know what is required to meet them.

Trainees need good teachers as role models, but maybe your school has a limited number of people you would put in that category. This can cause bad feeling in the staffroom where having a trainee on teaching practice is seen as a bit of an 'easy ride'. Many teachers find letting go of their classes difficult. They do not want to see their routines and so on changed. They are very controlling and find it hard to let trainees develop and learn from mistakes. On the other hand, a few teachers see having a trainee as a chance to have a rest, to abdicate responsibility for their class, to get other things done.

Unless you are heavily involved in a SCITT or have someone on the GTP, you will get the trainee that you are given. Most are great but occasionally there are nightmares: people with a very different pedagogical philosophy from you who cause no end of difficulty for all concerned. Trainees are learning to be teachers so it is unlikely (but not impossible) that they will be as effective as experienced colleagues. Typically this will affect the behaviour and learning of pupils. This needs to be managed well to limit damage.

Being in partnership means having to rely on others and may mean compromising on judgements. Your school may think that a trainee should not qualify but others think otherwise, for instance.

And then there are the pragmatics. You will have lots of new people in the school. More is usually better – but not always. They will need somewhere to sit in the staffroom. What do you do about confidential matters? Are there any staff meetings that trainees should not attend?

POSITIVE ASPECTS

There are clear benefits to being involved in ITT. There is the philanthropic buzz that comes from the influence practising teachers have upon the quality of future entrants to the profession. On a more pragmatic level it means being able to hand pick your new teachers – many trainees obtain jobs in schools they do a teaching practice in.

It increases the adult to pupil ratio, which means that children get more attention and teachers should be less stretched. Kathryn Kabra believes:

> The children gain so much more adult contact in an average school day, experience so many different teaching styles that there has to be something to meet every learning need and they're guaranteed a teacher in front of them rather than the uncertainties of staff shortages and supply availability. It's a win-win situation for everybody. (Kabra, 2002: 36)

CASE STUDY 9.1: A TRAINING SCHOOL

Kathryn Kabra describes the opportunities that her school has been offered through gaining training school status, and the many ways in which it has made a difference.

Having had a regular stream of PGCE trainees passing through our doors over the last decade many staff had already received quality mentor training from our HEI partner, and had experienced the highs and lows of mentor life and trainee morale boosting. We were, as a staff, very aware of what was to be gained from contact with enthusiastic, innovative individuals who implicitly demand that we draw upon the strengths of our own experience and re-acquaint ourselves with those convictions which first drew us into teaching. To rediscover the extent of our expertise and find that it is recognized and valued is no small spin off for a workforce, which can feel jaded and finely tuned to criticism. So raised morale and self-affirmation have had a significant impact on the energy generated within the school. Being selected to be a training school was a powerful recognition of the quality and value of the mentoring that staff have provided over the years.

The reflective practice that mentoring and modelling good practice entails, and the opportunity to disseminate their skills and knowledge through leading INSET both in school and at the HEI, have made significant contributions both to their professional portfolios and to a general 'can-do' culture. Four people have applied for assessment this term as advanced skills teachers (ASTs). We are hoping to set up two research projects during the next academic year, one to evaluate innovations to the organization of Foundation Stage classes and the other as part of a wider research project looking at the educational needs of children of Pakistani origin. Two of the staff have acted as professional tutors for the HEI and have been involved with supporting mentors of PGCE trainees in other schools. Through this an incidental effect has been the formation of closer links with neighbouring schools and an opportunity to learn from other teachers.

Training school status has brought together many of the school's ongoing developmental initiatives under one umbrella and made economies of scale possible. In the best practice of good teaching and learning we have been able to step back from an activity led training curriculum into a cycle of needs analysis, target audience identification, identification of the best person for the job, identification of the best method of presentation and evaluation of its effectiveness, leading to modification and improvement. A training school co-ordinator post was created, and a second member of staff appointed to tutor PGCE trainees in this and other HEI partnership schools for one day a week. The training school, like Jack's beanstalk, is growing and reaching for the sky! (Kabra, 2002: 33–5)

Having lots of enthusiastic beginning teachers around gives schools a buzz and may influence those experienced colleagues who might be described as 'professionally stagnant' (Child and Merrill, 2002). Trainee teachers bring to schools the benefits of up to date subject and pedagogical knowledge.

Effective mentoring is at the heart of ITT. In supporting and assessing trainees, mentors have to reflect on their own performance and often become better teachers themselves as a result. This is recognized in the new kind of advanced skills teachers for ITT (ASTITT) who are recognized as successful mentors/trainers. A major benefit for schools involved in ITT is the transferability of mentoring skills to other aspects of the school's life and work, specifically in working with NQTs and performance management. Mentoring trainees is good practice for working with other teachers – ones who are perhaps less willing to develop! Two schoolteachers (Butler and Geeson, 2002) seconded to work on PGCE courses state, 'mentoring has become an increasingly significant mode of professional development'. They continue: 'where mentoring has been an integral part of the school's ethos, there is likely to be greater collaboration amongst staff in sharing ideas, schemes of work and practice'.

Teachers who have a trainee working with them will eventually be able to leave the classroom, enabling them to support others. In Child and Merrill's research only three out of 53 mentors thought that ITT took up too much teacher time: just over a quarter claimed that trainees taking classes generated meaningful 'free' time for teachers, whereas two-thirds took the view that they created 'quality' time for other staff. They conclude that 'free time is considered an inappropriate phrase as it implies some kind of shirking of responsibility; quality time is redolent of something professional, a time in which CPD might be occurring' (Child and Merrill, 2002b: 20).

CPD NEEDS OF MENTORS

How schools organize their training role will be looked at further in the next chapter on induction. It is important to ask mentors what they need. Common areas are observation and feedback skills.

OBSERVATION – GENERAL POINTS

Mentors may find observing stressful, because they feel inexperienced and uncertain of the best way to go about it. The year group and area of the curriculum to be taught may not be familiar. They may feel that their observation and feedback will compare unfavourably to that of the university supervisor. As the person responsible for the trainee, they will also be mindful of the need to move them forward while maintaining a good relationship. This can lead people to be too kind, and to not bite the bullet. Trainees sometimes feel that they are not being sufficiently challenged. This is particularly true of the most successful ones, but they too need to be helped to develop professionally.

Observation and giving feedback are very complex skills, for which training and practice are required. The important thing to remember is that the whole process needs to be useful for the trainee. It is for their benefit that it is being done. To this end it is essential that mentors, ITT and induction tutors consider the context of the observation. This includes:

- the stage of the trainee (is this an early or final teaching practice?);
- how they are feeling;
- their previous experiences of being observed;
- the state of the mentor's relationship with the trainee or NQT;
- what part of the school year, week and day it happens in;
- the disposition of the class.

Mentors also need to recognize their own values, beliefs and moods. This is why it is important to concentrate on the progress the children make before judging the effectiveness of the teaching. The more we observe other teachers, the more convinced we are that there is no one way to teach.

Observers should also recognize their own feelings at the time of the observation. No one functions effectively when they are tired, stressed or irritable. People tend to be more generous and easygoing when feeling happy. Mentors should recognize their feelings, and in some way compensate for them, in order to be as objective as possible. They also need to recognize that their very presence in the classroom will affect the pupils.

BEFORE THE OBSERVATION

It is useful if not essential to have a focus – something the trainee is trying to get better at. This will not exclude you from noticing and commenting on other things but will ensure that you have information on the key area that you are working on. Discuss ground rules such as how your presence is to be explained to the class, what you are going to do, where you should sit, your exact time of arrival, what you will need before or at the beginning of the observation, such as the lesson plan and access to the planning file. Agree a time and place to discuss the lesson, giving yourself time to reflect and write notes, ideally within 24 hours of the observation.

DURING THE OBSERVATION

It is essential to look at teaching in relation to learning. One must always be thinking about cause and effect. Why are the pupils behaving as they are? The cause is often related to teaching. Thus, the observer needs to look carefully at what both the teacher and the pupils are doing. Read the lesson plan, paying particular attention to the learning objective. Is it a sensible objective, and is it shared with the pupils? If you have a photocopy it is useful to annotate the plan, for instance showing what parts went well, when pace slowed, and so forth. Look at the planning file and pupils' work to see what the lesson is building on.

If the student teacher has not given you a place to sit, choose one which is outside the direct line of the teacher's vision, but where you can see the pupils and what the teacher is doing. When the pupils are doing activities, move around to ascertain the effectiveness of the teacher's explanation, organization and choice of task. Look at different groups (girls and boys; high, average and low attainers; and students with English as an additional language or special needs) to see whether everyone's needs are being met.

Make notes about what actually happens, focusing on the agreed areas but keeping your eyes open to everything. Make clear judgements as you gather evidence. Refer to the criteria you agreed to use – have a copy with you. Try to tell 'the story' of the lesson, by noting causes and effect. For instance, what was it about the teacher's delivery that caused students' rapt attention or fidgeting? Think about the pupils' learning and what it is about the teaching that is helping or hindering it. Note what they actually achieve. Teachers are not always aware that some students have only managed to write the date and that others have exceeded expectations, for instance. Look through books to get a feel for their progress and marking.

Avoid teaching or interfering in any way. This is very tempting but will distract you from your central purpose, which is to observe the teaching and learning. It is not wise to intervene in controlling the class unless things get out of hand, because it can undermine the teacher's confidence and may confuse the pupils, who will see you as the one in charge rather than their teacher. However, letting pupils get away with things may undermine your role. As far as possible be unobtrusive.

■ WRITTEN NOTES

Before you write observation notes you need to remind yourself of their purpose and audience. Are they aiming to develop someone or be brutally honest? Some things are easier to approach orally or in an oblique way. There are two sorts of writing from an observation: the notes you make during the lesson and the summary of strengths and areas for development for feedback. We think both should be used. That way the observer can make informal jottings during the lesson knowing that they will be pulled together in a tidy summary afterwards.

Written feedback should contain praise and acknowledgement of success, identify strengths and weaknesses or areas to develop, that will be useful in future lessons. Finally, they may have ideas for improvement.

There is a range of sorts of comments in observation feedback:

- Descriptive – what happens but without any evaluation. This is not very helpful.

- Questioning/reflective – there are two sorts of questions:
  - those designed to stimulate thought and get people thinking about an area that could be improved, for example, 'how could you have avoided the arguments over pencils?'
  - genuine questions for clarification – for example, 'why are you ignoring Paul's behaviour?'

- Evaluative – judging, for example, 'very well planned'; 'shouting simply raises the noise and emotional level'.

- Advisory – suggestions, for example, 'Dean and Wayne might behave better if they were separated'.

What features can you see in the notes written by Sara Bubb in Figures 9.2 and 9.3?

■ AFTER THE OBSERVATION – DISCUSSING THE LESSON

Take some time to reflect. Think about the teaching and learning you have seen, focusing on strengths and a few areas for development. Be clear about your main message – this will take some thinking about. There is no point listing every little thing that went wrong. You need to have 'the big picture' in your mind in order to convey it to the beginning teacher. Remember it needs to be useful to them – aim to help them develop. You want to avoid the extremes of crushing them or giving the impression that things are better than they really are. It is a very fine line to tread, but your knowledge of the context and the person will help you.

Attend to the physical setting of the discussion. Choose a place where you will not be disturbed – you never know how someone is going to react in a feedback. Position chairs at right angles for the most conducive atmosphere. This enables you to have eye contact but not in the formal direct way that sitting opposite someone across a desk would ensure but sometimes such a setting may help get a message across.

Good feedback is:

Prompts:	Comments and evidence. What impact does teaching have on pupils?
Planning Groundrules	Pupils come in calmly and settle down – clearly know expected behaviour. Good to have Yvette go through homework straight away while you get your things organized.
Behaviour management Expectations Organization Resources Shares learning objectives Subject knowledge Explanations Teaching strategies Voice Pace Use of time Questioning	Wonderful snappy start. Lovely smile – real warmth that the students react well to. Good to ask the difference between biog and autobiography, though you didn't pick up on the boy's use of the term 'story' which would have been useful. I don't think you shared learning objs or told the class the big picture of the lesson. These things really help students cue into what you want them to and aids their learning. It's also school policy. I like the way you hook the children's interest by asking them whose autobiography they'd like to read. It does however take a while. Could you use talk partners to make even more of this part of the lesson? V good choice of text – prob appealing to all boys and girls. A good hook – shows you have thought about what will motivate the students. Good, snappy getting of the chapter headings from a range of students – again perhaps you could do some pair work for this to get more out of more of them. Ordering was done efficiently and democratically, but to get where you want. Lovely humour and lively style, in getting them to articulate why they know it's David Beckham's autobiography. Good use of Yvette to read paragraph. How could she be more involved at other times? Good changing of tenses as a class, and coping with errors e.g. bring – branged. Lovely to get the class to clap the boy for reading aloud – really celebratory and boosting. The students seemed to cope well with the activity of writing out a paragraph in a different tense. It would have been brilliant if there'd been a purpose for doing so. Could you have differentiated this to challenge students more? It was good to get them working though they had little time to do so (5 mins?). Could they have done more individual/paired work throughout the lesson?
Motivating Differentiation Add. adults Feedback Activities Plenary	You told them what to do for homework – finish off drafts. Shame there wasn't a plenary to pull together what they've learned. What did they learn? What did you expect them to? Students packed up and left sensibly. Time: 1.50 Pupils on task: all……… off task:…… Time: 2.15 Pupils on task: all off task: but some looking a bit switched off

FIGURE 9.2 OBSERVATION NOTES MADE DURING A LESSON (BUBB 2003c)

- prompt – takes places as soon as possible after the lesson observation;
- accurate – based only on specific, observations/evidence which can be readily shared with the teacher;
- balanced – the positive emphasized and points for development related to the focus chosen as an objective;
- respectful to the teacher's perspective – allows for input from the teacher;
- related to objectives set for review and directly actionable by the teacher;
- conducted in a quiet and private space.

Be aware of your body language and notice the teacher's. A large proportion of communication is non-verbal. Try to ask questions to guide the trainee's thinking, but not

---

SUMMARY OF CLASSROOM OBSERVATION

Strengths of the lesson

Well done, Juliet, this was a lesson that I enjoyed. You have so many talents as a teacher! In particular the strengths of this lesson were:

- Your clear enjoyment of teaching and self-confidence
- Strong voice, good intonation – clear explanations
- Warmth towards the students – your smile, eye contact, facial expressions and body language all work to encourage and give students the confidence to take risks. V positive feedback & use of praise to boost self confidence
- Good questioning especially stretching EAL pupils to explain what they mean
- Excellent control – all the above contribute help in this area but you are also very confident yourself and this helps. You expect them to behave in a certain way, and they do. You handle the odd misbehaviour briskly with a change of tone ('don't call out, Michael') and good use of body language (turning away, not giving attention) but then you catch M being good – brilliant!
- Well resourced and organized
- Clear plan, with timings
- Good use made of the OHP
- Good use of support teacher at start of lesson and in reading out a paragraph to emphasize the tense difference
- Good choice of text that motivates and is part of their culture

---

Areas for further development

Try to increase the learning of more of the students more of the time, e.g.:
- Share learning objectives
- Big picture of the lesson
- More paired work: discussing whose autobiography they'd like to read, writing and maybe ordering chapter headings
- Having a plenary for them and you to evaluate learning and progress
- Make even more use of support teacher

Objectives

Plan lessons to increase the learning of more of the students more of the time

---

FIGURE 9.3 SUMMARY OF OBSERVATION (BUBB 2003c)

in a way that intimidates or implies criticism. Encourage reflection and listen well by asking open-ended questions, such as:

- How do you think the lesson went?
- What were you most pleased with? Why?
- What were you trying to achieve?
- What did the pupils learn?
- What did the lower attaining pupils learn?
- What did the higher attaining pupils learn?
- Why do you think the lesson went the way it did?
- Why did you choose that activity?
- Were there any surprises?
- When you did … the pupils reacted by … Why do you think that happened?
- Help me understand what you took into account when you were planning?

- If you taught that lesson again, what, if anything, would you do differently?
- What will you do in the follow up lesson?

Be aware of what you say, and how you say it. Focus on the teaching and learning that took place, using specific examples of what pupils said and did. Avoid talking about yourself or other teachers you have seen, unless this will be useful to the trainee. Comments such as 'I wouldn't have done that' or 'I would have ... ' are inappropriate and can irritate and alienate the beginning teacher. It is sometimes tempting to talk about your most awful lesson. This can be comforting, but can detract from the purpose of the discussion. Aim for the beginning teacher to do most of the talking and thinking.

Paraphrase and summarize what the person says. It involves reflecting back your interpretation of what you have heard, which can be very useful for the teacher. Use phrases such as 'So what you mean is ... , 'In other words ... ' Be positive and upbeat throughout. Be sensitive to how the trainee is taking your feedback, and ease off if necessary.

CONCLUSION

Involvement in initial teacher training can bring many benefits to the school and can help to develop that all-important learning and development culture, but it should not be entered into lightly. This chapter has highlighted some of the pros and cons of such involvement and tried to throw some light on what is for many a complex and confusing situation regarding the routes to achieving qualified teacher status. It has also concentrated on the training needs of tutors and school-based mentors, focusing particularly on observation and feedback skills. Many of these skills are, of course, generic and can be used for both performance management and for the induction of newly qualified teachers – the subject of our next chapter.

CHAPTER TEN

Newly Qualified Teachers and their Induction

- The induction entitlement
- How schools organize induction
- Induction programmes

Most people would agree with the aims of England's policy – that induction should ensure that the future professional and career development of individual teachers is built upon a firm foundation. It helps develop informed professionalism by providing newly qualified teachers with significant opportunities to:

- show their potential;
- make rapid advancement towards excellence in teaching;
- begin to make a real impact on their school's development (DfES, 2003e: 4).

The induction year is arguably the most formative period in a teacher's career. So we need to set high expectations and standards at this time of greatest receptiveness and willingness to learn and develop. However, support is crucial if new teachers are to develop the competencies, confidence and attitudes that will keep them happy in the job and serve as the basis for ongoing professional development.

THE INDUCTION ENTITLEMENT

All parts of Great Britain now have statutory induction arrangements. They are different, albeit similar, as illustrated in Table 10.1. Induction arrangements should be an incentive to a career in teaching. Newly qualified teachers should feel that they will be well supported especially when things do not go smoothly. Induction should be a carrot. Indeed, many aspects of England's induction policy are clearly attractive to new teachers. It is statutory so that they know that all schools by law have to comply with it, and they have the following entitlement:

1 A 10 per cent lighter teaching timetable than other teachers in the school.

2 A job description that does not make unreasonable demands, such as unduly difficult classes.

TABLE 10.1 THE FIRST YEAR – DIFFERENCES BETWEEN ENGLAND, SCOTLAND AND WALES

	England	Scotland	Wales
First year called	Induction	Probation	Induction
New teacher known as a	NQT	New teacher	NQT
Arrangements started	May 1999	Aug 2002	Sept 2003
Lead organization	General Teaching Council for England	General Teaching Council for Scotland	General Teaching Council for Wales
Timetable reduction	10%	30%	10%
Looked after by	Induction tutor	Supporter	Induction tutor
Time for their job	None	0.1	None
Judged against	Induction standards	The Standard for Full Registration	The End of Induction Standard
Assessment	3 times	2 times	3 times
How to get a job	New teacher finds it	New teacher placed in a school	New teacher finds it
Time limit between QTS and induction	None	Have to do probation straight away	None

3 Meetings with a school 'induction tutor', including half termly reviews of progress.

4 An individualized programme of support.

5 Objectives, informed by strengths and areas for development identified in the career entry profile, to help them meet the Induction Standards.

6 At least one observation of their teaching each half term with oral and written feedback.

7 Procedures to air grievances at school and local education authority level.

This entitlement should give NQTs protection against the worst of experiences that others have encountered during their first year.

However, England has built into its induction policy a rigorous assessment and monitoring system. This is seen by some NQTs as beneficial in that they like to be told that they are doing well and to know that if there are concerns they will be raised. For many, however, the assessment component of induction is a stick to threaten and potentially beat them with. Formal assessment reports are written at the end of each of the three terms, placing considerable demands on the headteacher and induction tutor as well as the teacher. Newly qualified teachers are judged on whether they meet the demanding standards for the end of the induction year. They have to demonstrate that they meet all the standards that they met during their initial training and the six additional Induction Standards (see Figure 10.1). These standards are demanding and the consequences of not meeting them severe. Unless they are successful on appeal, those failing to meet the standards will not be able to teach in a maintained school or non-maintained special school, despite still having qualified teacher status. These teachers would still keep QTS but are de-registered from the General Teaching Council. Thus, the only teaching they could do is in an independent school, a city technology college or as a private tutor. They cannot repeat induction or their initial training.

HOW SCHOOLS ORGANIZE INDUCTION

Professional support (see Figure 10.2) is key to the success of the induction year. Newly qualified teachers may need colleagues to take a range of roles.

Clearly, an induction tutor could not and should not take on all these roles. The whole staff is responsible for inducting a new teacher, and often people will take on certain roles naturally. Figure 10.3 shows how different schools have arranged induction support. Problems may arise when key roles are not taken by someone in the NQT's life. Equally problematic is when one person takes on too many roles or when people assume erroneously that someone else is taking a role.

Induction tutors have a crucial role. The DfES considers these to be their roles and responsibilities:

- Provide, or co-ordinate, guidance and effective support for the NQT's professional development.

- Have the necessary skills, expertise and knowledge to work effectively in this role. In particular, you should be able to make rigorous and fair judgements about the NQT's progress in relation to the requirements for satisfactory completion of the induction period.

- Play a key role in providing assessment throughout the NQT's induction programme. The support and assessment functions may be split between two or more teachers where this suits the structures and systems of the school. In such circumstances, responsibilities should be clearly specified at the beginning of induction and arrangements should be put in place to ensure that monitoring and assessments are based on, and informed by, the NQT's teaching and professional development.

- Undertake most of the observations of the NQT's teaching. Professional reviews of progress, based on discussions between the NQT and the induction tutor, should take place at intervals throughout their induction support programme.

- Keep a dated copy of all reports on observations, review meetings and objectives until the Appropriate Body has decided whether the NQT has completed their induction support programme satisfactorily and any appeal has been determined. A note should be kept of the other evidence used. The NQT should receive copies of all such written records and the Appropriate Body should have access to them (from DfES, 2003e: 24).

Thus induction tutors, like mentors of trainees, will have specific professional development needs. Local education authorities, HEIs and consultancies run varying degrees of training, and some of the longer and more in-depth courses are accredited. Many of the skills required of ITT mentors and induction tutors are the same – observation, feedback, coaching, report writing. However, the similarities can disguise the differences, and a lot is at stake for NQTs who do not meet the standards so it is important that induction tutors have the necessary skills, expertise and knowledge.

NQTs must continue to meet the requirements of the Standards for the Award of QTS, and build on these by showing that, in the following areas, they also:

Professional Values and Practice
a. Seek and use opportunities to work collaboratively with colleagues to raise standards by sharing effective practice in the school.

Knowledge and Understanding
b. Show a commitment to their professional development by identifying areas in which they need to improve their professional knowledge, understanding and practice in order to teach more effectively in their current post, and with support, taking steps to address these needs.

Teaching
c. Plan effectively to meet the needs of pupils in their classes with special educational needs, with or without statements, and in consultation with the SENCO contribute to the preparation, implementation, monitoring and review of Individual Education Plans or the equivalent.
d. Liaise effectively with parents or carers on pupils' progress and achievements.
e. Work effectively as part of a team and, as appropriate to the post in which they are completing induction, liaise with, deploy, and guide the work of other adults who support pupils' learning.
f. Secure a standard of behaviour that enables pupils to learn, and act to pre-empt and deal with inappropriate behaviour in the context of the behaviour policy of the school.

FIGURE 10.1 THE INDUCTION STANDARDS (DfES, 2003e: 43)

Planning partner	Helper	Expert practitioner
Colleague	Disciplinarian of pupils	Organizer
Friend	Adviser	Monitor of progress
Supporter	Critical friend	Trainer
Counsellor	Facilitator	Protector
Assessor	Motivator	Parent

FIGURE 10.2 ROLES TO SUPPORT NQTs (BUBB, 2000: 11)

More than anything, NQTs value someone who can give them time. This is a very precious resource. Induction tutors often have many other time-consuming roles and their time spent on induction is rarely funded. As ever, much has to be done on goodwill or it does not happen. Induction tutors should want to do the job and be suited to it, otherwise the NQT will suffer. Here are positive comments that a group of NQTs made about their induction tutors.

1 They were always available for advice.

2 They gave me a regular meeting time, even though they were busy.

3 They were genuinely interested in how I was doing.

4 They were honest and open, which encouraged trust.

5 They listened to me – and did not impose their own views.

6 They made practical suggestions.

Primary School 1 (mono-support)
Induction tutor: Member of the senior management team.

Primary School 2 (mono-support)
Induction tutor: Headteacher.

Primary School 3 (bi-support)
Induction tutor: Member of the senior management team.
Mentor: The parallel class teacher.

Primary School 4 (tri-support)
Induction co-ordinator: Member of the senior management team.
Induction tutor: Year group leader.
Buddy mentor: A recently qualified teacher.

Secondary School 1 (mono-support)
Induction tutor: Senior member of staff.

Secondary School 2 (bi-support)
Induction co-ordinator: Senior member of staff in charge of all NQTs in the
                                      school.
Induction tutor: The head of department.

Secondary School 3 (tri-support)
Induction co-ordinator: Senior member of staff in charge of all NQTs in the
                                      school.
Induction tutor: The head of department.
Buddy mentor: A recently qualified teacher.

Secondary School 4 (tri-support)
Induction tutor/co-ordinator: A senior teacher who organizes the induction
                                      programme, meetings, assessment reports, etc.
Academic mentor: The head of department who advises on all subject
                                      related matters.
Pastoral mentor: A head of year who gives guidance on behaviour
                                      management and pastoral issues.

Secondary School 5 (multi-support)
Staff Development Officer: In charge of co-ordinating the induction programme for
                                      all NQTs and organizes contracts, job descriptions, staff
                                      handbook and the pre-induction visits before the NQTs
                                      start work.
Subject mentor: Head of the department that the NQT works in:
                                      supervises planning and teaching and gives subject
                                      specific input.
Pastoral mentor: A head of year who gives guidance on behaviour
                                    management and pastoral issues.
Buddy mentor group: A group of recently qualified teachers who provide a
                                      shoulder to cry on.

FIGURE 10.3 ORGANIZATION OF INDUCTION PERSONNEL (BUBB et al., 2002: 29)

7   They shared their expertise, ideas and resources.

8   They were encouraging and optimistic – they made me feel good.

9   They stopped me working myself into the ground by setting realistic objectives.

10   They were not perfect themselves, which was reassuring!

11   They looked after me, keeping parents and the head off my back.

12   Their feedback after observations was useful. Good to get some praise and ideas for improvements.

13   They were well organized, and if they said they would do something
      they did it (Bubb, 2000: 14)

VARIABILITY OF INDUCTION EXPERIENCE

There is still variability of new teachers' experiences in spite of statutory regulations. One of the benefits of England's induction policy is that it should help standardize the provision that new teachers receive across and within schools. Though induction provision appears to have improved, there are still too many NQTs (20 per cent) who do not get their 10 per cent reduced timetable (Totterdell et al., 2002). This reduction is a crucial part of induction without which other elements, such as observing other colleagues, cannot be achieved. Schools' interpretation of what is a 'good enough' meeting of the induction standards varies and this is felt to be unfair by NQTs. It seems a flaw in the system that decisions are made so subjectively by induction tutors and headteachers with only limited input from LEA, university or Ofsted specialists in this field.

There needs to be a balance between support, monitoring and assessment as indicated in Figure 10.4. Although the induction circular makes clear that NQTs are responsible for raising concerns with their school and Appropriate Body, this is hard to do in practice. Complaining is always uncomfortable, and NQTs are in a particularly tricky situation, since the headteacher is responsible for recommending whether they pass or not. As one NQT wrote:

> It is very difficult to discuss problems. I want to pass my induction year and, if this means keeping my head down and mouth shut, that's what I'll do. The alternative is to highlight problems with my support and then have to face awkward times with my induction tutor or head, with the implications that might have on whether they pass or fail me. (Bubb, 2001: 19)

SCHOOL INDUCTION POLICY

If schools have an induction policy, everyone will know about procedures, rights and responsibilities. The most effective policies we found were those in which there had been input from the people they affect, and which were regularly updated in the light of experience.

School policies should be based on an understanding of good practice, to ensure that procedures can be followed quickly, consistently and effectively by reference to agreed practices and principles. A school induction policy should serve to ensure that a structured induction programme is followed; individuals involved in induction are aware of their role and responsibilities; individuals are aware of each other's roles and responsibilities, and NQTs are treated fairly and consistently. So a school policy on induction should cover three main areas:

- why the senior management team regards induction as beneficial for the school;
- the procedures staff should follow in order to support, monitor and assess NQTs;
- how NQTs can make best use of opportunities offered to them (Bleach, 2000: 100).

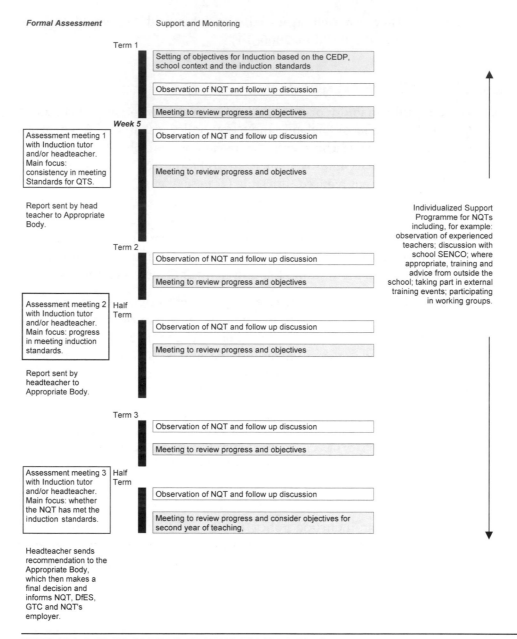

Formal Assessment

Support and Monitoring

Term 1

Setting of objectives for Induction based on the CEDP, school context and the induction standards

Observation of NQT and follow up discussion

Meeting to review progress and objectives

Week 5

Observation of NQT and follow up discussion

Assessment meeting 1 with Induction tutor and/or headteacher. Main focus: consistency in meeting Standards for QTS.

Meeting to review progress and objectives

Report sent by head teacher to Appropriate Body.

Term 2

Observation of NQT and follow up discussion

Meeting to review progress and objectives

Assessment meeting 2 with Induction tutor and/or headteacher. Main focus: progress in meeting induction standards.

Half Term

Observation of NQT and follow up discussion

Meeting to review progress and objectives

Report sent by headteacher to Appropriate Body.

Term 3

Observation of NQT and follow up discussion

Meeting to review progress and objectives

Assessment meeting 3 with Induction tutor and/or headteacher. Main focus: whether the NQT has met the induction standards.

Half Term

Observation of NQT and follow up discussion

Meeting to review progress and consider objectives for second year of teaching,

Headteacher sends recommendation to the Appropriate Body, which then makes a final decision and informs NQT, DfES, GTC and NQT's employer.

Individualized Support Programme for NQTs including, for example: observation of experienced teachers; discussion with school SENCO; where appropriate, training and advice from outside the school; taking part in external training events; participating in working groups.

FIGURE 10.4 OVERVIEW OF THE INDUCTION PROCESS (TTA 2002a: 6)

Procedures that staff should follow can be outlined in induction policies through describing:

- the roles and responsibilities of individuals involved including headteacher, induction tutor, induction manager if appropriate, other people involved in induction, the governing body and LEA staff;
- the induction programme which will be provided;
- guidance for assessment and monitoring of the NQT.

A procedure for review should also be included in the policy, to ensure that the school's intentions and procedures continue to be effective. Figure 10.5 is an example of an induction policy for the first term.

Your Induction Year: Who does what and when in the first term

The school will:

By the end of the first month:
- Negotiate an agreed Individual Action Plan with you, identifying objectives for professional development for the first term based on the Career Entry and Development Profile (TTA, 2003a).
- Ensure that the induction tutor observes you.
- Provide an appropriate weekly support programme for you.

During the term:
- ensure that the induction tutor maintains a written record of all support,
- monitoring and assessment evidence carried out in relation to your progress.
- ensure that half-termly review sessions take place between your induction tutor and you.

By the end of the term:
- ensure that the induction tutor carries out a formal assessment of your progress according to national guidelines and criteria.
- ensure that the induction tutor conducts the first formal assessment meeting with you, providing well-founded feedback on your progress.
- Return the appropriate Record of Assessment to the LEA Induction team.

You will:

By the end of the first month:
- Negotiate an agreed Individual Action Plan with the induction tutor.
- Attend the weekly NQT meeting (Tuesdays, 3.30 p.m.–4.30 p.m.).

During the remainder of the term:
- Develop your professional practice to meet the objectives agreed in your Individual Action Plan.
- Respond to feedback from lesson observations.
- Keep a written record of all support, monitoring and assessment carried out by the college.
- Meet each half term with your induction tutor to review progress.
- Attend the first LEA conference for NQTs.

FIGURE 10.5 INDUCTION POLICY FOR TERM ONE (BUBB et al., 2002: 25)

INDUCTION PROGRAMMES

The DfES guidance says that schools must, 'provide a programme of monitoring, guidance and support which is tailored to individual needs and will help the NQT meet the requirements for satisfactory completion of induction' (DfES, 2003e: 6). This is easier said than done. Schools need to be prepared to cater for the full range of people who go under the NQT umbrella. The ease with which teachers settle into their first job will depend on:

- how well they met the QTS standards during training;
- the type and calibre of their initial teacher training and school placements;
- their motivation;
- the new context of the school and class;
- how reflective they are in completing the Career Entry and Development Profile (TTA, 2003a);
- the quality of the school's induction programme.

For those who only just scraped through their teaching qualification, a deficit model of induction is just what they need – an opportunity to develop from a low base. However, schools may be grateful for the protection of the assessment system to weed out people whose flaws identified during training turn out to have a detrimental effect on pupils' learning when tested in the workplace. At the other extreme, there are NQTs who are highly effective early on in their first year. Induction should meet their needs too. The Fast Track programme (see Chapter 9), which those who meet the rigorous entry requirements can join either on starting a PGCE or in the first few years of teaching, does just that. It enables teachers to work in a school for two years with a particular remit in addition to class teaching. This should be a worthwhile task that moves the school on and which provides appropriate challenge to the teacher.

Schools need to treat NQTs in a professional manner and to provide a high-quality induction from which people will benefit not only in the first year of teaching, but which will form a foundation for future professional development. Everything known about effective professional development needs to be considered carefully when drawing up induction programmes, that should be individualized but which exploit opportunities for NQTs to work together (see Chapter 2). A clear picture of the NQT's strengths and development needs at the end of their initial training course is an essential foundation stone. This picture comes from the Career Entry and Development Profile and discussions with the NQT about their experiences, strengths and needs.

In relation to planning and reviewing the NQT support programme, induction tutors need:

- full access to, and knowledge of, the school's policies and procedure, and a clear picture of how induction fits into the wider context of teachers' professional development;

- to be familiar with the standards for the award of qualified teacher status;

- a thorough understanding of the Induction Standards and the requirements for satisfactory completion of induction;

- an ability to work with the NQT to set, use and review appropriate development objectives;

- a knowledge of the resources available to support NQTs both within and beyond the school (TTA, 2001b: 6).

A primary induction tutor, for instance, planned the programme from her analysis of NQTs' initial needs. She made sure she covered the important areas relating to the induction standards. Courses were identified and the NQTs met with all the curriculum co-ordinators, the SENCO and staff from outside services. The NQTs also undertook observations of experienced teachers modelling good practice, in their own school and then others. There were meetings on parents' evenings, classroom management and with the link inspector. Figures 10.6 and 10.7 give examples of an induction programme for a secondary school and an individual primary NQT programme.

A secondary induction tutor reported on working with one of her ex-NQTs for input into what makes a programme work from the NQTs' point of view. 'I want to find out for next term what they want from the course. They might have individual needs or they

Professional review meeting	
Date and time: *October 15 3.30 p.m.*	
Agenda *Progress*	
Things that are going well *Behaviour management and classroom organization improving*	
Things to improve *Marking* *Pace*	

Progress on current objectives
    1. *Parents – successfully completed a parents' evening; detailed interview with Mrs B. Still needs to be professionally assertive in informal contacts.*
    2. *Classroom organization – trays labelled and things looking tidier. Pupils and assistants know where things are. Still needs to consider rearrangement of some pupils.*	

Date of next meeting *10 December 3 p.m.*	

FIGURE 10.6 PROFESSIONAL REVIEW MEETING

Date	Topic
Sep 5	Welcome to the school
Sep 12	NQT information session and get together
Sep 19	Settling in – what you can expect
Sep 26	Pastoral care – working with parents – LEA
Oct 10	First half-term review
Oct 17	SEN and student support for learning and behaviour - LEA
Nov 7	A proactive approach to classroom management
Nov 14	Gifted and talented initiative
Dec 5	Raising the attainment of girls
Dec 12	End of term review
Jan 16	Assessment: serving learning
Jan 23	EAL/Partnership teaching – LEA
Feb 13	End of half-term review
Mar 6	Literacy and numeracy strategies – LEA
Mar 27	Accessing and using school data
Apr 2	End of term review
May 1	ICT across the curriculum – strategies – LEA
May 8	To be decided by NQTs
May 22	End of half-term review
Jun 12	To be decided by NQTs
Jul 3	Evaluation session and congratulations social
Jul 10	End of year review: what's next?

FIGURE 10.7 AN EXAMPLE OF A SECONDARY SCHOOL GROUP INDUCTION PROGRAMME (BUBB et al., 2002: 72)

might collectively choose something' (Bubb et al., 2002: 74). She offers them a menu of possible activities such as classroom management, working with the industry links co-ordinator, the SENCO, the primary–secondary liaison officer.

PRE-EMPLOYMENT INDUCTION

An induction visit before starting work, is very valuable. Some schools organize an unpaid or paid induction day or week in July for all new teachers, including those who are newly qualified. (Some also get paid over the summer holidays!) One school that paid for new staff to be put up in a local hotel felt that the expense was justified in terms of the valuable bonding that took place. It also helped to prepare new staff adequately for the start of the new year. One NQT said: 'It was good to met people properly, spend some time with the head of department, get schemes of work' (Bubb et al., 2002: 70). Another NQT said: 'We got all the information and had a couple of months to go away and mull it over and work out what it all meant' (Bubb et al., 2002: 70).

REGULAR MEETINGS WITH INDIVIDUAL NQTs

The majority of induction tutors in our national research project for the DfES (Totterdell et al., 2002) said that they held meetings lasting 30 minutes or more with an NQT at least fortnightly – 27 per cent held them weekly, 26 per cent fortnightly and 37 per cent half termly. However, we found that NQTs thought that meetings were taking place less regularly than did the induction tutors. We believe there is a lesson to be learnt here about clear communication over the programme of activities, and sticking to an agreed schedule. Publishing the schedule in advance is good practice.

Most NQTs had scheduled weekly or fortnightly meetings to discuss issues and progress. The most common topics of these meetings were:

- feedback after lesson observation;
- behaviour management;
- the curriculum;
- schemes of work and lesson planning;
- school development;
- parents' evenings.

It is useful to record key points from meetings with NQTs, particularly those for the half-termly reviews. They provide a useful record and focus discussion and reflection – and provide evidence that procedures had been fully followed. Figure 10.8 is an example of notes from a half termly review meeting.

GROUP MEETINGS FOR ALL THE NQTs

Where there are several NQTs in a school, it is useful to hold group meetings on topics of interest to all. Figure 10.6 shows one secondary school's general programme, which co-ordinated with the LEA's induction programme. An induction manager explains:

> One night a week for the first term we look at issues that are pertinent to school, then in the second and the third term we just do it a bit more ad hoc and look at various issues as they come up. For example, this week it's their very first parents' evening. But they meet as a group because then they can also say, 'I had a terrible time this week and I can help them or they can help each other, which is very important'. (Bubb et al., 2002: 71)

Newly qualified teachers need support of a very practical nature to deal with issues such as behaviour management. It seems to be the most common reason why teachers leave the profession in their first year and so must be addressed early on in any induction programme.

Objectives: To write clear and informative reports for parents
To conduct parents' evening confidently
To plan an outing

Week beginning... Observation of NQT	NQT release time for induction	Induction tutor meetings	Staff meetings and inset
5 June	Observe Y4 Written reflection	Plan the induction programme	Report writing formats, tips and agreed procedures
12 June Observation by induction tutor	Observe Y1 & Y2 in Beacon school, focusing on good practice Written reflection	Feedback from observation Reading reports	Moderation of science investigations for Years 1–6.
19 June	LEA induction course: professional development – being a curriculum co-ordinator		School trips and outings – health and safety procedures incl risk analysis
26 June Observation by headteacher	Preliminary visit to farm to prepare for class trip – risk assessment	Feedback from observation	Mathematics – the mental and oral starter
3 July	Prepare for class trip, using school policies	Discuss planning for the outing	Mathematics – purposeful plenary ideas
10 July Final assessment meeting	Gathering evidence for the final assessment meeting	Final assessment meeting	Sports Day arrangements
17 July	Looking at new class and their records		Planning for next year

FIGURE 10.8 A PRIMARY NQT's INDIVIDUAL INDUCTION PROGRAMME – 2ND HALF OF SUMMER TERM (BUDD et al., 2002: 73)

INFORMAL MEETINGS

Informal meetings are also important. Over 80 per cent of induction tutors said they met informally and often daily with their NQTs, initiated by either party and covering a wide range of immediate concerns.

WHOLE-SCHOOL INSET

Staff meetings and INSET days make a valuable contribution to NQTs' development. Figure 10.8 shows how this can be recorded alongside other more individual activities.

INDUCTION PROVISION FROM OUTSIDE THE SCHOOL

Although the school is a valuable source of specific support for NQTs, outside help brings expertise and fresh perspectives. Local education authorities, universities and private consultancy firms run NQT courses and conferences. Newly qualified teachers value the opportunity to meet with other NQTs outside their school. Peer group support plays a key role in validating NQTs' experiences and helps them to succeed in the induction year: 'It's lovely when you speak to other reception teachers and they say exactly the same things and you think, that's super, because I know it's not just my children, it's not just me' (Bubb et al., 2002: 71). Some schools involve LEA induction staff or outside consultants in reviewing objectives, observing NQTs and conducting formal assessment.

CONCLUSION

Newly qualified teachers are a precious resource who have invested much time and effort into getting where they are – and the government has invested heavily in their training. They need to be treated well. They are agents of change and the profession's new generation – millions of children's teachers and the school leaders of the future. Their early experiences and the foundation that is laid in the all-important first year have important consequences, not only for the rest of the NQTs' career in teaching but also for staff retention, motivation and morale. We ignore them at our peril!

CHAPTER ELEVEN

Supply and Overseas-Trained Teachers

- Why temporary teachers need CPD
- Analysing their needs
- Meeting their needs
- Professional development – getting QTS

This chapter looks at CPD and supply/temporary teachers, and issues around their induction, as well as the intricacies of helping those who trained overseas gain qualified teacher status in England and Wales. It starts by stating why supply teachers need CPD before presenting a case for meeting their training needs. It is argued that schools should be prepared to devote some of their limited CPD funds to temporary and overseas-trained teachers (OTTs), especially as national statistics show that schools, particularly those in the inner-city, are making increasing use of their services and, for all schools, the cost of employing temporary teachers is not insignificant.

WHY TEMPORARY TEACHERS NEED CPD

The main reasons why temporary or supply teachers need CPD are because:

- they form a 'vital and substantial component of the teaching workforce' (Hallgarten, 2002);
- their teaching is not always effective;
- they cost schools a lot;
- they get little professional development at the moment;
- many professional development opportunities involve supply teachers taking regular teachers' classes, so it is important that pupils are taught well;
- many people who come on supply stay with the school;
- CPD is a good way to retain supply teachers.

The cost of employing temporary teachers is a significant element in the budget of schools. It has been estimated by the DfES's own Value for Money Unit that schools spend on average £43.00 per pupil from their budget on supply teachers (£50.78 for primary schools and £32.80 for secondary schools) (DfES, 2002h). One recruitment analyst estimates that schools are now spending more than £600 million annually on supply teachers, including both agency and non-agency teachers. If this estimate is accurate, it would amount to 3.4 per cent of the entire expenditure of LEA-maintained schools in England, 5.3 per cent of the entire expenditure on teachers and twice the amount spent by schools on ICT for teaching and learning in 2000 (Hallgarten, 2002). Data from almost 3,000 schools inspected in 2000–01 show that on average primary schools had spent a yearly 3.4 per cent of their budgets, while the average in inner London was 4.6 per cent (Ofsted, 2003d). On average, secondary schools spend 2.2 per cent of their budgets with the average of inner London schools again higher at 4.3 per cent. London schools have a greater reliance on supply teachers than England as a whole – 5.6 per cent of London's teaching workforce is made up of supply, while in England the figure is 4.6 per cent (DfES, 2002h). Naturally, these difficulties are more pronounced in some schools than others and for the worst-hit schools development has been severely inhibited by the time-consuming tasks of recruiting and inducting new teachers.

The Ofsted report, *Schools' Use of Temporary Teachers*, found that temporary teachers required to teach unfamiliar classes after only very limited briefing by the school are faced with a very challenging task. As a result, they teach a higher proportion of unsatisfactory or poor lessons than permanent teachers. Inspectors found that the quality of some pupils' work had declined in approximately half of the secondary schools surveyed, as a result of being taught by temporary teachers for a significant period of time. Impact on behaviour was also significant. In just over half the secondary schools, and about one-quarter of the primary schools, pupils' attitudes to their work and their behaviour were of a lower standard to those in lessons taught by permanent teachers (Ofsted, 2003d).

Unfamiliarity with schools and pupils and having to teach age groups and subjects for which they have not been trained are common problems for temporary teachers. A lack of understanding of the National Curriculum, the National Literacy and Numeracy Strategies or examination syllabuses, along with a lack of continuity and poor briefing on teaching programmes impact on standards.

Joe Hallgarten of IPPR believes that improvements in the quality, professionalism and retention of the permanent teaching profession need to be extended to supply teachers so that they are not seen as 'expensive babysitters'. They would also benefit from the extension of CPD opportunities. 'The increase in the use of supply teachers seems here to stay and progressive policies, based on thorough research, are necessary to take account of that change'. Professional development would help the status of supply teaching. Hallgarten suggests that this should be two-way, with supply teachers giving advice on behaviour management.

Schools appreciate the need for training supply teachers but no schools felt that they could allocate their own training budget towards supply teachers. However, long-term supply teachers were often treated as permanent staff for training purposes (DfES, 2002h). Supply teachers may end up staying longer than some of the 'permanent' staff they have worked alongside. It is not unusual for someone recruited to fill a week's absence to remain at the school for two years.

ANALYSING NEEDS

Current practices for identifying and meeting CPD needs are not constructed in a way that takes account of supply teachers. For example, the national arrangements for performance management do not have to include supply teachers. This leaves a significant proportion of the teaching workforce untouched.

Definitions of supply teachers are confused: occasional, temporary, floating, emergency cover and others terms are used interchangeably. A whole range of different people with very different professional development needs are employed as supply teachers:

- newly qualified teachers who are trying to find a full-time job, or having a taste of several schools before committing themselves;
- people with young families who are returning to teaching after a career break. They may be 'testing the water' before finding a full-time job or may just wish to have flexible part-time work;
- teachers (often very experienced and knowledgeable) who have taken early retirement;
- overseas-trained teachers – from a range of countries but mainly South Africa, Australia, New Zealand, Canada and the West Indies.

Teachers who are new to the country can provide a particular challenge to CPD co-ordinators. Margaret Craig, headteacher of an inner London secondary school, considers: 'No teacher who has joined the school from overseas has been able to achieve their own potential performance level without a markedly greater degree of support than would be given to a British trained newly qualified teacher' (Craig, 2002: 29).

The CPD needs of supply teachers and the amount of additional support required is difficult to predict. Certainly overseas-trained teachers' needs can be hard to gauge. Those from English-speaking countries with similar educational systems will normally need less CPD than those from other contexts. Most schools consider, however, that a disproportionate allocation of CPD and other resources needs to be put into programmes for new staff, and that this is only worthwhile if the people stay. A key to the success for all appears to relate to the adaptability of the individual.

Common needs include:

- up-to-date information about the education system as a whole;
- teachers' legal liabilities and responsibilities;
- understanding provision for pupils with special needs;
- subject knowledge – for instance the primary history curriculum has proved difficult for OTTs who do not know about life in Victorian England;
- curriculum – schemes of work need to be very detailed and easy to understand;
- pedagogical philosophy – it is easy to underestimate the importance of this;

- planning – many OTTs are not accustomed to planning in the detail required in schools, and so expectations have to be clear and monitored;

- health and safety – conforming to recognized good practice;

- teaching strategies – many of the strategies that are taken for granted in England nowadays may not be in the repertoire of supply teachers. For instance, Margaret Craig noted a tendency for OTTs to tell students answers rather than draw out knowledge from them;

- behaviour management – some supply teachers are very skilled but others have a limited range of strategies for dealing with difficult behaviour. Cultural differences need to be understood. Some pupils are 'in your face' and OTTs may interpret their forthrightness as lack of respect. Pupils become bewildered by inconsistency of expectation across classrooms;

- differentiation – meeting the needs of all, including the highest and lowest attaining pupils;

- assessment procedures – it is often only when assessments are analysed that misunderstandings and gaps in subject knowledge become apparent;

- communication problems – these include not understanding pupils' vernacular language (for example, 'wicked', 'hot'), pupils not fully understanding OTTs' accents and style of speech, and the grammatical and spelling differences of people from different countries. This is true even of English-speaking countries.

This may seem like an intimidating list but there is 'great benefit for students of attracting and retaining a culturally diverse staff, many of whom provide role models of success over difficulty' (Craig, 2002: 30).

MEETING NEEDS

KNOWLEDGE OF THE EDUCATION SYSTEM

All supply teachers but especially newly arrived overseas teachers need quick and easy access to information about the English education system and the 'big picture' of the curriculum, such as how the strategies map onto the National Curriculum. People who have not had an introduction to the big picture of the education system find that they have gaps and misunderstandings in knowledge that are hard to address once embedded. Explanations of the many abbreviations and acronyms used in education are very useful – and not just for OTTs! This need is perhaps best met through courses organized at a regional level, such as the Institute of Education in London's courses for overseas-trained teachers (see example below), leaving people at school to explain the specific scheme of work to be taught.

Knowledge and Understanding of the Curriculum in English schools

Intended outcome: by the end of the session participants will know more about how the whole education system is organized in England.
Programme:
- How education is organized for 3–18-year-olds;
- The National Curriculum – values, aims and purposes;
- The SEN Code of Practice;
- SATs – the end of key stage tests;
- The strategies for literacy, numeracy and Key Stage 3;
- Understand the many acronyms and abbreviations used in education.

Such courses give participants an opportunity to see all the curriculum documents in one place and to make links between them. Booklets, such as the DfES parents' guides to the school system (DfES, 2002i), give information in an easy to access format too.

Certain concepts that are taken for granted within our education system may be problematic for those brought up in cultures with different sets of values. For instance, some OTTs find the notion of the inclusion of pupils with special needs difficult. 'Why aren't they kept down a year?' they ask. Socialization into a country's education culture can be difficult. Some schools have an induction for all new staff before they start teaching. Margaret Craig aims for her OTTs to join the school in July and undertake a three-week observation and teaching practice in the school

The DfES has published five books of free self-study materials for use in the professional development of supply teachers (DfES, 2002j). There is a dedicated part of the Teachernet website for supply teachers (http://www.teachernet.gov.uk/supplyteachers). This includes the materials in full, plus an online library of useful websites to help them keep up to date with current best practice in the classroom and with educational initiatives that affect their teaching. The five books are very useful and cover the following:

1 Getting Started

Teacher learning and development

Meeting the needs of all pupils

Professional responsibilities and legal liabilities

Educational initiatives and issues

2 Core Subjects in Primary Schools

The National Curriculum

Assessment, recording and reporting

Other adults in the classroom

English, mathematics and science

3 Core Subjects in Secondary Schools

The Key Stage 3 national strategy

The National Curriculum

English, mathematics and science

4 Classroom and Behaviour Management

Effective teachers and learners

Planning and managing for effective work in the classroom

Behaviour management

5 Filling the Gaps

The curriculum 3 to 19

Personal, social and health education and citizenship

Information and communications technology

▓ TRAINING BY SUPPLY AGENCIES

The government, the GTC and Ofsted have all called for further professional development for supply teachers, while the unions have produced a charter calling for supply teacher parity with permanent staff members. One supply agency, Hays Education Personnel, provides free professional training for supply teachers on Saturdays.

They also offer an Advanced Professional Certificate in Effective Supply Teaching. The Edexcel accredited course will offer supply teachers the chance to achieve a Business and Technology Education Council (BTEC) Professional Development qualification. As the qualification is funded by the Learning and Skills Council (LSC) and Hays Education Personnel, supply teachers can embark on a CPD programme without having the financial burden normally associated with it. The certificate not only enables teachers to enhance their classroom practice and education knowledge, but also allows them to produce clear evidence of continuous professional development. This portfolio can be used to support their future career, in interviews for permanent posts or as evidence for Performance Management and Threshold Assessment. The certificate takes two years to complete during which teachers will need to attend ten one-day courses, five each year.

▓ INDUCTION INTO THE SCHOOL

In 2003, Her Majesty's Chief Inspector (HMCI), said:

> There is a need for careful induction of temporary teachers into schools. Supplying necessary information about pupils' abilities and curriculum targets will enable the temporary teacher to focus on providing an adequate challenge to learners. It is also essential that schools provide temporary teachers with clear and simple information that defines teaching expectations … Schools should provide the guidance and support of a senior mentor especially with regard to managing classes and maintaining discipline. (Ofsted, 2003c)

Furze Platt Senior School in Maidenhead does just this. A senior teacher is responsible for supply teachers. She gives them a folder containing key information in an accessible, concise way. Figure 11.1 shows the Contents page. The DfES suggests that schools make use of a format such as that in Figures 11.2 and 11.3 so that supply teachers are clear as to what has to be done.

As we explained in Chapter 6, monitoring and evaluation are key aspects of any training and development process. Thus, it is useful for schools to get feedback on supply teachers' experiences so that systems can be refined. Figure 11.4 is an evaluation sheet used at Furze Platt Senior School.

Contents

Welcome
Management Structure
Internal telephone extensions
 1. Cover requirements (example sheet) – loose sheets will be provided daily
 2. Pupil school day
 3. Useful information in brief
 4. Furze Platt Senior School aims
 5. Some particular expectations
 6. Registers of attendance
 8. Pupil code of conduct
 9. School rules
 10. School uniform and dress codes
 11. First aid information
 15. Protection of children from child abuse
 16. Reward, punishment and discipline
 17. Pupil record books/common marking scheme
 18. Assemblies and collective worship
 21. Referrals of difficulties – NB Heads of department should always be contacted
     in the first instance. Please report any problems to Mrs W at the end of the day
 22. Pupil incident report forms and detention forms
 25. Health and safety in school
 26. Fire extinguisher information
 27. Fire notices and procedures
 28. Fire assembly points
 29. Map of the school
 30. Sample form for LEA supply teachers
 31. Sample evaluation sheets (a loose sheet will be provided for you to complete).

FIGURE 11.1 FURZE PLATT'S FOLDER FOR SUPPLY TEACHERS

• School begins at 8.50. It would be helpful if you could arrive at school by 8.20.
• You will be taking .... Class
• This is the class normally taken by
....
• It is a mixed ability class of year................... and contains ....
children.
• I have attached a class list (with photos where possible).
• You will have...............................(teaching assistant) working in the class between
9 a.m. and lunchtime. She will make sure you can find everything you need.
• .... , the special needs support assistant will inform you about
the requirements of any students with special educational needs.
• Individual Pupil Information (i.e. for special needs, health problems or behavioural
problems):
Name of
pupil:..

Nature of
problem:...

• Line management: During the day
....
Key stage Co-ordinator, will give you any help and support you need.
...., has the parallel class, situated next door to your own and
will be able to help with curriculum issues if...(Key Stage
Co-ordinator) is unavailable.
• A lesson plan is attached/will be available on your arrival in school (delete as
necessary).
• A map of the location of the school can be provided on request.
• Additional events occurring that day are:
....

FIGURE 11.2 INSTRUCTION PROFORMA FOR PRIMARY SCHOOLS TO GIVE SUPPLY TEACHERS

School Name:
....
....
School Phone Number: ....
Contact:
....
....
Date(s) of Cover: ....
School begins at 8.50. It would be helpful if you could arrive by 8.20.
Details of class (es) to be covered.
Class: .... Period: .... Subject
....
Class: .... Period: .... Subject
....
Class: .... Period: .... Subject
....
Class: .... Period: .... Subject
....
Class: .... Period: .... Subject
....
Class: .... Period: .... Subject
....
• Line management will be provided by:
....
• Lesson plans will be in the classroom/provided by the Head of Department
(delete as necessary).
• A map of the location of the school can be provided on request.
• Individual Pupil Information (i.e. for special needs, health problems or
behavioural problems):
Name of
pupil:...
....
Nature of problem:
....
• Additional events occurring that day are:
....
....
....
....

FIGURE 11.3 INSTRUCTION PROFORMA FOR SECONDARY SCHOOLS TO GIVE SUPPLY TEACHERS

PROFESSIONAL DEVELOPMENT – GETTING QTS

One of the best forms of professional development for overseas-trained teachers is to get qualified teacher status. Overseas-trained teachers do not need to be qualified here in order to work – they can teach for four years without QTS and many are understandably resentful when they realize that the qualification from their own country does not fully qualify them to teach in England. However, people become more effective teachers in English schools through gaining QTS (Bubb, 2003d), and it gives them a focus for their professional development – and another qualification for their CV. They can also be assessed for exemption from induction at the same time as for QTS, if they have been teaching for more than two years in this country or elsewhere.

Unless people are qualified to teach in a country that is part of the European Economic Area, they will need to get QTS here in order to be classed as fully qualified – and to be paid accordingly. Headteachers usually pay them on the unqualified teacher pay scale. Those lucky enough to be on the qualified teacher pay scale (often working in schools

Your name   *A.N. Other*   Your specialist area/s *Maths/ICT*

Dates of supply work

Teaching agency name   *SSA*

Please indicate in the boxes below the number of times you have been on supply with us

1ˢᵗ visit ☐ 2–5 2–5 ☒ 5–8 6–9 ☐ More 10+ ☐

1   How would you rate your welcome at school?   *Good* Satisfactory   Poor
    Comments?

2   How useful did you find the information pack for   *Good* Satisfactory   Poor
    supply teachers?
    Comments?

3   Did you have any difficulty finding the work for the classes you had to cover?
    Yes   *No*
    Comments?
    One lesson unclear. Sought help from another class teacher

4   Was the work left for your classes you had to cover   Good *Satisfactory*   Poor
    Comments? (suitability of work, adequate for the time etc.)
    RE – Good
    Science – easily finished by some pupils
    French –Some pupils had difficulties
    Science – Students needed help with Question 1 of test

5   Were registers made available for your cover lessons?   *Yes*   No

6   Do you have any general comments, observations or suggestions you would
    like to make?
    The Pupils: (punctuality, discipline, settling down, remaining on-task and so on)
    Some students arrived very late to P5 Science

    The Staff: (support within the department, friendliness at break/lunchtimes etc.)
    HOF – French called in to check everything OK
    HOF – Science quick to respond to unruly student request for help

    The arrangements/information:

    The overall ethos of the school:
    Good

Please write the subject area/s you were asked to cover during your day.
RE, Science, French, Maths, Science

Would you be happy to work here again?   *Yes*   No   (if no, would you please
indicate why)

Thank you for your work today. I hope you enjoyed your day and that I may call upon your services again.

FIGURE 11.4 EVALUATION BY SUPPLY TEACHERS OF THEIR EXPERIENCE AT FURZE PLATT SENIOR SCHOOL

which do not fully understand the regulations) find that they cannot apply to cross the threshold without QTS.

However, there is much more to getting QTS than being a good teacher. The initial step is to contact the OTT Advice Line (01245 454321) who will send a pack of useful materials and the application form. *How to Qualify as a Teacher in England* (TTA, 2003b) contains all the necessary information, but needs careful reading. The steps are summarized here:

1 Check their command of spoken and written English, and their qualifications and experience.

2 Carry out police and medical checks.

3 Request OTT pack from OTT Advice Line.

4 Find out whether the OTT wants to get QTS – when they have looked at the information in the pack so that they understand what is involved.

5 Make contact with someone listed in the OTT pack that can act as a recommending body (RB).

6 Check eligibility – degree, English and mathematics GCSE, standard English.

7 Ask the OTT Advice Line for an Advisory Visit voucher.

8 Arrange the advisory visit with someone from a RB, and prepare for it by reading TTA documentation.

9 Complete the pages on the application form that refer to the school and to the OTT's qualifications and experience and send to the RB.

10 Collect original certificates for RB to see.

11 During the advisory visit the RB will probably want to observe the OTT and discuss their work in relation to the standards. It is useful for the school to have an informed view.

12 The RB will draw up a training plan so that the OTT is helped to meet the standards. The application form needs the headteacher's and chair of governors' signatures.

13 The application form is submitted to the TTA – check all parts are complete as over half are queried.

14 The TTA sends a letter saying that the OTT is registered for QTS.

15 OTT applies for, takes and passes the literacy, numeracy and ICT skills tests, having practised online.

16 Assessment – over one and a half days for QTS only and two days for QTS plus exemption from induction.

17 Assessor recommends the OTT for QTS.

18 QTS is awarded by the DfES and then they can register with the General Teaching Council (Bubb, 2003d).

■ ENTRY REQUIREMENTS

The first thing to check is qualifications. The TTA insists that all people applying for QTS need to provide their *original* – not photocopied – proof of qualifications. It would make sense for schools to insist on seeing original certificates and to check their equivalence with the National Academic Recognition Information Centre (NARIC) before contracts are signed. Many schools find out too late that employees they assumed were well qualified do not, in fact, even meet the QTS entry requirements. Degrees from other countries are not always equivalent. Beware, for instance, the New Zealand diploma in education – only the higher diploma is equivalent to a UK degree.

To be eligible to apply for QTS, OTTs need to meet the same criteria (TTA, 2002a) as any homegrown prospective teacher:

- A qualification equivalent to a UK degree. NARIC (01242 260 010) can provide information on the comparability of qualifications to UK qualifications.

- Secondary OTTs need to be at degree standard in the subject they are being awarded QTS in by the time they are assessed – not when they apply. However, if their degree bears little relationship to the subject they are teaching they will need to study to gain additional knowledge.

- The equivalent to a GCSE pass at grade C or above in English and mathematics and, if they were born after 1 September 1979 and wish to teach the primary age range, science. If they do not have suitable qualifications they will need to take the GCSE or an equivalence test at an ITT provider.

- To communicate clearly in spoken and written standard English. You can get a feel for this by asking for them to handwrite you a letter of application and talking to them over the phone. Look out for grammatical errors, especially tenses and plurals.

Many fall at this first hurdle, as you can imagine, but if you know these requirements problems can be avoided. They also need experience of teaching in at least two schools and at two consecutive key stages.

■ APPLICATION FORM

The application form is an off-putting 26 pages long. Before filling it in, get some expert advice. The TTA give schools vouchers for advisory visits to explain the procedures and advise on options. The OTT Advice Line organizes these on request from a school. The person carrying out the advisory visit will explain to the headteacher or their representative and the OTT the:

- standards for qualified teacher status;

- induction standards and pros and cons of applying for exemption from induction if the teacher has two years' experience;

- assessment process;

- skills tests in literacy, numeracy and ICT that have to be taken online at designated centres.

You may want someone from a teacher training institution to act as the 'recommending body', who knows the QTS and induction regulations well and who can audit the OTT against the standards and suggest ways to address gaps in their knowledge, experience and skills. They take responsibility for ensuring that the application is completed correctly – the TTA has to query about half of the forms at the moment. Alternatively schools can be the RB, if there are members of staff who are very familiar with the QTS and induction standards and regulations – and who have time to audit, train and mentor the OTT.

Overseas-trained teachers can opt for assessment only, without any training, but it would be a rare teacher that did not need to do anything extra to prepare for the assessment and skills tests. The £750 from the TTA for training does not go very far. Schools will need to finance any more from their own resources.

■ ASSESSMENT

The assessment is in two parts. Like anyone training to be a teacher nowadays, OTTs must pass the infamous online skills tests in numeracy, literacy and ICT before they can be awarded QTS. To have other qualifications in these subjects is not enough. The TTA website (www.canteach.gov.uk) has downloadable practice tests, links to the registration and test booking pages, and email advice lines to help with specific areas of knowledge. Once applications have been approved, OTTs are sent a registration number and can apply to take the tests at one of the designated centres. Those whose mother tongue is not English can apply for a 25 per cent extension to the time limit.

The main assessment takes place in school and is carried out by a TTA external assessor or someone from the RB if it is accredited for a day and a half (or two days for induction and QTS). During this time OTTs have to *demonstrate* that they meet the standards. Being a good teacher is not enough. The assessor will need evidence of the knowledge and teaching experience in two consecutive key stages. There are three sorts of evidence:

- documentation – CV, planning, assessment, reports, notes from observations carried out by others, pupils' work from two key stages, and so on;

- observation of the OTT teaching – a minimum of two hours for QTS only and three hours for QTS plus exemption from induction;

- discussion with the OTT and others who know his or her work.

CONCLUSION
■

Schools get frustrated when supply teachers in whom they have invested a great deal of professional development time and money, leave. John Sanderson's school, for instance, put a lot of effort into getting a South African teacher qualified teacher status: 'he was successful and then moved on so the school had no benefit and there was no reward for the school's efforts' (Sanderson, 2002). This issue is an important one for government to address.

CHAPTER TWELVE

Early Professional Development

- Why is it important?
- The EPD pilots
- EPD activities
- Threshold assessment
- Advanced skills teachers

This chapter focuses attention on teachers in their first five years of teaching, traditionally a time when many feel a little lost and neglected after the intensity of the training and induction years. Early professional development (EPD) is a term which because of the EPD pilots, which had earmarked government funding, has become associated with the second and third years of a teacher's career. However, our use of 'early' professional development is broader, covering the first four years after induction. After considering why EPD is important we will look at the lessons learned from the EPD pilots. Then we will consider the CPD implications of people wishing to cross the threshold and those who decide to apply to be advanced skills teachers.

WHY IS IT IMPORTANT?

So why do teachers in their first five years need help with their professional development? Ofsted's reports (2003c) say that because the quality of training has improved schools now have the best NQTs ever. Excellent! However, not all who train end up working as teachers. Only 83 per cent of those who get QTS through primary PGCEs in London are teaching in the year after their course (TTA, 2002b) – and this percentage includes those working abroad, in the independent sector and on supply. So it looks as if for every 100 people who start a primary PGCE in London only 85 qualify and 71 work as teachers. Similarly, for every 100 people who start a PGCE in secondary mathematics only 78 qualify and 69 end up teaching when they finish (Bubb, 2003c).

But the picture gets worse. Smithers and Robinson's research (2003) into why teachers leave the profession found that it is the very newest teachers who are leaving. Only about 70 per cent of teachers stay in the profession for more than five years. So of the 100 people who start a PGCE primary course, only 49 are teaching after five years. What a waste!

Teachers have often felt a little at sea in the years immediately after induction. They get lots of attention (or should do) when training and during induction, and then it suddenly stops. They are meant to be experienced and know what they are doing, and no longer have allowances made for them. But in reality learning to teach confidently takes years so having early professional development can be a bit like being able to drive with P plates on – it is a safety net. Teachers also feel that they are in CPD limbo: neither entitled to NQT courses nor ready for leadership and management type development. They are no longer observed regularly and do not get stimulated. As a result some teachers go off the boil. A typical pattern emerges: if they do not get a tonic they do not teach so well, then they do not enjoy the job so much, so they leave.

Although many people have long seen the need for giving teachers special support after induction, it is fairly new as a formal notion. It was first mentioned in England's *Learning and Teaching: A Strategy for Professional Development* (DfEE, 2001a). However, Northern Ireland has recognized it for some time and in Wales induction is seen as the first year of a three-year long EPD, but in Scotland there is no named period of EPD as such.

The Ofsted report (2003a) on teachers' early professional development found little differentiation in the CPD offered to second- and third-year teachers in at least half of the schools inspected, so that their particular needs remained unrecognized and, consequently, were not addressed. In the schools where EPD was effective, Ofsted found a raft of benefits including stronger teaching, a clear contribution of second- and third-year teachers to the work of their colleagues, and more commitment to a career in teaching.

THE EPD PILOTS

In response to the sorts of concerns above, the DfES and GTC (England) set up a pilot project of early professional development for teachers in their second and third years of teaching. The pilot programmes ran from 2001 to 2004 in 12 LEAs at a cost of £25 million. There was to be a national roll-out of funds for EPD but that has been cancelled or postponed due to the funding crisis of 2003.

The DfES's (2002e) aims for teachers involved in EPD were:

- to have made significant progress towards the threshold standards – increasing their pedagogical skills and their ability to apply them effectively to a wide range of children and a wider range of situations;

- to have strengthened their ability to learn from the knowledge base in schools, professional networks, research and enquiry;

- to have increased the ability to contribute, as professionals, to immediate colleagues, their school and the wider education community;

- to be more strongly committed to teaching as a career.

The NFER evaluation considered the pilot successful and analysed key factors. Classroom observations and being mentored by an experienced colleague were rated highly by second-year teachers. Teachers were also more positive if they had chosen their mentor and their own training programme. The more involvement teachers had in selecting their EPD programme, the more likely they were to feel their professional development needs had been met, and record higher ratings for the effects of EPD on their teaching practice and professional attitudes.

In Wakefield, one of the pilot LEAs, teachers appreciated having a bursary to support professional development. They emphasized the importance of having quality time with a mentor to discuss professional and career development because this 'focuses on asking the right questions about what I need to do' (Thompson, 2002: 24). They liked the opportunity to network with teachers from other schools but overall the real benefit was that professional development was a clear priority.

However Minnis (2003) in her small-scale research into EPD in one secondary school in another pilot LEA, considered that only two teachers out of the group of ten made 'significant' progress towards threshold standards because their EPD was linked to performance management targets. Because the mentoring system broke down, the remaining eight teachers did activities that bore little relationship to what they needed to get better at in the classroom. Some spent their funds on computers, printers and software which may have made their job easier but did not really make them better teachers. Others made visits or went on courses to develop extracurricular activities such as school trips and clubs. This made them happier but did not make them any better at or more committed to teaching.

EPD ACTIVITIES

Teachers have done a wide range of things with their EPD funds. Teachers were encouraged to 'be creative' with their EPD funding, and some have considered career moves to alternative forms of educational provision as a result. One such example is a drama teacher who attended a course on drama and movement therapy with her third-year money, and is now considering specializing in drama therapy in education, a long-term goal:

> The EPD fund gave me an opportunity to get this plan into action and let me know that I hadn't been forgotten. My needs are as important as the students' but we often forget this as teachers. When I feel creative and inspired, as I certainly did after this course, it has an effect on students and colleagues. (*TES*, 2003: 8).

Someone posted this on the *TES* staffroom website:

> I'm hoping to spend mine on a MPhil programme with the aim of getting out of the classroom and developing a career in research and uni work. Not sure if this is realistic (and it's the opposite of what the government have set the scheme up for) but I can't go on as I am.

One mainstream secondary school teacher wanted to work with children with emotional and behavioural problems. So she went on behaviour management courses, visited another school's unit, studied inner-city schools in New York state, and now wants to shadow a youth offending team and visit local special schools. It all helped prepare her for her current post, as second in charge of her school's social inclusion unit.

Someone else wanted to work on pastoral issues and is now acting head of Year 9. Her EPD fund went on training, working with a head of year, buying resources and developing a project on attendance. She was delighted: 'I have friends teaching in other boroughs who feel they haven't progressed as they would have liked to, yet I have gone through the roof. It's motivated me because I was able to get extra training in areas I was interested in' (*TES*, 2003).

■ PROFESSIONAL BURSARIES

There are also 'professional bursaries' for teachers in their fourth and fifth years. These are worth £500 per year, which is not a lot but some people have used these very well. Some teachers have spent the money on professional development directly related to their current post and teaching. Others have put it towards the fees for a higher degree, to further their own subject knowledge or to explore places to take pupils on educational visits. Others have done things that seem a little self-indulgent such as the English teacher who is buying guitar lessons on the grounds that it is a good stress buster and that he will run a guitar club. A science teacher has had a weekend in Paris to see the Pasteur Institute.

There are some more examples on the Teachernet website (www.teachernet.gov.uk/bursaries):

> After being appointed to a new job as Music Co-ordinator, a teacher wanted to use the summer break to develop his skills as a music teacher. He had already established contacts with a summer camp in New Jersey that offered music courses for children with severe behavioural problems. Using the funding provided through the bursary scheme, he was able to arrange a visit to the camp, where he spent the two weeks observing music sessions, exchanging ideas with camp instructors with extensive experience in the field and leading sessions himself. He acquired a wealth of new ideas and techniques to draw on.

> A head of the French department was looking for ways to support a move from head of department to head of year. Using his bursary as a fourth year teacher, he attended a course entitled 'Becoming a Pastoral Leader'. He intends to use the remainder of the money, plus the further bursary he will be entitled to as a fifth year teacher, towards funding a post-graduate diploma in Education Leadership.

Overall, the most successful EPD activities have had the same constituents as any effective form of CPD (see Chapter 2). They have taken into account preferred learning styles, had a great deal of autonomy and addressed areas that have been carefully considered with someone in a mentoring role. However, teachers need to be accountable for their EPD activities to ensure that authentic teacher development impacts on pupils' learning. The use of CPD portfolios during EPD is a basis for establishing teachers' adoption of a philosophy of career-long learning – and also helps teachers prepare for passing the threshold.

THRESHOLD ASSESSMENT

Early professional development is meant to help teachers make progress towards the threshold standards. The threshold is the next assessable point after induction. Crossing the threshold is not an automatic process. To be eligible people must have qualified teacher status, be working in a state school and be at the top of the main scale – M6.

There are eight threshold standards (see Figure 12.1). They cover five main areas, all of which relate directly or indirectly to classroom teaching: knowledge and understanding; teaching and assessment; pupil progress; wider professional effectiveness; and professional characteristics.

The standard 'Take responsibility for their professional development and use the outcomes to improve their teaching and pupils' learning' will require evidence that teachers:

1. Knowledge and Understanding: Teachers should demonstrate that they have a thorough and up-to-date knowledge of the teaching of their subject(s) and take account of wider curriculum developments, which are relevant to their work.

2. Teaching and Assessment: Teachers should demonstrate that they consistently and effectively:
☐ plan lessons and sequences of lessons to meet pupils' individual learning needs
☐ use a range of appropriate strategies for teaching and classroom management
☐ use information about prior learning to set well-grounded expectations for pupils and monitor progress to give clear and constructive feedback.

3. Pupil Progress: Teachers should demonstrate that, as a result of their teaching, their pupils achieve well relative to the pupils' prior attainment, making progress as good or better than similar pupils nationally.

4. Wider Professional Effectiveness: Teachers should demonstrate that they:
☐ take responsibility for their professional development and use the outcomes to improve their teaching and pupils' learning
☐ make an active contribution to the policies and aspirations of the school.

5. Professional Characteristics: Teachers should demonstrate that they are effective professionals who challenge and support all pupils to do their best through:
  • inspiring trust and confidence
  • building team commitment
  • engaging and motivating pupils
  • analytic thinking
  • positive action to improve the quality of pupils' learning.

FIGURE 12.1 THE THRESHOLD STANDARDS (DfES, 2001b)

■ identify and take advantage of such opportunities for professional development as will enhance the effectiveness of their teaching and the pupils' learning;

■ apply the outcomes of these opportunities to their teaching;

■ share the outcomes of their professional development with colleagues.

Evidence to support this standard will include such things as school staff development logs, personal records of professional development undertaken, certificates of attendance, minutes of staff meetings or reports to governors where staff attendance at professional development opportunities are recorded, and so on. Keeping the threshold standards in mind during one's career and maintaining a professional portfolio will make this process easier.

Teachers are responsible for applying for threshold assessment. This involves summarizing evidence – in the form of concrete examples from day-to-day work – to show that they have worked at broadly the standards indicated over the last two to three years. Filling in forms is something that most people hate and CPD co-ordinators may wish to organize some support for them. Kevan Bleach, assistant head at Sneyd School in Wolverhampton, runs sessions where he outlines the process, shows them exemplars and talks through different approaches that others have taken in completing the forms.

Headteachers make the assessment because they have a legal and professional responsibility for evaluating the standards of teaching and learning in the school and ensuring that proper standards of professional performance are established and maintained. However, people who manage staff have to assist the head to carry out threshold assessments.

The head has to send all the threshold applications to Cambridge Education Associates (CEA) who manage the process for the DfES. All applications go forward for a second professional opinion. The external assessor's role is more to ensure that proper procedures have been followed than to re-examine every application in detail. There will be two types of assessor verification for Round 4 (2003–04), distance verification and on-site verification. The majority of schools will receive distance verification. Assessors will telephone headteachers to seek clarification or to obtain additional information. Visits will be made where the headteacher has not been through the threshold process before or where there are issues. If an on-site verification is required, assessors will ask for a range of evidence from a sample of applicants so that they can be clear that the standards have been demonstrated.

■ CHECKLIST FOR THRESHOLD ASSESSMENT FOR HEADS AND CPD CO-ORDINATORS

1 Cascade details of threshold assessment procedure, standards and deadline for applications to teachers.

2 Read threshold assessment support pack for schools.

3 Ensure confidentiality of process at all times by restricting access to completed forms to those involved in assessing the application.

4 Check the eligibility of all applicants in the *School Teachers' Pay and Conditions* document (DfES, 2002a).

5 Notify number of applications to CEA by the deadline. Acknowledge receipt of each application form.

6 Check the validity of evidence presented on each application and complete the headteacher sections.

7 Send assessed forms and contextual information to CEA by deadline.

8 If a visit it to take place, ensure that teachers in the sample are given copies of the assessor's written request for evidence in good time.

9 Promptly notify each applicant of the outcome of their application.

10 Give written and oral developmental feedback to all teachers.

ADVANCED SKILLS TEACHERS

If people want to stay in the classroom, becoming an advanced skills teacher is a financially viable alternative to taking the promotion route into management. The salary range is, at the time of writing, £29,757–£47,469 (£35,700–£53,412 in London). The government wants 3–5 per cent of the teaching workforce to be ASTs. The main duty of ASTs is to be an excellent teacher in their own school for four days a week. For one day a week they have to share their good practice with other teachers and help other people's professional development – not only in their own schools but also in others (see Chapter 2). They offer an area of specialism which could be a subject (for example, music, PE, science), age phase (for example, Early Years) or both (for example, literacy in Key Stage 1). Some ASTs have been appointed to support initial teacher training –

ASTITTs! Also, in London there are plans to establish a group of 'London Commissioner's Teachers' – comprising ASTs, mainly those teaching the core subjects, and ready to work in the most challenging schools (DfES, 2003c: 36).

If there is an excellent teacher on the staff they can apply to become an AST when they are still on the main pay scale (MPS). There is no minimum period of time that teachers have to have worked before they can apply to be an AST, and they do not have to have passed the threshold. However, the application form is gruelling and the applicant has to provide supporting evidence under each of the AST standards (see Figure 12.2) on the lengthy application.

---

1. Excellent results/outcomes
As a result of aspiring AST's teaching, pupils show consistent improvement in relation to prior and expected attainment; are highly motivated, enthusiastic and respond positively to challenge and high expectations; exhibit consistently high standards of discipline and behaviour; show a consistent record of parental involvement and satisfaction.

2. Excellent subject and/or specialist knowledge
Aspiring ASTs must keep up to date in their subjects and/or specialism(s); have a full understanding of connections and progressions in the subject and use this in their teaching to ensure pupils make good progress; quickly understand pupils' perceptions and misconceptions from their questions and responses; understand ICT in the teaching of their subject or specialism(s).

3. Excellent ability to plan
Aspiring ASTs must prepare lessons and sequences of lessons with clear objectives to ensure successful learning by all pupils; set consistently high expectations for pupils in their class and homework; plan their teaching to ensure it builds on the current and previous achievement of pupils.

4. Excellent ability to teach, manage pupils and maintain discipline
Aspiring ASTs must understand and use the most effective teaching methods to achieve the teaching objectives in hand; display flair and creativity in engaging, enthusing and challenging groups of pupils; use questioning and explanation skilfully to secure maximum progress; develop pupils literacy, numeracy and ICT skills as appropriate within their phase and context; are able to provide positive and targeted support for pupils who have special educational needs, are very able, are from ethnic minorities, lack confidence, have behavioural difficulties or are disaffected; maintain respect and discipline and are consistent and fair.

5. Excellent ability to assess and evaluate
Aspiring ASTs must use assessment as part of their teaching to diagnose pupils' needs, set realistic and challenging targets for improvement and plan future teaching; improve their teaching through evaluating their own practice in relation to pupils' progress, school targets and inspection evidence.

6. Excellent ability to advise and support other teachers
Aspiring ASTs must provide clear feedback, good support and sound advice to others; are able to provide examples, coaching and training to help others become more effective in their teaching; can help others to evaluate the impact of their teaching on raising pupils' achievements; are able to analyse teaching and understand how improvements can be made; have highly developed inter-personal skills which allow them to be effective in schools and situations other than their own; provide a role model for pupils and other staff through their personal and professional conduct; know how to plan and prioritise their own time and activity effectively; are highly respected and able to motivate others.

FIGURE 12.2 THE AST STANDARDS (DfES, 2001b)

In most cases, excellent teachers will have plenty of evidence for most of the standards but the last standard may be harder to find evidence for simply because they have not had the opportunity to provide clear feedback, good support and sound advice to others, to provide examples, coaching and training to help others become more effective in their teaching, or to help others evaluate the impact of their teaching on raising pupils' achievements. This is where CPD co-ordinators can deploy prospective ASTs to mutual advantage. They will need training and practice in these skills.

Heateachers have to agree to the application and verify each standard, perhaps with other people's advice. If the application meets the requirements, an assessor may spend a day in school watching the person teach, interviewing them and others who know their work, and looking at the portfolio of evidence of how the standards are met.

In the next chapter we look at an alternative to becoming an advanced skills teacher: becoming a middle manager or middle leader.

CHAPTER THIRTEEN

Emergent Leaders and Middle Managers

- Role definitions
- Training and development needs
- Training programmes

This chapter looks at the training and development needs of emergent leaders, subject leaders and middle managers, and at the various ways in which they can be met. After briefly defining its terms, and outlining the key role that middle managers can play in teaching and learning, it draws on data (Earley et al., 2002) to examine training and development needs with reference to the *National Standards for Subject Leaders* (TTA, 1998). Reference is also made to the range of training programmes currently available, including the recently launched course for middle leaders from the National College for School Leadership entitled 'Leading from the middle'.

Middle managers, of which there are said to be around 220,000 in English schools (NCSL, 2003a), have a variety of names or labels in schools: subject leaders, heads of department, year heads, pastoral heads, curriculum co-ordinators, Key Stage managers, special educational needs co-ordinators, heads of ICT or literacy, or numeracy, to name the most common. Middle managers – or middle leaders as they are increasingly called – have long been recognized as crucial to a school's success but it is only comparatively recently that their importance has attracted the attention of policy-makers and educational researchers, particularly those interested in school effectiveness and school improvement. This is perhaps surprising given that middle managers/leaders are uniquely placed to have a major impact on a school and the quality of its teaching and learning.

Middle managers have long been seen as 'kingpins', 'the boiler house' or 'the hub of the school'. The NCSL has stated that effective middle leaders are at 'the heart of the matter' representing 'a critical base of knowledge and expertise for schools' noting that heads 'talk about them as "the engine room of change" and a repository of expert, up-to-date knowledge capable of transforming and energising learning and teaching' (NCSL, 2003b: 1).

One of the first activities of the NCSL when it was established in late 2000 was to design and publish a leadership development framework that consisted of five stages of leadership development. The first stage, that of *emergent leadership*, was when 'a teacher is beginning to take on management and leadership responsibilities and perhaps forms an aspiration to become a head teacher' (NCSL, 2001: 7). It is the management training and leadership development needs of emerging and established middle leaders that is the main focus of this chapter. But it is first necessary to consider briefly the nature of the role in both primary and secondary schools.

ROLE DEFINITIONS

The definition of middle management is problematic. All teachers are managers in that they are responsible for the management of pupils and resources, and the management of the learning process. Increasingly teachers manage support staff too, but only some have responsibility for the work of other teachers – the key factor in any definition of management. Management is often defined as the achievement of organizational aims and goals through the collaborative efforts of groups of people. Management, at senior or middle management level, is about getting things done by working with and through other people and it is likely to consist of a combination of activities such as planning, organizing, resourcing, controlling, monitoring and evaluating. It will also involve leading.

Middle managers are now seen as having a leadership role – as *middle leaders*. It is not the case that previously leadership was unimportant – it has always been necessary to lead a subject or a department or a year group – rather it is more a matter of emphasis. The importance of leadership is reflected in the national standards, which as we will see, are for subject leaders. Before their publication in 1998 'subject leader' was not a standard term with (in primary schools) subject or curriculum co-ordinator, or (in secondary schools) department head being more commonly used. The NCSL also prefers to use the term 'middle leader' rather than 'middle manager'. This reflects the dominant discourse which is about leadership not management, and distributed or shared leadership where anyone in an organization can function as a leader outside their formal position as such.

Middle managers have always had a pivotal role in passing ideas and information 'up the line' to organizational leaders. Senior managers rely heavily on middle managers to keep them informed of what is going on at the 'chalk face' and to alert them to problems and opportunities. The ability to take on a wider organisational perspective and not be restricted to a departmental or sectional viewpoint, is highly valued and encouraged by senior staff. Middle managers as key brokers within organizations are, therefore, potential agents of change through their ability to control and influence the flow of information.

NATIONAL STANDARDS FOR SUBJECT LEADERS

Various models or conceptualizations of middle managers' roles have been developed over the years, both for primary (for example, West, 1995) and secondary schools (for example, Earley and Fletcher-Campbell, 1992) but these have been superseded or taken over by the 'subject leader' standards developed by the Teacher Training Agency and published in 1998 (TTA, 1998). As noted earlier, the *National Standards for Subject Leaders* were developed as part of a much wider initiative to establish a professional development framework for teachers (Green, 2004) and to define standards of performance within the profession at a number of key points, (DfES, 2001b; TTA, 1998). In the description of the role (for both primary and secondary schools) offered by the TTA, the term 'subject leader' is preferred to either middle manager or curriculum co-ordinator.

The TTA defines the core purpose for subject leadership as: 'to provide professional leadership and management for a subject to secure high quality teaching, effective use of resources, and improved standards of learning achievement for all pupils' (TTA, 1998: 4). It goes on to state that:

> A subject leader provides leadership and direction for the subject and ensures that it is managed and organised to meet the aims and objectives of the school and the subject. While the headteacher and governors carry overall responsibility for school improvement, a subject leader has responsibility for securing high standards of teaching and learning in their subject as well as playing a major role in the development of school policy and practice. Throughout their work, a subject leader ensures that practices improve the quality of education provided, meet the needs and aspirations of all pupils, and raise standards of achievement in the school. (TTA, 1998: 4)

Most importantly, it is assumed that subject leaders work within a school-wide context, are able to identify subject needs but recognize these have to be weighed against the overall needs of the school.

The national standards discuss the key outcomes of subject leadership and the *professional knowledge and understanding* that subject leaders should possess (for example, the characteristics of expert teaching in the subject; relevant research and inspection evidence; the use of comparative data to establish benchmarks and set targets; health and safety requirements; the relationship of the subject to the curriculum as a whole; school governance).

In addition to the above, the TTA lists four broad categories of *skills and attributes* which subject leaders should possess. These are:

- leadership skills, attributes and professional competence: the ability to lead and manage people to work towards common goals;

- decision-making skills: the ability to solve problems and make decisions;

- communication skills: the ability to make points clearly and understand the views of others;

- self-management: the ability to plan time effectively and to organize oneself well.

Attributes listed as required for the successful enactment of subject leadership include: personal presence, adaptability, energy and perseverance, self-confidence, enthusiasm, intellectual ability, reliability and integrity and commitment.

The key areas of subject leadership and management are set out in detail under the four headings of:

- *Strategic direction and development of the subject* (within the context of the school's aims and policies, subject leaders develop and implement subject policies, plans, targets and practices);

- *Teaching and learning* (subject leaders secure and sustain effective teaching of the subject, evaluate the quality of teaching and standards of pupils' achievements and set targets for improvement);

- *Leading and managing staff* (subject leaders provide to all those with involvement in the teaching or support of the subject, the support, challenge, information and development necessary to sustain motivation and secure improvement in teaching);

- *Efficient and effective deployment of staff and resources* (subject leaders identify appropriate resources for the subject and ensure that they are used efficiently, effectively and safely) (TTA, 1998: 9).

Although the national standards have been generally welcomed by the profession (Field and Holden, 2004) it has become apparent that they cannot cater for all those who fulfil a subject leadership role. For example, there are crucial differences as to what can be expected from a middle manager (with four responsibility points) who has been teaching for over ten years and is in charge of a large faculty of 15 specialist teachers, and a primary school teacher (with no extra points or allowance) in their second year in the profession and responsible for a subject (for example, ICT) throughout the school. The national standards are generic, cross-phase and meant to apply to all subject leaders.

▇ IMPROVING TEACHING AND LEARNING

A key aspect of the role as outlined in the national standards and one where both leadership and management skills come to the fore is in relation to teaching and learning – how can middle managers influence effective teaching and learning outcomes?

Turner (1996) outlined several ways in which department heads influence teaching and learning outcomes. These included discussion of department vision and how to achieve it; encouragement of teamwork; informal discussions; use of meetings to plan curriculum, share good practice, discuss marking policy and teaching methods used; engage in staff development; feedback on performance; direct classroom observation and classroom appraisal.

The question of monitoring performance, feedback and classroom observation is an interesting one and it is generally recognised that this is in an area where practice is often less than rigorous. Turner (2003: 14–15) suggests that the reasons for this 'reluctance' might be the desire not to damage team morale or upset relationships amongst colleagues or because of the fear that observational evidence might be used at a later stage in any formal procedure relating to decisions about pay or performance. It may also be due to lack of time to engage in such activities as it is known that middle managers are given little non-contact time (NCT) to devote to the management and leadership responsibilities of their respective areas.

But attitudes towards monitoring and evaluation of colleagues are changing. This has been brought about by a number of factors, most significantly external (Ofsted) school inspection (Ferguson et al., 2000), but performance management and the drive to raise standards (school improvement) have also had a role to play. Wise (2001) highlights the tensions or internal role conflict that this can cause to subject leaders who find themselves caught between a strong expectation from senior staff that monitoring of teaching and learning will take place and team members who may feel uncomfortable about their teaching being monitored by their line manager. Much will depend on the culture of the department and the school and the extent to which observation is mutual and seen as being primarily for *developmental* purposes and not for accountability (Earley and Fletcher-Campbell, 1992).

In the summer of 2003 the National College for School Leadership published a practical guide to what middle leaders can do to improve learning in secondary schools (NCSL, 2003b). It states that the guide, entitled *The Heart of the Matter*, 'confirms a shift of role from managers of resources to leaders of people' and sets out to:

- illuminate the relationship between effective middle leadership and school improvement;
- recognize the practical ways in which schools can harness the potential of middle leaders and develop their capacity to work as a team;
- explore how senior leaders can provide support and enable middle leaders to be as good as they can be (ibid.: 1).

The message of the guide is that schools need clarity, consensus and senior staff support 'in identifying what makes a difference in building schools' capacity to improve learning for all' (ibid.: 1). It asks how can middle leaders be enabled to have maximum impact on the quality of learning in schools? The practical guide sets out eight areas in which middle and senior leaders can make a difference to learning. These are:

- a focus on learning and teaching;
- generate positive relationships;
- provide a clear vision and high expectations;
- improve the environment;
- provide time and opportunities for collaboration;
- distribute leadership: build teams;
- engage the community;
- evaluate and innovate.

For each area a list is provided of what middle leaders can do and how senior leaders can support and enable them to work effectively. At the end of the first area – teaching and learning – are some comments from practitioners:

> In our school we felt there were three key tasks that we needed middle leaders to fulfil:
> - *Teaching* – make sure that the teaching delivered by those you line manage is of the highest possible quality;
> - *Learning* – make sure that pupils achieve at least to their potential as established by baseline testing, and preferably, beyond;
> - *Becoming involved in, or initiating, a whole school activity related to school improvement* – help to drive the school forward (NCSL, 2003b: 10).

The message is to focus on these three essentials – 'deliver well in these key areas and you'll be doing a good job' (NCSL, 2003b: 10).

TRAINING AND DEVELOPMENT NEEDS

It is generally acknowledged that over the years the training and development needs of middle managers and middle leaders have not been thoroughly addressed. Adey and Jones (1998) identified subject leaders' needs and found the two most frequently mentioned areas where training was requested were general management skills, and financial matters and budgeting, especially in relation to planning. The whole area of preparation, training and professional development of middle managers and emergent leaders was also the subject of the DfES baseline study (Earley et al., 2002).

In the baseline study middle managers were asked (using a four-point adequacy of preparation scale) to indicate, in general terms, how well prepared professionally they were *prior* to taking up their current position. The results of the questionnaire survey are shown in Table 13.1.

TABLE 13.1 PERCEPTIONS OF PREPARATION FOR MIDDLE MANAGEMENT

	Very prepared (1) (%)	(2) (%)	(3) (%)	Not prepared at all (4) (%)
Middle managers (n = 229)	22 (15)	47 (26)	21 (39)	10 (20)
LEAs (n = 100)	2	39	54	5

Note: Figures in brackets refer to sufficiency of training

As can be seen from Table 13.1, although over one-fifth (22 per cent) reported being 'very prepared', one in ten regarded themselves as 'not prepared at all'. The group of middle managers was also asked (using a four-point sufficiency scale) whether in their view they had received a *sufficient* amount of leadership and management training before taking on their current role. Fifteen per cent of the sample perceived that training as 'quite sufficient', whilst 20 per cent regarded it as 'not at all sufficient' (see figures in brackets in Table 13.1). Adding together points 3 and 4 on the scale indicates that a significant percentage of the sample (59 per cent) was less than happy with the amount of leadership and management training they had received before taking on their current role.

Table 13.1 also shows the responses from the questionnaire sent to LEAs and completed by chief advisers. Local education authority respondents were asked to indicate how well they thought the majority of middle managers and team leaders within their LEA were professionally prepared *prior* to taking up their leadership positions. As can be seen from the table, the percentages were very low at both ends of the scale (2 per cent = 'very prepared' and 5 per cent = 'not prepared at all') with the highest number (54 per cent) selecting point 3 on the adequacy of preparation scale. In other words, the LEAs were indicating there was significant room for improvement.

As noted earlier, the *National Standards for Subject Leaders* (TTA, 1998) define the role in relation to four key areas and in terms of the skills and attributes applied to each of the areas. The sample of middle managers was asked to note in which of these they would welcome further or new training and development opportunities. The results, shown in Table 13.2, indicate that with the exception of 'decision-making' and 'communication' skills, approximately one-half of the sample of middle managers would welcome further training and development opportunities in *all* of the specified areas. *Leading and managing staff* was the key area mentioned most frequently (59 per cent), with *leadership skills* (55 per cent) and *self-management* (55 per cent) the second highest scorers.

TABLE 13.2 FURTHER TRAINING OPPORTUNITIES WITH REFERENCE TO THE *NATIONAL STANDARDS* FOR SUBJECT LEADERS (n = 233)

Key area	% of sample
Strategic direction and development of the subject (within the context of the school's aims and policies, subject leaders develop and implement subject policies, plans, targets and practices)	48
Teaching and learning (subject leaders secure and sustain effective teaching of the subject, evaluate the quality of teaching and standards of pupils' achievements and set targets for improvement)	51
Leading and managing staff (subject leaders provide to all those with involvement in the teaching or support of the subject, the support, challenge, information and development necessary to sustain motivation and secure improvement in teaching)	59
Efficient and effective deployment of staff and resources (subject leaders identify appropriate resources for the subject and ensure that they are used efficiently, effectively and safely)	45

Key skills and attributes	% of sample
Leadership skills – the ability to lead and manage people to work towards common goals	55
Decision making skills – the ability to solve problems and make decisions	39
Communication skills – the ability to make points clearly and understand the views of others	33
Self-management – the ability to plan time effectively and to organize oneself well	55

A higher percentage of primary than secondary school respondents stated that they would welcome further or new training and development opportunities, particularly in the second key area 'Teaching and learning' (64 per cent of primary respondents compared with only 43 per cent of secondary respondents), and the third key skill 'Communication skills' (38 per cent of primary respondents compared to 27 per cent of secondary respondents).

Significant on-the-job or in-school experiences were noted with many middle managers making reference to working with others (good and poor role models), including a good head; promotion or taking up a management role; and working in a good school; everyday work experience and school development planning or involvement in whole-school initiatives. When presented with a list of possible sources of ideas and inspiration, middle managers most frequently referred to other school leaders (76 per cent), headteachers (52 per cent), books and other publications(49 per cent), senior management teams (44 per cent) and local education authorities (40 per cent). Clearly, their work experiences were crucial in shaping their thinking and their practice.

The baseline questionnaire survey also asked middle managers to indicate which external providers they had personally used to access professional development opportunities in relation to their leadership role. The findings, as shown in Table 13.3, point to the significant role of the LEA as a provider. Individual consultants and HEIs were also important. Middle managers were also requested to state what professional development activity (in relation to leadership and management) they had undertaken *over the past three years*. Nearly one-fifth of those providing comments made reference to LEA courses and programmes, one in eight to school-based INSET and about one in ten to HEIs where they were undertaking higher degrees.

TABLE 13.3 EXTERNAL PROVIDERS USED BY MIDDLE MANAGERS FOR PROFESSIONAL DEVELOPMENT OPPORTUNITIES IN RELATION TO LEADERSHIP ROLE

n = 233	% of sample
Local education authorities	63
Professional associations	25
Individual consultants	29
Higher education institutions	22
Organizations in the private sector with industrial connections	9
Organizations in the private sector without industrial connections	0
NPQH providers	6
Other	7

TRAINING PROGRAMMES

What then might an effective training programme for subject leaders and middle managers look like? Research into the current state of school leadership for the DfES (Earley et al., 2002) found that some training providers considered that middle managers did not need an overly prescriptive training and development framework, but rather one that invited the providers to respond with programmes that helped build a scaffold for future development. Several felt it would be important to accredit such training and development, perhaps in partnership with a higher education institution, as part of a postgraduate qualification. Training providers proposed the development of a spiral curriculum framework in which similar concepts were introduced, but at different levels, and developed to different degrees of complexity and depth. It was suggested that people should be identified early on in their careers and nurtured for the role in a 'fast track' kind of way.

An overriding theme emerging was the urgent need to see put in place a map of leadership development ensuring coherence, continuity, some common themes, and some choice at different stages. There was strong support for regional provision and a modular approach, beginning from early in the teacher's career. Middle managers and subject leaders, it was felt, would benefit from this approach with those who aspired to headship being better prepared for the position.

A follow-up to the DfES baseline study, funded by the NCSL, explored further the training and development opportunities provided by LEAs with a view to producing a good practice guide (Earley and Evans, 2002). Two examples (from many) were included in the guide to illustrate the kind of training programmes available for middle managers and subject leaders. The first example was for subject leaders or curriculum co-ordinators in primary schools. The small size of most primary schools meant that, in many cases, teachers became responsible for a curriculum area as soon as they had completed their induction year. Along with the requirement to have an in-depth knowledge of the curriculum area for which they were responsible, these emergent leaders also needed to acquire the skills of people management, including leadership and delegation. Often, these newer teachers were working with more senior and more experienced staff and needed to be able to engage those staff in curriculum development in their area of expertise. There were therefore two aspects of the role where development was needed:

- subject knowledge – to enhance credibility with staff;

- people management – to empower curriculum or subject co-ordinators to be leaders within their curriculum area.

Buckinghamshire LEA, for example, offers a one-day course in conjunction with a local university for primary school subject leaders, key stage and curriculum co-ordinators and deputy head teachers. Topics covered include:

- vision and values;
- teams and team building;
- leadership styles;
- motivating colleagues;
- school improvement planning.

It also offers a more extensive course in school improvement planning for key stage and subject co-ordinators.

Programmes for secondary middle managers (the term 'middle leader' was rarely used) were frequently provided by LEAs and these took a variety of forms but nearly all were underpinned or informed by the *National Standards for Subject Leaders*. For example, in Wiltshire LEA, a 20-hour course – 'the manager in the middle' – was offered. This very popular and well-regarded course had accreditation options with a local university. In Sheffield LEA a programme for middle managers, which also had accreditation options, made use of a variety of teaching and learning methods, including face-to-face teaching, learning sets, online support and mentoring. Middle managers and senior staff were trained to run learning sets and to act as mentors to others in their schools.

Effective training programmes for subject leaders have the following features:

- an emphasis on collaboration;
- involvement and support of senior management;
- flexible and intermittent training points;
- external agency;
- context related planning and development;
- necessity of enquiry and reflection;
- use of research to inform practice;
- evaluation and data analysis (Busher and Harris with Wise, 2000).

One of us (Sara Bubb) runs a four-day (spread over a term) course for subject leaders in Lambeth LEA that covers all elements of the role but uses local expert practitioners. It has activities to do back at school in the two weeks between each session that helps people to apply the learning through their own actions within their subject and context (see Figure 13.1). A growing number of university staff have worked as consultants with individual schools and helped them to devise their own in-house management development programmes for emergent leaders, middle managers and others who perhaps have aspirations to become a deputy or assistant headteacher (for example, Day, 2003). SercoQAA's six-day programme for subject leaders has been offered in different parts of the country (Field and Holden, 2004).

Day 1

9.00 – 10.30	Introduction – The national standards for subject leaders
10.50 – 12.15	Group task – bringing the standards to life
13.15 – 15.15	Ways to monitor and audit. Observation techniques

Task: Observe a small amount of teaching using the sheet demonstrated, even if it's only someone taking assembly. Bring the notes you made and prepare to tell us about it.

Day 2

9.00 – 10.30	Case study school – headteacher and a subject leader
10.45 – 12.15	Observation techniques (cont.)
13.15 – 15.15	Giving feedback – the post observation discussion

Task: Observe someone teaching and give her/him feedback. Bring the notes you made and be prepared to talk about how it went. Bring some planning for your subject from at least two teachers for a month. Bring your school's statistics booklet.

Day 3

9.00 – 10.30	Presentation on your observation. Monitoring planning.
10.45 – 12.15	Learn how to analyse data. Analyse your school's.
13.15 – 15.15	Monitoring planning from your school

Task: Feedback the results of your monitoring of planning and analysing of data to your school. Be prepared to tell us how it went. Bring some samples of your subject's work to monitor.

Day 4

9.00 – 10.30	Monitoring through sampling
10.45 – 12.15	Case study school: target setting
13.15 – 15.15	Action planning and course evaluation

FIGURE 13.1 PROFESSIONAL DEVELOPMENT FOR SUBJECT LEADERS IN LAMBETH

All the above developments are, however, likely to be affected by the NCSL's 'Leading from the Middle' training programme, which came fully on-stream in September 2003. This new programme is likely to have a considerable impact and many LEAs and schools may choose to re-evaluate their own provision for subject leaders in its light.

■ 'LEADING FROM THE MIDDLE'

'Leading from the Middle' (LftM) is a leadership development or learning programme designed for subject leaders from all school phases and forms part of the NCSL's development programme that includes, *inter alia*, NPQH, Headteacher Induction Programme (HIP) and LPSH.

The LftM programme was designed to take account of how adults best learn and what constitutes effective professional development. The programme represents a central commitment to distributed leadership – 'devolving responsibilities for leadership away from the head and involving leaders at many levels in the organisation' (NCSL, 2003a: 2) – and is intended to give middle leaders a broader understanding of the school context which will help them to combine teaching and management responsibilities with a more strategic role. It is intended that the programme will encourage 'middle leaders to work with and through other people, equipping them to manage change and creating a culture of leadership designed to bring about improvements in pupil learning' (NCSL, 2003a: 2).

The purpose of the 'learning' programme is to develop participants' leadership expertise and capability by:

- increasing their confidence and competence in collaborative leadership and management;

- equipping them with the knowledge and understanding, skills and attributes for learning-centred leadership within a school setting;

- enabling them to find, make and take their role in leading the transformational agenda.

A unique aspect of the programme is the requirement for teams rather than individuals to take part. School teams consisting of two or three subject leaders and a senior leader in a coaching role enrol on the programme. 'Leading from the Middle' takes place over three terms and is delivered at a number of regional centres. The programme employs what NCSL calls a 'blended' learning technique that combines face-to-face and online learning. The elements of the programme include a virtual school providing a simulation of leadership-centred learning activities; learning-centred leadership materials provided online, which incorporate the knowledge understanding, skills and attributes outlined in the *National Standards for Subject Leaders*; online communities; face-to-face tutoring (three full days – two in term 1 and one in term 2 – and two twilight sessions) and leadership coaching. It also includes a school leadership project that is at the heart of the learning model (NCSL, 2003a).

It is an exciting development and a central plank of the College's efforts to develop the leaders of English schools. It is hoped that some of the participants will wish eventually to take up more senior leadership positions in our schools.

CHAPTER FOURTEEN

Leadership Development for Heads and Deputies

- What we know about leaders' needs
- Professional development for leaders at different stages
- What universities and professional associations offer
- What LEAs offer

Heads and deputies have important needs, yet Her Majesty's Inspectorate have found that provision is patchy. For instance, 'the support programme offered by LEAs for new headteachers is characterized by inconsistency, with no LEA having good practice in all aspects and one-quarter of LEAs providing unsatisfactory support' (Ofsted, 2002d).

One of the first activities of the National College for School Leadership when it was established in late 2000 was to design and publish a leadership development framework that consisted of five stages of leadership development (NCSL, 2001). The first stage, that of emergent leadership, was considered in Chapter 13. It is the management training and leadership development needs of the other stages of leadership that is the main focus of this chapter.

The importance of careful and accurate needs identification has been referred to on several occasions in this book. This also applies to school leaders and more attention has been given to this recently, including the growing use of tools and techniques to ascertain feedback on performance, sometimes called 360-degree appraisal or feedback. Many of the NCSL's national programmes for example now include elements of needs identification. In this section we look at leaders' needs and wants drawing on two major studies – the DfES baseline study (Earley et al., 2002) and the work of HMI (Ofsted, 2002d). We also look at current provision and forms of support for school leaders from universities, professional associations and LEAs. The NCSL's good practice guide (Earley and Evans, 2002) is drawn upon to provide examples of the latter.

Further details of all NCSL programmes including 'Leading edge' seminars and specialist courses (such as leadership of schools in challenging circumstances) are found on the College's website at www.ncsl.org.uk. Information can also be found about the various online communities (such as Talking Heads, Virtual Heads and Talk2learn), networked learning communities and opportunities to undertake overseas visits and conduct research.

WHAT WE KNOW ABOUT LEADERS' NEEDS

NEEDS RELATED TO THE *NATIONAL STANDARDS FOR HEADTEACHERS*

As part of the DfES baseline study on the state of school leadership, heads, deputy heads and NPQH candidates (deputies aspiring to headship) were asked about their development needs matched to the *National Standards for Headteachers*. Table 14.1 shows the findings for the three groups. The numbers in brackets represent the top five priorities in each group where people said they would welcome further or new training and development opportunities. School leaders will find the national standards beneficial as an audit tool, and the results of the national survey are useful to compare themselves against.

TABLE 14.1 FURTHER TRAINING OPPORTUNITIES WITH REFERENCE TO THE NATIONAL STANDARDS FOR HEADTEACHERS

Element of the National Standards	Heads (n = 612) (%)	NPQH candidates (n = 151) (%)	Deputy Heads (n = 226) (%)
Develop an educational vision and the strategic direction for your school.	15	24	27
Secure the commitment of others to the vision.	23	26	19
Implement the vision through strategic planning, operational planning and target-setting.	25	33 (4)	31
Keep the work of the school under review and account for its improvement.	44 (3)	28	32 (5)
Promote and secure good teaching, effective learning and high standards of achievement.	58 (1)	28	49 (1)
Monitor, evaluate and review the quality of teaching and learning.	41 (4=)	32 (5)	37 (4)
Agree, develop and implement positive equal opportunities strategies.	10	10	10
Agree, develop and implement systems to meet the learning needs of all pupils.	47 (2)	30	32
Develop and maintain the trust and support of all members of the school community.	25	29	24
Plan, allocate, support and evaluate work undertaken by teams, groups and individuals.	25	29	19
Lead, support and co-ordinate high-quality professional development for all staff, including your own personal and professional development.	41 (4=)	21	30
Determine, implement and sustain effective systems for managing performance of all staff.	41 (4=)	26	24
Ensure that the curriculum, management, finance, organization and administration of the school support its vision, aims and values.	26	51 (2)	43 (3)
Work with governors to recruit, induct, develop and retain staff of the highest quality.	11	17	19
Manage time, finance, accommodation and resources and ensure value for money.	24	66 (1)	44 (2)
Lead and enable innovations and changes to take place appropriately and effectively, including ICT.	27	35 (3)	27

Note: The numbers in brackets represent the top five priorities for further training.

The standards where further or new training and development opportunities were most commonly welcomed, were to 'promote and secure good teaching, effective learning and high standards of achievement' (58 per cent of headteachers and 49 per cent of deputies) and to 'manage time, finance, accommodation and resources and ensure value for money' (66 per cent of NPQH respondents). The latter standard was also ranked highly by deputy heads, but not by headteachers, with less than a quarter noting it as a priority. Headteachers considered the standard 'agree, develop and implement systems to meet the learning needs of all pupils' as a key developmental area. This was

not the case for either NPQH candidates or deputies. On the other hand, 'ensure that the curriculum, management, finance, organization and administration of the school support its vision, aims and values' was given a high priority by the deputies and NPQH candidates but not by the headteachers.

Interestingly, the only standard where there was considerable difference between secondary and primary headteachers was 'lead, support and co-ordinate high quality professional development for all staff, including your own personal and professional development'. Primary heads (49 per cent) much more than their secondary colleagues (30 per cent) identified this as a priority area and as one in which they would welcome further or new training opportunities. When asked about other training and development requirements, time management, personnel issues, conflict management and financial planning were mentioned.

■ MOST POWERFUL DEVELOPMENT OPPORTUNITIES

School leaders were asked what they perceived to be the *single* most powerful development opportunity of their career, both on the job and off the job, in helping to forge their understanding of leadership. The responses have interesting implications for CPD co-ordinators and others within schools.

On-the-job activities included (in order):

- working with an effective headteacher;
- working in an effective leadership or management team;
- everyday work experience;
- working in a good school;
- being an acting headteacher.

Off-the-job opportunities included (in order):

- postgraduate study (for example, an MA in leadership and management);
- involvement in the national programmes, such as NPQH and LPSH (see later for details);
- CPD or INSET courses in general;
- visiting other schools;
- networking (which involves a range of activities, both informal and formal);
- working with other headteachers;
- being a parent and 'general life experience';
- working on specialist tasks (such as for the LEA or professional association).

The main sources of professional development opportunities and activities in which school leaders had participated over the last three years are shown in Table 14.2. They ranked the three activities or opportunities that had been most effective in their own development as school leaders. The top three for each group are shown in brackets in Table 14.2.

TABLE 14.2 PROFESSIONAL DEVELOPMENT OPPORTUNITIES PARTICIPATED IN OVER THE PAST THREE YEARS

Opportunities provided by:	Heads (% of sample) (n = 613)	NPQH (% of sample) (n = 151)	Deputy heads (% of sample) (n = 226)
Mentoring from other headteachers/colleagues	39 (3)	54 (1=)	48 (2)
Business and other mentors	22	8	13
Conversations with other educationalists	70 (1)	58 (1=)	63 (3)
Higher education institutions	26	37	30
Local education authorities	61 (2)	66 (3)	67 (1)
Education consultants	48	38	48
Professional associations	36	17	22
Private sector organizations	17	9	16
Public sector organizations	12	10	12
Involvement in Investors in People	34	30	35
Any other opportunities	19	15	13

Note: The numbers in brackets represent views of the three most effective activities.

Opportunities provided by LEAs, conversations with other education professionals and mentoring from other headteachers and colleagues were ranked as most effective. The services of education consultants were frequently called upon. Professional associations were prominent in the case of headteachers, but less so for NPQH candidates. Although all phases made extensive use of LEAs for professional development, primary and special school headteachers were found to be more likely to make use of this provision than their secondary school colleagues. Primary heads more commonly used mentoring from other colleagues, although its take up was high amongst heads in all school phases.

The DfES baseline study (Earley et al., 2002) also interviewed various people who train heads and deputies. This group considered that leaders needed more help with ICT development and performance management. They felt there was a need for leadership development that stressed instructional leadership – what the NCSL prefers to call learning-centred leadership – and personal and interpersonal development. Providers stated that mentoring, coaching and shadowing schemes should be more widely available and systematic, and that there should be more international opportunities for development. They were concerned to learn more about ways to enable and empower school leaders to have the courage to be creative and flexible. They felt that deputies and heads concentrated too much on developing skills for particular tasks and were unable to see how their role relates to others in the school.

PROFESSIONAL DEVELOPMENT FOR LEADERS AT DIFFERENT STAGES

THE FIVE STAGES OF LEADERSHIP

The model of continuous professional development underpinning this book is that learning is lifelong – 'from the cradle to the grave'. This model or continuum obviously also applies to leadership development and learning and the NCSL's five stages of school leadership (NCSL, 2001) provides a useful means of analysing different groups in schools and their training and development needs.

Provision of training and development and other support mechanisms can be discussed around the five stages in a school leader's career, namely:

1   *Emergent leadership*, when a teacher is beginning to take on management and leadership responsibilities and perhaps forms an aspiration to become a headteacher (see Chapter 13).

2   *Established leadership*, comprising assistant and deputy heads who are experienced leaders but who do not intend to pursue headship.

3   *Entry to headship*, including preparation for and induction into the senior post in a school.

4   *Advanced leadership*, the stage at which school leaders mature in their role, look to widen their experience, to refresh themselves and to up-date their skills.

5   *Consultant leadership*, when an able and experienced leader is ready to put something back into the profession by taking on training, mentoring, inspection or other responsibilities (NCSL, 2001: 7).

We have organized the CPD opportunities for each stage, identifying the appropriate NCSL programmes and examples of what LEAs offer, since they are the main providers.

STAGE 2: ESTABLISHED LEADERSHIP

This comprises assistant and deputy heads who are experienced leaders but who do not intend to pursue headship. The NCSL has designed the 'Established Leader Programme' for assistant and deputy headteachers who have chosen not to become a headteacher. It acknowledges the importance of their role as experienced leaders and seeks to support their professional development through consideration of five broad themes that relate directly to NCSL's Leadership Development Framework – vision and values; learning; leadership for learning; sharing leadership; and future(s) leadership. The programme is delivered in single-phase regional groups of 16 who undertake one two-day residential course and four further face-to-face days over a 12-month period. Approaches to train-ing include: action learning sets; peer support through the development of mentoring, coaching and critical friendship; study group work on think pieces and case studies from successful practice elsewhere; visits to other schools; and self-reflection. Online materials and an online community provide important further dimensions to the pro-gramme. The expectation is that candidates will become involved in dialogue with others to develop professional understanding and mutual learning.

Deputy head networks, personal career guidance and counselling for deputy heads are in place in some LEAs. Essex, for instance, offers development modules in coaching, men-toring, managing the performance of others, working in other schools (interim manage-ment), the art of consultancy, managing yourself (personal effectiveness), developing training skills, project management, information management and recruiting staff.

In some LEAs opportunities are available for staff to train together and for leadership teams to have 'away days'. Courses specifically for senior management and leadership teams are available. Warwick LEA has a programme entitled 'Leading change – devel-oping effective leadership teams'. This gives SMTs and leadership teams the chance to work together intensively on the theme of change management. Its focus is on school improvement and teamworking; it is cross-phase and consists of two residential workshops plus one and a half days' follow-up. Buckinghamshire is developing (with a private partner) a bespoke programme that examines the effectiveness of leadership teams. Although such programmes are expensive, their impact is high as they are designed to meet a school's specific needs. The NCSL is currently developing a 'top team' programme for leadership teams which is part of the leadership strategy of the London Challenge (DfES, 2003d).

STAGE 3: ENTRY TO HEADSHIP

As noted earlier, acting headship has been found to be a very good source of on the job professional development. Some LEAs make regular use of deputies as acting heads, and these positions are seen as practical placements for professional development, but only a few run workshops specifically for them.

The NCSL's National Professional Qualification for Headship – mandatory for all headship applicants since April 2004 – is for those in the 'entry to headship' stage who are seeking to become headteachers. The training is focused on candidates' development needs and the programme is underpinned by the *National Standards for Headteachers*. It includes online learning, school-based assessment and visits to successful schools. The programme takes between four months and two years to complete, depending on candidates' training and development needs. Participants can use the NPQH for credits towards a higher degree, but those who already have a Master's degree (in leadership and management) and a whole-school role, are permitted to 'fast track' NPQH.

There are different types of support offered to new heads:

- needs assessment;
- an induction training programme;
- mentoring;
- networking;
- link adviser support.

NEEDS ASSESSMENT

Her Majesty's Inspectorate (Ofsted, 2002d) found that it was often assumed that needs assessment had been done via NPQH or as part of Headteacher Leadership and Management Programme (HEADLAMP) training. Even when it had been, it was not necessarily used to inform LEA programmes. Needs assessment was often informal and conducted with the school's link adviser. Where it was done well:

- heads assessed themselves against the national standards;
- the assessment was informed by NPQH outcomes;
- the identified development needs took account of the school's context;
- a written report was produced, leading to a personal development plan.

Headteachers found needs assessment most useful when it was conducted one to two terms after taking up their posts, and they welcomed the opportunity to involve the leadership team or SMT in this and elements of the induction programme.

INDUCTION PROGRAMME

Her Majesty's Inspectorate found that good headteacher induction programmes included:

- early contact, including meeting with the head before taking up post;
- useful information packs and documentation;
- effective introductory meetings;
- use of needs assessment to inform subsequent training;
- regular meetings and training opportunities;
- additional support from the school's link adviser;
- involvement of experienced heads in the process, and not just as mentors;
- opportunities for heads to include senior staff in elements of the programme;
- monitoring and evaluation of the programme leading to improved provision.

Weaknesses to avoid included:

- insufficient recognition of the needs of particular phases and types of school;
- a programme tied to September only starts (not January or Easter);
- insufficient guidance and information on opportunities available (for example, heads were often unclear about the potential uses of HEADLAMP funds) (Ofsted, 2002d).

The National College has a 'Headteacher Induction Programme' (HIP), which from 2003 has replaced HEADLAMP. It provides new heads with a grant of £2,500 that can be used with a range of training and development providers. The HIP is an entitlement for all new headteachers appointed to their first permanent post. It builds on the good practice of HEADLAMP but addresses the shortcomings that were identified during the HEADLAMP review. The grant is available for up to three years from taking up post (or from the award of NPQH if heads are undertaking this when taking up headship).

The NCSL's 'New Visions Programme for Early Headship' is open to those in their first two years of headship and can be funded through the HIP grant. It is a year-long programme rooted in an innovative model of learning based on enquiry and reflection into the practical experiences of headship.

MENTORING

Her Majesty's Inspectorate found that mentoring or one-to-one 'executive coaching' was rarely well developed and its effectiveness extremely variable. Most conceptions of a mentor were as 'critical friend' but some examples were found where it was linked to a planned programme for school improvement. Her Majesty's Inspectorate considered that effective mentoring had:

- a selection process with formal training for mentors;

- written guidance for new heads and their mentors;
- structured and purposeful meetings, that have a clear agenda;
- careful costing, including funding for supply cover;
- monitoring and evaluation of the process, leading to improvement (Ofsted, 2002d).

Mentoring practices include formal arrangements and informal 'buddy' relationships. In Warwickshire, for example, this is arranged locally and, unlike formal mentors, buddies are often colleagues from local schools. In Wiltshire the whole process is managed by an executive group of heads 'to enable a new head to feel comfortable and supported in their first year of their new post through a professional relationship with a colleague' (cited in Earley and Evans, 2002: 19). The mentor is funded for three days of supply cover. Heads choose a mentor from a booklet that contains names and profiles. The purposes of mentoring include: acting as a confidential sounding board; to help plan professional development; to reduce stress; and to help meet needs. In another LEA, all new heads are approached by the school's link adviser who discusses pairings mentioned by the mentor steering group, which also quality-assures the process.

Where it works well, headteacher mentoring is often highly valued by both mentees and mentors: 'What worked was having a very experienced head from a similar school that could provide professional and personal support' (headteacher); 'We don't have a problem finding heads to work as mentors; they see it as part of their continuing professional development' (LEA inspector, quoted in Earley and Evans, 2002: 19). Most LEAs offer training for those heads wishing to become mentors of new heads. Specialist mentoring for acting heads and for those operating in challenging circumstances is found in a few LEAs.

NETWORKING

Although heads report good support through networks (for example, phase, cluster, diocese), these rarely focus on induction and tend not to be developmental. Very few new headteacher groups exist (if they do they tend to be via HEADLAMP – now HIP – or NPQH). These groups can be very useful for discussing common issues, identifying needs, and so on.

LINK ADVISER SUPPORT

Overall, HMI found support from LEA link advisers to be good and more consistent than induction programmes. Heads value the support and see it as focused on their own and the school's needs. Good features include:

- link advisers being involved in the head's appointment;
- careful matching of link advisers to headteachers;
- additional entitlement of link advisers' time for new headteachers;
- differentiated support which depends on school and head's needs;
- effective needs assessment by the link advisers, leading to the development of a planned induction programme (Ofsted, 2002d).

'Vision to Reality' is an aide-memoire developed by Warwickshire LEA to help incoming primary heads to establish their vision for the school. It takes the form of a structured discussion with an LEA adviser or associate and the results are reviewed at the end of the year. A similar exercise is available for secondary schools but here the focus is on leadership and management and on one further characteristic, selected by the school using a quality checklist.

■ STAGES 4 AND 5: ADVANCED LEADERSHIP AND CONSULTANT LEADERSHIP

The NCSL's Leadership Programme for Serving Headteachers (LPSH) helps heads in the advanced leadership stage to reflect on their personal leadership effectiveness and impact. Evaluations of this four-day programme have found it to be a challenging, revealing and personally motivating experience, and many heads have referred to it as the best leadership training they have ever had (NCSL, 2003c: 9). The programme includes self-directed learning where headteachers support and challenge each other in co-coaching groups. The programme design enables headteachers to embed the change and developments into everyday school leadership practice. It offers headteachers: online learning opportunities and access to NCSL's web-based support; 360-degree feedback from colleagues, including personal self-assessment; a three-day residential with follow-up sessions over planned intervals to ensure sustainability of learning. The LPSH provides opportunities for heads to learn collaboratively with others in a confidential setting, to focus on personal development and leadership styles and how they impact on school climate, and to experiment and test hypotheses in leadership and school development. The programme is staged over eight to ten months and includes pre-programme preparation and learning; a three-day residential; follow-up sessions and post-residential opportunities.

For experienced heads who have completed LPSH, some LEAs (such as Surrey) have devised 'Executive Headteachers' programmes or something similar. Surrey is also developing a 'buddy' scheme for experienced heads that are new to the authority. Hampshire offers a nine-day programme over the year for 24 primary heads on 'leadership and learning'. If the course is oversubscribed preference is given to those heads who have been in post for five years or more. The authority also offers a three-day residential training programme for Special school heads and deputies (which is in the LEA's EDP).

The NCSL's 'Strategic leadership of ICT' programme was devised jointly with BECTA. It helps heads to take a strategic lead of ICT with the aim of improving school effectiveness and teaching and learning. It is not a skills-based course but is based around the principles of vision, audit and planning and is a self- and peer-review learning programme. Self-assessment and reflection are key throughout.

The NCSL's 'Leading Small Primary Schools' programme is intended for heads in the advanced leadership stage and was created with the help of LEAs and heads, drawing upon recent research in this area. The programme focuses on leadership for learning, the impact of different leadership approaches, collaborative leadership and the importance of reflection for both staff and pupils.

The 'Consultant Leader Development Programme' enables experienced school leaders to take responsibility for the future development of the profession while remaining in post (NCSL, 2003c: 10). The NCSL sees such leaders as fundamental to building leadership capacity in schools and throughout the education system. Since autumn 2003 the programme has been developed for experienced advanced skills teachers, experienced deputy heads and for primary head consultants as part of the primary national strategy leadership programme.

The two most common ways that these two stages of leadership are supported in LEAs are through mentoring (and buddying), and acting as 'associate heads'. Mentoring is available to provide assistance for heads (temporary or permanent) of schools in need of support. In such circumstances heads often acted as consultants. Formal links between headteachers officially lasted six months, although informally they lasted much longer.

In some LEAs a register of expertise is kept and there are lists of heads and deputies who would be willing, if approached, to operate as acting or temporary heads. This is generally recognized as powerful professional development and, in the case of deputies, the best preparation for headship. Associate heads and consultant heads are being used in a variety of ways but usually to assist other heads or to take over the headship of failing and weak schools. In secondary schools consultant heads have been used to support schools in receipt of the Leadership Incentive Grant.

WHAT UNIVERSITIES AND PROFESSIONAL ASSOCIATIONS OFFER

Higher education institutions have traditionally provided leadership development and management development opportunities for teachers and school leaders, whether accredited or not. These will vary from place to place and depend on the offerings of your local university and HEIs but Table 14.2 shows that a significant number of heads (about a quarter) and deputies (about a third) have been involved with them over the past three years. The NCSL has been working closely with a group of ten universities – the providers' group – to ensure continuity and complementarity between the national programmes (such as NPQH and LftM) and higher degrees such as MAs and MBAs. As earlier noted it is now possible to use the possession of an NPQH for credits towards a Master's degree, and for those individuals with a higher degree in leadership and management to 'fast-track' (route 3) NPQH. The providers' group is also looking at ways to accredit other NCSL offerings within a national accreditation framework.

Master's programmes are usually studied over a minimum of two years (or one year full time) and often consist of a modular framework made up of core and optional modules. The MA in Educational Leadership and Management at the Institute of Education in London, for example, which can be taken via distance learning or face to face (or a combination of the two), has three core modules each of a term's duration:

- Leading and managing educational change and improvement.
- Leadership for the learning community.
- Understanding education policy.

In addition to the core modules a number of options are available (for example, human resource management; finance and budgeting for schools; developing management skills and insights). Finally, to complete the MA a research-based report or dissertation is required.

■ PROFESSIONAL ASSOCIATIONS

Like universities, the various professional associations but especially the heads' associations (Secondary Heads Association [SHA] and National Association of Head Teachers [NAHT]), have traditionally provided courses and conferences which cover management and leadership issues as well as current concerns. An example of the NAHT's programme for 2003–04 is given below. (Table 14.2 shows that school leaders but especially heads – over one-third – have made use of such professional development opportunities over the last three years.)

NATIONAL ASSOCIATION OF HEAD TEACHERS' COURSES PROGRAMME FOR 2003–04

Induction
- On track for successful headship
- Induction and development for deputy head teachers

Performance Management
- Headteachers experienced in Performance Management
- Team leader training for Performance Management
- Leading and managing teachers in challenging circumstances
- Effective coaching skills for team leaders
- Developing people through coaching
- Vital Statistics – Primary

Personal and School Development
- Dealing with difficult people
- Interpersonal leadership and leading learning
- A headteacher's guide for professional well being
- Monitoring, evaluation and School Self-Assessment

WHAT LEAs OFFER

Many LEAs have devised extensive programmes for primary, secondary and special school leaders. The LEA, it will be recalled, is still a major provider of CPD for most schools (see Table 14.2 and Chapter 5). In 2002 the NCSL produced a good practice guide entitled *LEAding Provision* and this gives many examples of provision (see Earley and Evans, 2002) some of which are reproduced below.

The programme in Essex LEA, for example, is structured around role focus, professional focus and course objectives. The programme differentiates between induction, development and progression, and outlines the key themes and skills that individual school leaders are expected to develop. These include:

- mentoring and coaching;
- consultancy skills;
- training skills;

- intervention strategies;
- recruitment and selection;
- developing personal effectiveness;
- developing organizational effectiveness;
- career development and management.

Local education authorities are encouraging the use of portfolios and professional development records (DfES, 2001a) and some have developed the use of the World Wide Web to produce progression charts for all school leaders which record the training individuals have received, identifies training needs, and helps to select appropriate programmes to ensure continual progression and career development.

In Bedfordshire LEA specific training opportunities for school leaders include:

- 'Aspiring heads of department' (two half-days for newly appointed heads of department)
- 'Effective middle management' (three-day course for middle managers)
- 'Preparing for primary deputy headship' (two-day course for potential heads)
- 'Developing primary deputy headship' (one-day course for recently appointed deputy heads)
- 'Developing an effective senior management team' (three half-days for members of management and leadership teams)
- 'Preparing for headship' (one day for senior staff in all phases)
- 'Primary leadership conference' (one day for primary heads and deputies)
- 'Current issues in leadership' (one day for heads from all phases)
- 'Leadership – developing your style' (one day for seniors in all phases).

No matter at what stages of leadership individuals are placed, LEAs are able to support their school leaders in a variety of ways. These include providing support groups and networks, disseminating good practice and offering opportunities to be involved in a variety of initiatives and programmes.

■ NETWORKS AND SUPPORT GROUPS

Headteachers, other school leaders and teachers have always made good use of networks and found them a valuable form of support when and where they exist. In Warwickshire, for example, a range of networks are currently on offer with local patch meetings seen as an effective self-supporting network, with colleagues from different phases meeting to discuss common concerns and issues. A number of LEAs are supporting applications from groups of schools to join the NCSL's Networked Learning Communities (NLC) initiative (see Chapter 2).

Opportunities for subject and curriculum specialists to get together are particularly difficult in small LEAs and some have entered into partnerships with others in order to make such provision. For example Bracknell Forest, a small unitary authority, offers termly meetings for its secondary school heads of departments, but has maintained links with its six LEA neighbours (also small unitary authorities) to offer joint sessions for science subject leaders. A similar arrangement has been made for its Special School heads. In Wiltshire a support network for clusters of small schools has been established, which provides opportunities to network with colleagues in similar schools and to share expertise and resources.

GUIDANCE AND ADVICE

Many documents and working papers are available to support school leaders on such topics as utilizing data to support school improvement, school improvement planning, and target-setting at Key Stage 3. Local education authorities have traditionally been good at offering advice and guidance to their schools. They produce a wide range of helpful documents and guides available on all aspects of school leadership and management. In themselves these can be useful professional development tools. In Warwickshire a school self-evaluation course for heads has led to the production of a guidance document on the usage of various quality models of self-review and evaluation. Another LEA (Hampshire) offers a programme for heads and deputies entitled 'School Improvement through Self Evaluation' which attempts to go beyond the Ofsted framework and examines different approaches to school evaluation. Wiltshire has produced a self-evaluation audit (based on the Ofsted framework), which is to be completed prior to the link adviser's visit to the school.

WORK–LIFE BALANCE AND WELL-BEING

Warwickshire LEA provides a free health check for its employees and, like a growing number of LEAs, is concerned about issues to do with work–life balance and general well-being. For example, a one-day workshop 'Self first for a change' is being offered.

In Wiltshire two initiatives are attempting to tackle these concerns. 'Peer counselling for heads' was a small-scale pilot research project involving eight primary headteachers who met for a day's training to consider such matters as peer counselling, how it relates to self-esteem, good communication, constructive feedback and building peer support. This one-day conference was followed by the heads pairing up, visiting each other's schools, and then meeting a term later to evaluate and write up their findings. The heads spoke positively of the experience.

'Pastoral support for heads' was a related project on how to ensure primary heads remained enthusiastic. Heads were carefully selected for this initiative. To participate they had to be successful heads who had been in post for five years or more, in schools with 200 pupils or more and, crucially, to have managed to maintain their morale and enthusiasm for the job. The programme consisted of four half-day sessions. Heads formed pairs but they could not be from the same area. Each pair had to share a success, 'walk' their schools and discuss with each other what it was that helped them to maintain their enthusiasm and motivation for the job. The whole group met at the end of the year to evaluate the value of the experience and write up their findings. They were asked how the LEA could help to support heads in reducing stress, managing time better and providing for their overall well-being.

ASSISTANCE FOR ETHNIC MINORITY GROUPS AND WOMEN LEADERS

The London Leadership Centre has a programme called SHINE, which is designed specifically to support staff from black and ethnic minority backgrounds to reach leadership positions. It is for aspiring heads but the SHINE programme for middle leaders has recently been developed as part of the leadership strategy of the London Challenge (DfES, 2003d). Only a few LEAs are providing opportunities for minority groups and women – one set up a 'centre for women leaders' whilst another, in conjunction with a university, is investigating the possibility of providing mentors for ethnic minority teachers in their second and third years in the profession. Another appointed a race equality officer and was looking at what needed to be done to help such staff manage career progression.

■ COMMUNICATIONS

Effective communication, both between school leaders and LEAs, and between head-teachers themselves, is crucial. In most cases advisory and consultative groups have been established which help to inform LEA strategy and policy and CPD provision. Such groups provide opportunities for all involved to have a direct input on the issues they feel to be important. Ownership of the process was key, the groups could set their own agendas whilst establishing and maintaining networking opportunities and providing a useful mechanism for dissemination. Such experiences can provide powerful learning opportunities.

■ DISSEMINATION OF GOOD PRACTICE

Local education authorities are well placed to disseminate the good practice within their schools. Involvement in the NCSL's national initiative, Networked Learning Communities will also help disseminate good practice (see Chapters 2 and 7).

Wiltshire LEA has a dissemination strategy which aims to support improvement and the development of a learning culture in all its schools by developing partnerships and 'identifying, capturing and disseminating good practice'. Strategies for the latter include:

- making good use of Beacon and specialist schools;
- using heads and deputies as coaches and mentors;
- naming and acclaiming publications;
- undertaking research and publication;
- producing training videos;
- providing opportunities for CPD;
- benchmarking with family groups and identifying good practice;
- encouraging school self-evaluation;
- promoting quality circles and networking groups;
- setting up research and development groups and Action Research projects;
- developing HEI partnerships;
- devising a good practice website;
- promoting quality standards, for example, IiP, EFQM, Basic Skills quality mark;
- appointing advanced skills teachers and leading teachers (for literacy, numeracy and early years).

This LEA has its own publication The *Wiltshire Journal of Education*, whose aim is to disseminate good practice and celebrate achievement in the county.

Another authority, Bedfordshire, has established a 'good practice identifier' who devotes 30 days each year to this activity. A termly newsletter (with six mini case studies on good practice within the LEA) is produced and a website, which includes 400 case studies of good practice, has been established (the learning zone at www.bedfordshire.gov.uk).

Dissemination of good practice was however, said to be made more difficult by the 'inverse proportionality principle' (DfES, 2001a) whereby LEAs are discouraged from going into good schools (one visit per annum to effective schools was the norm) and to focus their efforts on underperforming, seriously weak and failing schools.

RESEARCH-BASED ENQUIRY

Some LEAs are heavily committed to encouraging school-based research and enquiry and are promoting action research in schools – what Graham Handscomb in Chapter 7 refers to as the self-researching or the 'research-engaged school'. For example, Buckingham LEA has linked together ten schools that successfully applied for Best Practice Research Scholarships. A common theme is being investigated across the projects and an action learning set has been established, in partnership with a HEI, for all those involved.

CONCLUSION

This chapter has examined the range of CPD opportunities or leadership development provision that is currently available for school leaders using the NCSL's model or framework of the five stages of leadership. Performance management was mentioned in Chapter 4 as one way of ascertaining training and development needs and ensuring that they are met. For teachers this takes place with their team leader or line manager. For heads it involves the governing body who is assisted in the process by an external adviser (who often is a consultant head). As with the performance management of teachers, heads are expected to draw up at least one target in the professional development area. This has been significant, as previously heads have had a tendency to put the CPD needs of others before themselves (Barthes, 1990). However, as we argued in Chapter 2, it is crucially important for all school leaders, to demonstrate that they are learners too, and to work towards developing a culture that attaches great importance to continuing professional development and personal growth.

CHAPTER FIFTEEN

Governors' Training and Development

- Why training, development and support are so important for governors
- Diagnosing governors' needs
- How to meet needs

This chapter aims to demonstrate why CPD co-ordinators should be as interested in the training and development of members of their school's governing body as they are in that of their professional (and paid) colleagues. Governors, like staff, are part of the school's human resource, and as such their training, development and support are very important if they are to fulfil their responsibilities effectively.

Governors play an important role in relation to continuing professional development and training in several ways. They are, or should be, concerned about their own training and development, but equally important is the priority they give, and show they are giving, to CPD within the school as a whole. Most schools will have policies and procedures that relate, for example, to staff development and training, induction, the use of supply teachers and performance management. More specifically, 'appointed' governors have responsibility, with the help of an external adviser, for the performance management of the headteacher when the head, like teachers, will be asked to agree on at least one professional development objective.

All these 'people' or human resource matters are the concern of the governing body, which is responsible for developing and ratifying such policies and also for ensuring that they are successfully implemented. When a school is applying for Investors in People status, for example, assessors will want to seek the views of governors and ascertain the importance that the governing body attaches to the development of its people resource. But assessors will also be interested in exploring how governors' training and development needs are being met, if there is a training and development plan for the governing body, and whether or not this is an integral part of the school's development or improvement plan.

This chapter explores these issues further. First, it considers why training, development and support are so important for governors. What do governors do that is so significant to warrant such concern and interest from busy CPD co-ordinators? What role does training, development and support play, and what do we know about what works in relation to both whole-school governing body development and training to meet the needs of individual governors? How are new governors inducted into their roles and what part can school self-evaluation play in governing body development?

WHY TRAINING, DEVELOPMENT AND SUPPORT ARE SO IMPORTANT FOR GOVERNORS

KEY ROLES

Training, development and support are important for governors because without them the governing body is unlikely to operate as effectively as it might. It is important for the governing body to work well because it performs a number of key roles and responsibilities that help the school ensure it is an effective and an improving school. This is not the place to go into these in great detail and they have been discussed elsewhere (see, for example, Earley and Weindling, 2004). Briefly their key responsibilities have been encapsulated in terms of three roles:

1 To provide a sense of direction for the work of the school (strategic role).

2 To support the work of the school (critical friend role).

3 To hold the school to account for the standards and quality of education it achieves (monitoring and accountability role).

Training materials produced by the DfES and available for LEAs to use with newly appointed governors, have centred explicitly on the three key roles of governing bodies (DfES, 2001b).

This way of conceptualizing the governing body's role has been enshrined in legislation (Education Act 2002) and inspection. The most recent inspection framework, which has applied to schools since September 2003, has given further emphasis to the governors' role. Under the section entitled 'How well is the school led and managed?' inspectors are instructed to assess the extent to which the governing body:

- helps shape the vision and direction of the school;

- ensures that the school fulfils its statutory duties;

- has a good understanding of the strengths and weaknesses of the school;

- challenges and supports the senior management team (Ofsted, 2003a).

But what do we know about how governors and headteachers perceive and enact these key responsibilities and how they conceptualise the governing body's roles?

> Governors in about 90 per cent of schools have a satisfactory or better understanding of the strengths and weaknesses of their school, but they are less effective in shaping the direction of the school … Where governors do not contribute effectively to shaping the direction of the school, they often have little knowledge of the school's main development priorities, agree plans and policies unquestioningly, and rely too much on the headteacher as the source of their information about the school. (Ofsted, 2002e: 10)

These key roles are therefore unlikely to be undertaken effectively without some form of training and support. Governors serve on governing bodies for a period of four years, and although it is known that many stay on for a further term of office (Scanlon et al., 1999) it is important to ensure that governors are 'fully functioning' as soon as possible. This is why induction of new governors is so important.

■ BENEFITS OF A GOOD GOVERNING BODY

Research into school governance (for example, Creese and Earley, 1999; Scanlon et al., 1999) shows there are a number of advantages to having a good governing body:

- a critical and informed sounding board for the headteacher;
- offering support for the school;
- helping to break down the isolation of the head;
- being a link with parents and the community;
- working with the staff to provide direction and a vision for the school;
- provide a forum within which the teachers can explain their work;
- bringing to the school a range of non-educational expertise and experience (Scanlon et al., 1999: 27).

One of the most important attributes of a governing body is that it is largely composed of individuals who bring different perspectives to the headteacher and the school and therefore the opportunity to learn from different people with different backgrounds. Sometimes the professionals were too close to the issues or had tunnel vision: 'you simply can't see the wood for the trees'. Having a group of people with a variety of skills and experience was an added resource for headteachers. This could enhance their role and make their jobs easier.

Overall headteachers are beginning more fully to appreciate the benefits of having a good chair and an effective governing body in what could, otherwise be a lonely and, at times, vulnerable position. They can find sympathy and understanding, as well as challenge and stimulus, from a body of hard-working and committed laypeople who had the best interests of the school at heart.

Effective schools and effective governing bodies make a difference – they add value. There is already a considerable body of research into what makes a school effective. Although there has been less research into the effectiveness of governing bodies, it is possible to identify (for example, Scanlon et al., 1999) a number of factors that are present in effective governing bodies. These include:

- a positive attitude towards governors on the part of the headteacher;
- efficient working arrangements;
- effective teamwork within the governing body;
- governors who are committed to the school.

Governing bodies which make a conscious effort to improve their performance in these areas *do* become more effective as can be seen from the case studies described in Creese (2000). In his study of governing bodies that became more effective Creese pointed to four common factors which were significant: teamwork, positive relationships, efficient working arrangements and the important input of the chair of governors.

Many research studies (for an overview see Earley and Creese, 2003a) have identified the key role which the headteacher plays in determining the effectiveness, or otherwise, of the governing body. The nature of the relationship between the headteacher and the chair of governors in particular is crucial. As noted by Joan Sallis the well-known governor trainer and agony aunt, schools will boast about their governing body's quality because the quality of the governing body, like the quality of the staff, gives evidence of the head's leadership and management (Sallis, 2001). Relationships between staff in general and the governors are also important. Governors should be encouraged to visit their schools regularly and so become well known to the staff who trust them and respect their input.

A useful way of conceptualizing governing bodies as regards their effectiveness is in terms of where they are located on the pressure and support spectrum (see Figure 15.1). Effective governing bodies are those that provide high pressure but with high support. Governing bodies have to offer both support and challenge to the schools, but getting the balance between these two is not always easy.

low	*SUPPORT*	*high*

1. Supporters club
'We're here to support the head!'

4. Partners or critical friends
'We share everything - good or bad!'

low	*CHALLENGE*	*high*

2. Abdicators
'We leave it to the professionals!'

3. Adversaries
'We keep a very close eye on the staff!'

How would you describe *your* governing body?

FIGURE 15.1 THE EFFECTIVE GOVERNING BODY (CREESE AND EARLEY, 1999: 8)

To work effectively as critical friends there is a need for trust, sensitivity and openness. This cannot be legislated for, or introduced overnight. What is more, once achieved there is no guarantee that such qualities will persist – changes of personnel mean that they have to be continuously re-established. Effective governing bodies are not heads' supporters' clubs, abdicators or adversaries but, as shown in Figure 15.1, the partners or critical friends offering 'high support – high challenge' (Creese and Earley, 1999: 8).

DIAGNOSING NEEDS

SELF-EVALUATION

Another common theme for whole governing body training, perhaps also partly brought about by Ofsted, has been school self-evaluation and in particular evaluating the effectiveness of themselves – how are they currently operating as a governing body and what are their strengths and weaknesses? Are their working arrangements efficient and are they able to ensure their limited time and efforts are focusing on those things that matter most? Considering that governors are unpaid volunteers, the demands on them are high – and some may not think that CPD is a priority.

A number of LEAs already have in place self-evaluation programmes for their governing bodies. Some LEAs and other bodies, such as the governor associations and training organizations, have published appropriate criteria against which governors can judge their effectiveness or have developed self-review procedures or good governance guides which ask a series of questions governors might want to ask about their schools: for example, questions on issues such as the curriculum, finance, premises, staff development, development planning and, perhaps most importantly, school performance. Self-review or evaluation against a set of criteria can have a marked effect on enhancing the effectiveness of school governing bodies. Those that take part in such activity (and it probably tends to be those who are already pretty effective) are able to build on their strengths and recognize those areas where development is needed.

One of us (Peter Earley) was involved in a self-evaluation exercise that identified governor's awareness of the school, and monitoring and evaluating as major weaknesses. Such identification was the first step in bringing about action to alter this state of affairs. Governing bodies that take part in such activities will tend to be more questioning of heads and other staff, and of themselves, and have developed better procedures for asking such questions as why, where, how, what and, perhaps most importantly, 'how well are we doing?'. These naive questions can make heads and senior school staff think very carefully about what they are doing and planning to do and why. The key question that an effective and efficient governing body will want to ask at all times is: 'Is the way we operate as a governing body allowing us to focus on making our school more effective?'

With the above in mind it is interesting to note the recent moves to promote a national (albeit voluntary) model of governing body self-evaluation (Little, 2002). This is known as the 4Ps framework (see Table 15.1) and the Index of School Governance, and has been piloted in over 30 LEAs in England. The framework – also known as 345 – consists of three key roles (strategic overview, accountability and critical friend), four aspects or Ps (strategic Planning, ensuring Progress, real Partnership and sound Practice), and five criteria for each of the four Ps (see below). The index, developed by Catherine Burt, is both a product and a facilitated process for governing body self-evaluation. It will be interesting to see how it develops and whether it becomes the preferred or dominant model but clearly self-evaluation for governing bodies is here to stay!

Good relationships between governors and staff are fundamental to improving the effectiveness of the governing body. Although finding the time is hard, governors need to visit the school during the day to see pupils at work and talking to, and getting to know, the staff. Governors benefit from being offered guidance on how to get the most out of their visits.

Jane Phillips of NAGM has drawn up this list to prompt governors into thinking about their school as a learning organization:

1   Are there regular opportunities for staff to examine and reflect together on classroom practice and pupil learning?

2   Are governors involved?

3   Is there dialogue across departments and within and between Key Stages?

4 Are governors informed of this dialogue?

5 Do staff actively turn to each other to solve problems?

6 Do governors actively turn to each other to solve problems?

7 Is there a common understanding between staff as to what counts as progress for pupils?

8 Do governors share this understanding?

9 Do pupils experience the same high expectations of their progress across departments and within and between Key Stages?

10 Do governors share these high expectations?

11 Does the school measure what it values – not those things that are easily measured?

12 Do the values of the staff and the values of the governing body coincide?

13 Do staff have opportunities to read about, examine and share 'best practices' within and beyond the school?

14 Do governors have an understanding of 'best practice' in teaching?

15 Is there feedback from pupils about the quality of their learning experiences in school?

16 Is this feedback shared with the governors?

17 Is the relationship between parents and staff a learning relationship – that is, do they learn from each other?

18 Are governors involved?

19 Is the relationship between governors and staff a learning relationship – that is, do they learn from each other?

20 What is the head's role in all of this? (Phillips, 1999)

TABLE 15.1 GOVERNING BODY SELF-EVALUATION – THE 4Ps

Planning	Progress	Partnership	Practice
1. Direction	1. Monitoring	1. Representation	1. Teamwork
2. Improvement	2. Target-setting	2. Participation	2. Relationships
3. Documentation	3. Efficiency	3. Communication	3. Meetings
4. Decision	4. Impact	4. Accountability	4. Organization
5. Statute	5. Equality	5. Advocacy	5. Development

■ INDIVIDUAL GOVERNORS' NEEDS

It is worth remembering that governors, who may be parents, support staff, teachers, members of the local community or businesspeople, come onto the governing body from a variety of backgrounds with a wide range of experience. Some will have an educational background – indeed, a recent study found that nearly 40 per cent of governors work in education or have an education-related occupation (Earley and Creese, 2003b). Most, however, will have limited knowledge of education, although all of course will recall their own school days!

NEW GOVERNORS

The first matter to be attended to therefore is how to induct new governors into their role and ensure they become knowledgeable about the school and about education in general. We should not aim to make them educational experts; that is not their role – the strength of the governing body as Joan Sallis and others have argued lies in the fact that it is made up of non-experts, its 'precious light of ordinariness'. But newcomers need to 'get up to speed' as quickly as possible. Most LEAs offer a programme of training for new governors, often based on the training materials developed by the DfES (DfES, 2001b), which focus on the aforementioned three key roles.

CHAIRS OF GOVERNORS

The relationship between the headteacher and the chair of governors is crucial and affects how the whole school operates. Chairs provide 'an ear to bash, a shoulder to cry on and someone to bounce ideas off' (Sallis, 2001). They require certain key qualities: they need to be accessible, keen and interested.

The chair of governors is often the prime mover in enhancing the effectiveness of the governing body and 'it is difficult for a governing body to improve or become more effective if the role of the chair is poorly enacted' (Scanlon et al., 1999: 5). It is not always easy to chair effectively meetings of a group of disparate volunteers, such as a governing body. It may include some governors with little or no experience of meetings, who find difficulty in expressing their views, whilst at the other end of the spectrum there are those with considerable experience of serving on committees. A good chair will be able to ensure that all governors are able to contribute to meetings which have clear objectives and outcomes achieved within a reasonable space of time.

Chairs need to set up efficient working arrangements, which allow governors time to concentrate upon the key issues for their school. The setting up of a pattern of meetings, and delegation to sub-groups, enables governors to give time to the important issues. Chairs need to run meetings well with all governors being given the opportunity to contribute. Including timings for the various items on agendas and indicating clearly specific responsibilities for follow-up in the minutes of meetings are two examples of good practice in this area.

The majority of LEAs offer training specifically targeted at chairs, in the form of briefings about forthcoming issues and/or guidance on how to run meetings, and so on. Greater stress may need to be laid upon the factors linked to the effectiveness of the governing body, and the steps necessary to enhance effectiveness. In particular, chairs may need reminding of the importance of good teamwork, and of having working arrangements which allow governors time to concentrate upon the key issues in their schools. These are aspects of the work of the governors that should be stressed in any evaluation of the effectiveness of the governing body.

HOW TO MEET NEEDS

There are many training opportunities for governors and a growing amount of support. The DfES produces a termly newsletter entitled *Governors* and there is lots of very useful information on their website (www.governornet.co.uk) as well as the websites of the governor organizations (nagm.org.uk; governors.fsnet.co.uk; and ngc.org.uk) and the *Times Educational Supplement* (www.tes.co.uk). The *TES* produces a weekly column for governors and Joan Sallis answers governors' questions. Also, there is a 24-hour hotline available for governors (on www.schoolgovernorline.info or 0800 0722 181) to answer any questions governors may have about any aspect of school life.

Much governor training provided by local education authorities focuses largely on what might be termed the 'nuts and bolts' of governance – issues such as governors' legal responsibilities, budget management and so on. Here is one LEA's list of courses:

Admissions Briefing – New Arrangements and Regulations;

Briefing: School Governance Procedures Regulations;

Briefing on School Workforce Remodelling;

Briefings – Reconstitution Regulations;

Clerks' Accreditation Training Day;

Clerking Pupil Discipline Committees;

Chairing Matters;

Development for Training Liaison Governors;

Induction Course for New Governors.

The wider but more fundamental issue of governors' involvement may receive less attention. A further difficulty lies in the constant turnover of governors. With new governors being appointed on a regular basis, there is an ongoing need for induction programmes, a need that has been partly filled by a national programme which LEAs are free to use (DfES, 2001b). New governors inevitably take time, perhaps as long as two years, to get to grips with their role. If they only serve one four-year term, they can only offer two years when they are in a position to undertake the sort of tasks which effective governance requires.

In many LEAs, governor trainers already offer training sessions aimed at the whole governing body, on such matters as:

- preparing for an Ofsted inspection: what governors need to know;
- developing the governing body's strategic role;
- governors' school visits;
- being a good employer: staffing issues for the governing body;
- understanding your school performance data;
- the critical friend role in practice.

Such collective training sessions are invaluable as part of the essential team-building process. It is also worth noting that social events, of various sorts, contribute to helping governors get to know one another and to find a common sense of purpose. There is no reason why governing bodies should rely solely upon external agencies for developmental work in team building. Experienced headteachers and governors can gain in terms of their own development by organizing training sessions for their governing body. For example, headteachers have to explain more fully to laypeople what the professionals have too often taken for granted, to make things more explicit, translate the coded language and jargon of education, and fill in background details so that governors can make informed decisions.

TEAM BUILDING

There is no reason to suppose that governors will automatically form themselves into a team with shared beliefs and a common sense of purpose – indeed, the opposite is more likely to be the case. Some form of team-building process must take place if the governing body is to become an effective team. Many governing bodies arrange training sessions of one sort or another for the whole governing body, in addition to the training attended by individual governors. Good teamwork can be strengthened through having sound procedures and good communication systems, which are understood by all. Some LEAs have sessions run by an experienced trainer who will work with governing bodies in a series of challenges and problem-solving exercises designed to give you insights into the skills and behaviour deployed as a governor in meetings.

ROLE OF 'LINK' GOVERNORS

Most governing bodies appoint or select a 'link' or training governor whose responsibility is to bring to the attention of individual governors the various training opportunities available and encourage them to attend. This person will work with the CPD co-ordinator to manage the training budget, and if the school is signed up to the LEA's training and support programme, will wish to ensure the school is getting value for money for its annual subscription.

The link governor ensures that all new governors are provided with documentation about the school and the governing body, whilst being careful not to overload them. This school-based induction pack should be seen as complementing that provided by the LEA. In addition a growing number of governing bodies are setting up 'buddy' or mentoring systems whereby an experienced governor will be attached to a new one. The other essential feature of induction is arranging for the new governors to visit the school at the earliest opportunity. Indeed, all governors 'new' or 'old' should be encouraged to give high priority to visiting the school in order to see the pupils at work and to talk with the staff.

WHOLE GOVERNING BODY TRAINING

Training can also be an integral part of the way the governing body operates – for example, by having an item on the agenda of the full governing body meeting which allows those governors who have attended courses to feed back to others; or by having a five minute item which examines a particular topic (for example, school visits, sex education, equal opportunities, links with the school). Effective governing bodies are known to share information about recent developments in education and elsewhere which are likely to impact on the school. Headteachers, chairs of governors, link governors, indeed all governors may make copies and circulate relevant (short) articles and overviews. Matters are made easier as more governors and school staff acquire email addresses.

The training and development of individual governors, especially new ones, is very important but training for the whole governing body can be tailored more specifically to its needs. Research has found a strong link between perceptions of governing body effectiveness and involvement in whole governing body training (Scanlon et al., 1999). It also identified a trend where more and more governor training was of this kind and now nearly all LEAs (as part of the package that most schools purchase) offer such a service at least once a year to the school if requested. Effective governing bodies are likely to use their limited training funds carefully to ensure a balance between school-based training and off-site sessions for individual governors. Both are clearly needed and the role of the link governor and the CPD co-ordinator/headteacher is important here. Also important is that experienced heads, CPD co-ordinators and governors can gain in terms of their own development by organizing training sessions for their governing bodies. It can be even more valuable if it is occasionally held in conjunction with staff.

Another advantage of whole governing body training is that it promotes team building and teamwork. It can also help develop positive relationships between governors, the head and senior staff. As earlier noted, teamwork is a characteristic of effective governing bodies but there is of course no guarantee that this disparate (albeit well-meaning) group of governors will automatically form themselves into a team with shared beliefs and a common sense of purpose. Some form of team building process must take place if the governing body is to become an effective team. Some arrange events so as to bring governors together to get to know each other and to develop a common purpose thus enhancing their sense of identity as a team. These include meetings (some on Saturdays) and a variety of other working sessions and/or social events. Others arrange training events around a theme of concern to the governing body such as the school development plan or, commonly, preparation for inspection. If there is one thing Ofsted inspections have done for schools and governing bodies it is to get them to unite against a common foe – an unintended but positive consequence perhaps!

CONCLUSION

Governors need to access high-quality training to carry out their roles effectively, especially with regard to such difficult areas as monitoring and evaluating the work of the school. Training will help to raise governors' awareness of their roles and their statutory responsibilities as well as increase their confidence to play a full part in the life of the school and the governing body. Acting as critical friends or asking pertinent questions to heads and teachers is not easy and governors need lots of help and support – from within the school, the LEA and governor organizations – to do this effectively. Headteachers and CPD co-ordinators should therefore consider the training needs of governors in the same way they would those of paid employees of the school. As noted above, Creese (2000) in his study of governing bodies that became more effective pointed to four common factors which were significant: teamwork, positive relationships, efficient working arrangements and the important input of the chair of governors. Training can make a significant impact on all of these. The key to effective governance is therefore the development of a partnership between the school, its staff and governors, one built on positive relationships and trust which enables a supportive, yet challenging and questioning, culture to exist. For this to occur training is crucially important. It is also very important for governors to demonstrate by their actions that they are interested in the CPD of school staff and that they work towards being 'good employers' of people. As we said at the beginning of this book, people matter!

REFERENCES

Adey, K. and Jones, J. (1998) 'Development needs of middle managers: the views of senior managers', *Journal of In-service Education*, **24**(1): 131–44.

Balshaw, M. and Farrell, P. (2002) *Teaching Assistants: Practical Strategies for Effective Classroom Support*. London: David Fulton.

Barthes, R. (1990) *Improving Schools from Within*. San Francisco, CA: Jossey-Bass.

Baxter, G. and Chambers, M. (1998a) 'Setting the standard for coordinators', *Professional Development Today*, **1**(2): 79–84.

Baxter, G. and Chambers, M. (1998b) 'Evaluating staff development', *Professional Development Today*, **2**(1): 31–8.

Bentley, P. (2002/2003) 'Continuing professional development: views from the front', *Professional Development Today*, **6**(1): 57–62.

Berrill, D. and Whalen, C. (2003) 'Professional identity/personal integrity: towards a reflective portfolio teaching community'. Paper presented at AERA, Chicago.

Bezzina, C. (2002) 'Rethinking teachers' professional development: agenda for the 21st century, *Journal of In-service Education*, **28**(1): 57–78.

Bleach, K. (2000) *The Newly-qualified Teacher's Handbook*. London: David Fulton.

Bolam, R. (1993) 'Recent developments and emerging issues', in *The Continuing Professional Development of Teachers*. London: GTC.

Bolam, R. and McMahon, A. (2003) 'Recent developments in CPD', in C. Day and J. Sachs (eds), *International Handbook of the Continuing Professional Development of Teachers*. Maidenhead: Open University Press.

Boyle, B., White, D. and Boyle, T. (2003) A longitudinal study of teacher change: what makes professional development effective? Paper given to American Education Research Association, Chicago, IL, April.

Brereton, P. (2001) 'Harnessing DVD for staff development', *Professional Development Today*, **5**(1): 81–6.

Brown, S. and Earley, P. (1990) *Enabling Teachers to Undertake INSET*. Slough: NFER.

Bubb, S. (2000) *The Effective Induction of Newly Qualified Primary Teachers: An Induction Tutor's Handbook*. London: David Fulton.

Bubb, S. (2001) *A Newly Qualified Teacher's Manual: How to Meet the Induction Standards*. London: David Fulton.

Bubb, S. (2003a) *The Insider's Guide for New Teachers: Succeeding in Training and Induction*. London: TES/Kogan Page.

Bubb, S. (2003b) *A Newly Qualified Teacher's Manual: How to Meet the Induction Standards*. Reprint. London: David Fulton.

Bubb, S. (2003c) *The Insider's Guide to Early Professional Development: Succeed in Your First Five Years*. London: TES/RoutledgeFalmer.

Bubb, S. (2003d) 'Helping overseas-trained teachers get QTS', *Managing Schools Today*, **12**(4): 40–4.

Bubb, S. and Hoare, P. (2001) *Performance Management*. London: David Fulton.

Bubb, S., Heilbronn, R., Jones, C., Totterdell, M. and Bailey, M. (2002) *Improving Induction*. London: RoutledgeFalmer.

Busher, H. and Harris, A. with Wise, C. (2000) *School Leadership and School Improvement*.

London: Paul Chapman Publishing/Sage.

Butler, S. and Geeson, J. (2002) 'Why everyone needs mentoring', *Secondary English Magazine*, **5**(3).

Carnell, E. (2001) 'The value of meta-learning dialogue', *Professional Development Today*, **4**(2): 43–54.

Child, A. and Merrill, S. (2002) 'Making the most of ITT', *Professional Development Today*, **5**(2): 17–20.

Connor, D. (1997) 'Becoming a professional development co-ordinator – the challenge', *Professional Development Today*, **1**(1): 47–52.

Cordingley, P. (2001) 'CPD reformed? An interview with Carol Adams', *Professional Development Today*, **4**(2): 79–84.

Cordingley, P. (2003) 'Bringing research resources to school based users', *Professional Development Today*, **6**(3): 13–18.

Craig, M. (2002) 'Crisis for challenging schools', *Professional Development Today*, **5**(2): 29–34.

Creese, M. (2000) 'Enhancing the effectiveness of governing bodies', *Professional Development Today*, **3**(3): 49–58.

Creese, M. and Earley, P. (1999) *Improving Schools and Governing Bodies: Making a Difference*. London: Routledge.

Davey, J. (2000) 'Evaluating staff development: a case study', *Professional Development Today*, **3**(2): 33–40.

Day, C. (1999) *Developing Teachers: The Challenge of Lifelong Learning*. London: Falmer.

Day, C. (2003) 'Continuing professional development: views from the front', *Professional Development Today*, **6**(1): 51–6.

Day, C., Hadfield, M. and Kellow, M. (2003) *Schools as Learning Communities: Professional Development through Network Learning*. Paper presented at AERA conference, Chicago, IL, 21–26 April.

Dennison, B. and Kirk, R. (1990) *Do, Review, Learn, Apply: A Simple Guide to Experiential Learning*. Oxford: Blackwell.

Department for Education and Employment (DfEE) (1989), *Elton Report*. London: DfEE.

Department for Education and Employment (DfEE) (1998) *National Standards for Headteachers*. London: DfEE.

Department for Education and Employment (DfEE) (2000a), *Performance Management in Schools, Performance Management Framework*, 0051/2000. London: DfEE.

Department for Education and Employment (DfEE) (2000b) *Performance Management in Schools, Model Performance Management Policy*. London: DfEE.

Department for Education and Employment (DfEE) (2000c) *Supporting the Teacher Assistant: A Good Practice Guide*. London: DfEE.

Department for Education and Employment (DfEE) (2000d) *Teacher Assistant File: Induction Training for Teaching Assistants*. London: DfEE.

Department for Education and Employment (DfEE) (2000e) *Code of Practice on LEA/Schools Relations*. London: DfEE.

Department for Education and Employment (DfEE) (2001a) *Learning and Teaching: A Strategy for Professional Development*. London: DfEE.

Department for Education and Employment (DfEE) (2001b) *The Standards Framework*.

London: DfEE.

Department for Education and Employment (DfEE) (2001c) *Good Value CPD: A Code of Practice for Providers of Professional Development for Teachers.* London: DfEE.

Department for Education and Skills (DfES) (2001a) *Teachers' Standards Framework: Helping You Develop.* London: DfES.

Department for Education and Skills (DfES) (2001b) *National Induction Programme for Governors: Toolkit for Trainers.* London: DfES.

Department for Education and Skills (DfES) (2002a) *School Teachers' Pay and Conditions.* London: DfES.

Department for Education and Skills (DfES) (2002b) *Staff Health and Wellbeing.* London: DfES.

Department for Education and Skills (DfES) (2002c) *The EPD Pilots.* London: DfES.

Department for Education and Skills (DfES) (2002d) *Time for Standards: Reforming the School Workforce.* London: DfES.

Department for Education and Skills (DfES) (2002e) *Qualifications for Teaching Assistants.* London: DfES.

Department for Education and Skills (DfES) (2002f) *Looking for a Bursar?* London: DfES.

Department for Education and Skills (DfES) (2002g) *Developing the Role of School Support Staff.* London: DfES

Department for Education and Skills (DfES) (2002h) *Using Supply Teachers to Cover Short Term Absences.* London: DfES.

Department for Education and Skills (DfES) (2002i) *Parents' Guide to the School System.* London: DfES.

Department for Education and Skills (DfES) (2002j) *Self-Study Materials for Supply Teacher.* London: DfES.

Department for Education and Skills (DfES) (2003a) *Raising Standards and Tackling Workload: A National Agreement.* London: DfES.

Department for Education and Skills (DfES) (2003b) *School Workforce in England.* London: DfES.

Department for Education and Skills (DfES) (2003c) *Transforming London Secondary Schools.* London: DfES.

Department for Education and Skills (DfES) (2003d) *The London Challenge – Transforming London Secondary Schools: London Data.* London: DfES.

Department for Education and Skills (DfES) (2003e) *The Induction Support Programme For Newly Qualified Teachers.* Guidance 0458/2003. London: DfES.

Department of Education and Science (DES) (1972). *Teacher Education and Training* (James Report). London: HMSO.

Dixon, C. (2002) 'Investors in People and support staff: does it make a difference?' MA dissertation, Institute of Education, University of London.

Dreyfus, H. and Dreyfus, S. (1986) *Mind Over Machine.* New York: Free Press.

Earley, P. (1995) *Managing our Greatest Resource: The Evaluation of the Continuous Development in Schools project.* Oxford: CBI Education Foundation/NFER.

Earley, P. (1996) 'Introduction', in P. Earley B. Fidler and J. Ouston (eds) *Improvement through Inspection? Complementary Approaches to School Development.* London: David Fulton.

Earley, P. and Creese, M. (2003a) 'Governors and school improvement', *Research Matters.* London: Institute of Education, University of London.

Earley, P. and Creese, M. (2003b) 'Lay or professional? Re-examining the role of school governors', in B. Davies and J. West-Burnham (eds), *Handbook of Educational Leadership and Management*. London: Pearson.

Earley, P. and Evans, J. (2002) *LEAding Provision: School Leadership Development in LEAs: A Good Practice Guide*. Nottingham: NCSL.

Earley, P. and Fletcher-Campbell, F. (1992) *The Time to Manage? Department and Faculty Heads at Work*. London: Routledge.

Earley, P and Kinder, K. (1994) *Initiation Rights: Effective Induction Practices for New Teachers*. Slough: NFER.

Earley, P. and Weindling, D. (2004) *Understanding School Leadership, Management and Governance*. London: Sage/Paul Chapman Publishing.

Earley, P., Evans, J., Gold, A., Collarbone, P. and Halpin, D. (2002) *Establishing the Current State of School Leadership in England*. Nottingham: DfES.

Earley, P., Fidler, B. and Ouston, J. (eds.) (1996) *Improvement through Inspection? Complementary Approaches to School Development*. London: David Fulton.

enabling educational excellence (2002) Inset newsletter, Cheadle: Nord Anglia.

Ebbutt, D. (2003) 'The development of a research culture in secondary schools', *Education Action Research*, **10**(1).

Eraut, M., Pennycuick, D. and Radner, M. (1988) *Local Evaluation of INSET: A Meta-evaluation of TRIST Evaluation*. Brighton: University of Sussex.

Ferguson, N., Earley, P., Ouston, J. and Fidler, B. (2000) *Improving Schools and Inspection: The Self-inspecting School*. London: Paul Chapman Publishing/Sage.

Field, K. and Holden, P. (2004) 'National standards for subject leaders', in H. Green (ed.) *Professional Standards for Teachers and Headteachers: A Key to School Improvement*. London: RoutledgeFalmer.

Frost, D. and Durrant, J. (2003) *Teacher-led Development Work*. London: David Fulton.

General Teaching Council (GTC) (2003b) *Teachers' Professional Learning Framework*. Birmingham: GTC. Available at www.gtce.org.uk

General Teaching Council for England (GTCE) (2001) *A Professional Development Entitlement for Teachers*. London: GTC.

Green, H. (ed.) (2004) *Professional Standards for Teachers and Headteachers: A Key to School Improvement*. London: RoutledgeFalmer.

Guskey, T. (2000) *Evaluating Professional Development*. New York: Corwin Press.

Guskey, T. (2002) 'Does it make a difference? Evaluating professional development', *Educational Leadership*, March, 45–51.

Hallgarten, J. (2002) *Supply Teachers: Symptom of the Problem or Part of the Solution?* London: IPPR.

Handscomb G. (2002/03) 'Learning and developing together', *Professional Development Today*, 6(1): 17–22 Winter.

Handscomb G. and MacBeath J. (2003) *The Research Engaged School*. Forum for Learning and Research Enquiry, Essex LEA.

Hargreaves, D. (1998) Creative Professionalism: The Role of Teachers in the Knowledge Society. DEMOS Arguments series 22.

Harland, J., Ashworth, M., Atkinson, M., Halsey, K., Haynes, J., Moor, H. and Wilkin, A. (1999) *Thank You for the Days: How Schools Use their Non-contact Days*. Slough: NFER.

Harris, A. (2002) *School Improvement. What's in it for Schools?* London: Routledge/Falmer.

Harris, B. (2000) 'A strategy for identifying the professional development needs of teachers: a report from New South Wales', *Journal of In-service Education*, **26**(1): 25–47.

Haughton, E. (2002) 'Ride the training express', Learning Support Supplement, *Times Educational Supplement*, 6 December.

Hay McBer (2000) *Effective Teachers*, London: DfES.

Hobby, R. (2001) 'Virtuous circles', *Professional Development Today*, **5**(1): 71–80.

Honey, P. and Mumford, A. (1986) *The Manual of Learning Styles*. Maidenhead: Peter Honey Publications.

Honey, P. and Mumford, A. (2000) *The Learning Styles Helper's Guide*. Maidenhead: Peter Honey Publications.

Hopkins, D. (2002a) Presentation at the launch of the Networked Learning Communities initiative, National College for School Leadership.

Hopkins, P. (2002b) 'The role of video in improving teaching and learning', *Professional Development Today*, **5**(3): 37–44.

Hustler, D., McNamara, O., Jarvis, J., Londra, M., Campbell, A. and Howson, J. (2003) *Teachers' Perceptions of Continuing Professional Development*. Nottingham: DfES.

Investors in People UK (IiPUK) (2000) *The Investors in People Standard*. London: IiPUK.

Jackson, D. (2003) 'Building schools' capacity as learning communities', *Professional Development Today*, **5**(3): 17–24.

Jallongo, M. (1991) *Creating Learning Communities*. Indiana, National Education Service.

Jones, T. (2003) 'Continuing professional development in Wales: an entitlement for all', *Professional Development Today*, **6**(1): 35–42.

Kabra, K. (2002) 'From initial teacher training to a learning community', *Professional Development Today*, **5**(3): 31–6.

Kay, J. (2002) *The Teaching Assistant's Handbook*. London: Continuum.

Kellow, M. (2003) 'Developing learning: school and teacher development through networking learning communities', *Professional Development Today*, **6**(2): 6–12.

Kendall, L., Lee, B., Pye, D. and Wray, M. (2000) *Investors in People in Schools*. Research Report 207. Nottingham: DfEE.

Kerry, T. (2001) *Working with Support Staff*. London: Pearson.

Kerry, T. (2003) 'Releasing potential', *Managing Schools Today*, **12**(6): 25–7.

Kirkpatrick, D. (1959) 'The Kirkpatrick model for training evaluation', *The Journal of the American Society of Training Directors*, (3) August.

Knowles, M. (1984) *Andragogy in Action*. San Franciso, CA: Jossey-Bass.

Lee, B. (2002) 'What is effective CPD?', *Professional Development Today*, **5**(3): 53–62.

Lieberman, A. (1999) 'Networks', *Journal of Staff Development*, **20**(3).

Little, J.W. (1990) 'The persistence of privacy: autonomy and initiative in teachers' professional relations', *Teachers' College Record*, **91**(4): 509–36.

Little, R. (2002) 'Accelerated learning', *Governors' Agenda*, (22), April: 10–11.

Lorenz, S. (1998) *Effective In-class Support*. London: David Fulton.

MacBeath, J. (forthcoming) *Consulting Pupils about their Learning: A Toolbox* (working title). London: Pearson.

Madden, C. and Mitchell, V. (1993) *Professions, Standards and Competence: A Survey of Continuing Education for the Professions*. Department for Continuing Education, University of Bristol.

McIntyre, D. (2001) MEd presentation. Essex LEA/University of Cambridge.

Miliband, D. (2003) 'School improvement and performance management'. Speech to the Performance Management Conference, Bournemouth. Available at info@dfes.gsi.gov.uk

Minnis, F. (2003) 'Early professional development'. MA dissertation, Institute of Education, University of London.

Mortimore, P. and Mortimore, J. (1993) *Managing Associate Staff: Innovation in Primary and Secondary Schools*. London: Paul Chapman Publishing.

Mosley, J. (1996) *Self-esteem Builders*. Cambridge: IDS.

Moss, S. and Silk, J. (2003) 'What can coaching bring to continuing professional development in education?', *Professional Development Today*, **7**(1): 19–22.

National College for School Leadership (NCSL) (2001) *The Leadership Development Framework*. Nottingham: NCSL.

National College for School Leadership (NCSL) (2003a) 'Leading from the Middle, a supplement to *LDR*', May. Nottingham: NCSL.

National College for School Leadership (NCSL) (2003b) *The Heart of the Matter: A Practical Guide to What Middle Leaders can do to Improve Learning in Secondary Schools*. Nottingham: NCSL.

National College for School Leadership (NCSL) (2003c) *School Leadership*. Nottingham: NCSL.

National Education Research Forum (NERF) (2001) *The Impact of Educational Research on Policy and Practice*. Sub-group report of NERF.

Naylor, D. (1999) 'The professional development needs of midday assistants', *Professional Development Today*, **3**(3): 51–60.

O'Sullivan, F., Jones, K. and Reid, K. (1990) *Staff Development in Secondary Schools*. London: Hodder and Stoughton.

Office for Standards in Education (Ofsted) (2002a) *Continuing Professional Development for Teachers in Schools*. London: Ofsted.

Office for Standards in Education (Ofsted) (2002b) *Performance Management of Teachers*. London: Ofsted.

Office for Standards in Education (Ofsted) (2002c) *Teaching Assistants in Primary Schools: An Evaluation of the Quality and Impact of their Work* (HMI Report 434). Available online.

Office for Standards in Education (Ofsted) (2002d) *Leadership and Management Training for Headteachers: Report by HMI* (HMI 547). London: Ofsted.

Office for Standards in Education (Ofsted) (2002e) *The Work of School Governors* (HMI 707), report from HMCI, London: Ofsted. Available online.

Office for Standards in Education (Ofsted) (2003a) *Inspecting Schools*. London: Ofsted.

Office for Standards in Education (2003b) Early Professional Development.

Office for Standards in Education (Ofsted) (2003c) *HMCI Annual Report*. London: Ofsted.

Office for Standards in Education (Ofsted) (2003d) *Schools' Use of Temporary Teachers*. London: Ofsted.

Oldroyd, D. and Hall, V. (1991) *Managing Staff Development: A Handbook for Secondary Schools*. London: Paul Chapman Publishing.

Pachler, N. and Field, K. (2004) 'Continuing professional development', in S. Capel, M. Leask, and T. Turner, (eds), *Starting to Teach in the Secondary School*. London: Routledge/Falmer.

Phillips, J. (1999) 'Is your School a Learning Organisation?' St Albans: Phillips Associates.

Pitcher, J. (2003) 'To raise the status of visual arts in school and develop Emotional Literacy through creative approaches', *Wiltshire Journal of Education*, 4(3): 18–20.

PriceWaterhouseCoopers (PwC) (2001) *Teacher Workload Study Interim Report*. London: DfES.

Reynolds (2003) 'So near but yet so far', *Times Educational Supplement*, 20 June: 23.

Riches, C. and Morgan, C. (eds) (1989) *Human Resource Management in Education*. Buckingham: Open University Press.

Riley, K. (2003) *Redefining Professionalism: Teachers with Attitude!* GTCE website at http://www.gtce.org.uk/news/featuresDetail.asp?ezineID=107

Rosenholtz, S. (1989) *Teachers' Workplace: The Social Organisation of Schools*. New York: Teachers College Press.

Sallis, J. (2001) *Heads in Partnership: Working with your Governors for a Successful School*. London: Pitman.

Sanderson, J. (2002) 'Sink or swim? How are overseas trained teachers to stay afloat in English waters?'. MA dissertation, Institute of Education, University of London.

Scanlon, M., Earley, P. and Evans, J. (1999) *Improving the Effectiveness of School Governing Bodies*. London: DfEE.

Smithers, A. and Robinson, P. (2003) *Factors Affecting Teachers' Decisions to Leave the Profession*. Research brief and Research report no. 430. Nottingham: DfES.

Stoll, L. and Fink, D. (1996) *Changing our Schools*. Buckingham: Open University Press.

Stoll, L., Wallace, M., Bolam, R., McMahon, A., Thomas, S., Hawkey, K., Smith, M. and Greenwood, A. (2003) 'Creating and sustaining effective professional learning communities: questions arising from the literature', Universities of Bath and Bristol information sheet.

Swann, W. and Loxley, A. (1998) 'The impact of school-based training on classroom assistants in primary schools', *Research Papers in Education*, 13(2): 141–60.

Taylor, P. (2004) 'Effective performance management and professional development: a case study', *Professional Development Today*, 7(1): 4–10.

Teacher Training Agency (TTA) (1998) *National Standards for Subject Leaders*. London: TTA.

Teacher Training Agency (TTA) (2001a) *The Role of Induction Tutor*. London: TTA.

Teacher Training Agency (TTA) (2002a) *Qualifying to Teach: Professional Standards for Qualified Teacher Status and Requirements for Initial Teacher Training*. London: TTA.

Teacher Training Agency (TTA) (2002b) *ITT Performance Profiles 2001*. London: TTA.

Teacher Training Agency (TTA) (2003a) *The Career Entry and Development Profile*. London: TTA.

Teacher Training Agency (TTA) (2003b) *How to Qualify as a Teacher in England*. London: TTA.

TES Website – www.tes.co.uk/staffroom

Thompson, K. (2002) 'Early professional development', *Professional Development Today*, 6(1): 23–8.

Times Educational Supplement (TES) (2003) *On Course*. 21 March. London: *TES*.

Tomlinson, H. (1993) 'Developing Professionals', *Education*, 24 September.

Tomlinson, J. (1993) *The Control of Education*. London: Cassell.

Totterdell, M., Heilbronn, R., Bubb, S. and Jones, C. (2002) *Evaluation of the Effectiveness of the Statutory Arrangements for the Induction of Newly Qualified Teachers*. Research brief and report no. 338. Nottingham: DfES.

Turner, C. (1996) 'The roles and tasks of a subject head of department in secondary schools: a neglected area of study?', *School Organisation*, 16(2): 203–17.

Turner, C. (2003) 'A critical review of research on subject leaders in secondary schools', *School Leadership and Management*, 23(2): 209–27.

Waters, M. (1998) 'Personal development for teachers', *Professional Development Today*, 1(2): 29–38.

Watkins, J. and Drury, L. (1994) *Positioning for the Unknown: Career Development for Professionals in the 1990s*. Bristol: Centre for Continuing Education, University of Bristol.

Watkinson, A. (1999) 'The professional development of teaching assistants', *Professional Development Today*, 2(3): 63–9.

Watkinson, A. (2002) *Assisting Learning and Supporting Teaching: A Practical Guide for the Teaching Assistant in the Classroom*. London: David Fulton.

Watkinson, A. (2003) 'Using teacher assistants: an answer to the teacher recruitment crisis?' *Managing Schools Today*, 12(6): 29–33.

Wenger, E. (1998) *Communities of Practice: Learning, Meaning and Identity*. Cambridge: Cambridge University Press.

West, N. (1995) *Middle Management in the Primary School*. London: David Fulton.

West-Burnham, J. and O'Sullivan, F. (1998) *Leadership and Professional Development in Schools*. London: Pitman.

Williams, A. (2002) 'Informal learning in the workplace – a case study of new teachers'. Paper given at BERA conference, University of Exeter.

Williams, M. (1993). 'Changing policies and practices', in *The Continuing Professional Development of Teachers*. London: GTC.

Wise, C. (2001) 'The monitoring role of the academic middle manager', *Educational Management and Administration*, 29(3): 333–41.

Woods D. (2000) *The Promotion and Dissemination of Good Practice*, London: The Education Network, October.

Woodward, W. (2003) A third of teachers plan to quit, *Guardian*, 7 January.

Author Index

Adey, K 165
Balshaw, M 114
Barthes, R 17, 186
Baxter, G 36, 37, 78
Bentley, P 43, 45, 63
Berrill, D 31
Bezzina, C 23
Bleach, K 133, 157
Bolam, R 4, 29
Boyle, B 28, 29
Brereton, P 73
Brown, S. 28
Bubb, S. 54, 56, 58, 64–5, 80, 114–5,
    124–6, 131–40, 153, 169
Butler, S 121
Carnell, E 18, 21, 72
Chambers, M 36, 37, 78
Child, A 121–2
Connor, D 44, 48
Cordingley, P 9, 97
Craig, M 143–4
Creese, M 189, 190, 192, 196
Davey, J 49, 85–7
Day, C 5, 73
Dixon, C 109
Dreyfus, H & S 30
Drury, L 7
Durrant, J 83, 96
Earley, P 7, 29, 41, 162, 164, 166, 168,
    172, 175, 179, 182, 188, 190, 192
Eraut, M 84
Evans, J 168, 172, 179, 182
Farrell, P 114
Ferguson, N, 164
Field, K 14, 33, 164, 169
Fink, D 23
Fletcher-Campbell, F. 162, 164
Frost, D and Durrant, J 83, 96
Gardner, H 19
Geeson, J 121
Green, H 162
Guskey, T 32, 80–2

Hall, V 6
Hallgarten, J 141–2
Handscomb G 89, 93, 97, 99
Hargreaves, D 93–4, 97
Harland, J 11
Harris, A 94, 98
Harris, B 51
Haughton, E 111–2
Hoare, P 80
Hobby, R 73
Holden, P 164, 169
Honey, P 19
Hopkins, D 94
Hopkins, P 73
Hustler, D 35, 67, 69
Jackson, D 25
Jallongo, M 36
Jones, J 165
Jones, T 9, 10
Kabra, K 110, 119–21
Kay, J 114
Kellow, M 26–7
Kerry, T 107, 114
Kinder, K 29
Kirkpatrick 78–80
Knowles, M 17
Lee, B 28
Lieberman, A 25
Little, J. W 23
Little, R 191
Lorenz, S 108
Loxley, A 108
MacBeath J 89, 93, 97, 99
McMahon, A 29
Madden, C 4, 12
McIntyre, D 93
Merrill, S 121–2
Miliband, D 53
Minnis, F. 79, 155
Mitchell, V 4, 12
Mortimore, P & J 108
Mosley, J 45, 110

Subject Index